Confrontation
and Compromise

Confrontation and Compromise

Presidential and Congressional Leadership, 2001–2006

Jason D. Mycoff and Joseph A. Pika

ROWMAN & LITTLEFIELD PUBLISHERS, INC.

Lanham • Boulder • New York • Toronto • Plymouth, UK

ROWMAN & LITTLEFIELD PUBLISHERS, INC.

Published in the United States of America
by Rowman & Littlefield Publishers, Inc.
A wholly owned subsidary of The Rowman & Littlefield Publishing Group, Inc.
4501 Forbes Boulevard, Suite 200, Lanham, Maryland 20706
www.rowmanlittlefield.com

Estover Road
Plymouth PL6 7PY
United Kingdom

British Library Cataloguing in Publication Information Available

Library of Congress Cataloging-in-Publication Data:

Mycoff, Jason D., 1975–
    Confrontation and compromise : Presidential and Congressional leadership,
2001–2006 / Jason D. Mycoff and Joseph A. Pika.
      p. cm.
    Includes index.
    ISBN-13: 978-0-7425-4059-0 (cloth : alk. paper)
    ISBN-10: 0-7425-4059-6 (cloth : alk. paper)
    ISBN-13: 978-0-7425-4060-6 (pbk. : alk. paper)
    ISBN-10: 0-7425-4060-X (pbk. : alk. paper)
      1. United States—Politics and government—(2001–)—Case studies.
    2. United States—Politics and government—(2001–)—Decision making—
    Case studies. 3. United States—Social policy—(1993–)—Case studies. 4. Bush,
    George W. (George Walker), (1946–)—Political and social views—Case studies.
    5. United States—Congress—Decision making—Case studies. 6. Political
    leadership—United States—Case studies. 7. Political science—United States—
    Case studies. I. Pika, Joseph August, 1947– II. Title.
    E902.M93 2007
    973.931—dc22   2007003300

Printed in the United States of America

∞™ The paper used in this publication meets the minimum requirements of American National Standard for Information Sciences—Permanence of Paper for Printed
Library Materials, ANSI/NISO Z39.48-1992.

To Brandi, Madison, and Maya
To Mary, Kristen, Elizabeth, and Joseph

Contents

Preface

This book characterizes leadership in the U.S. policymaking system through six case studies of major policy initiatives undertaken during the Bush presidency. Our purpose is to help undergraduate students better understand the strategic interaction among policymakers that is essential for overcoming the many obstacles to action in a fragmented system. Writing new laws, reforming old laws, responding to crises, and creating new federal programs and agencies require coordinated action between Congress and the president. In our case studies, we focus on how the interpersonal relationships and policy negotiations between President Bush and other administration officials, congressional leaders like Speaker of the House Dennis Hastert (R-IL), and rank-and-file members of Congress like Senator Russ Feingold (D-WI) led to outcomes for six of the nation's most significant problems during the first six years of the twenty-first century.

This approach to studying Congress and the presidency is distinctive in several respects. Many books seek to explain the congressional-presidential relationship by analyzing the competition between the two branches for power and influence over the policymaking process and each other. This common approach explores constitutional roles while often treating policy outputs as the sum of institutional contributions rather than as the product of political strategies and tactics. As a result, individual policymakers and their contributions become a latent variable shrouded within a black box model. Instead, our experience in the classroom suggests that students achieve a deeper understanding of the policymaking system and its outputs by focusing on the individuals within each branch responsible for the planning, negotiation, and strategy. Our purpose in this book, therefore, is to explore the leadership exercised by individuals in both branches in fashioning national policy. Unlike many studies, ours examines leadership in both branches of national government.

This book includes a number of useful features for undergraduate instruction including, among others, detailed and timely case studies and profiles of individual leaders. First, the heart of the book is six case studies providing accessible examples of how the policymaking system works and why individual leadership is necessary to overcome contextual obstacles. The six case studies include issues from both terms of the Bush presidency leading into the 2006 midterm elections. The cases include examples of what are widely considered policy successes (education reform; intelligence redesign; creation of the Department of Homeland Security; and campaign finance reform), policy failures (Social Security reform), and a case that is so recent that we cannot yet determine if it is a success or failure (Hurricane Katrina). This selection of cases includes topics of great interest to students and provides examples of issues from the president's agenda, issues championed by both Democrats and Republicans in Congress, issues considered in the wake of national emergency, and issues considered over the course of multiple Congresses and administrations. When combined, these six cases provide a useful examination of the policymaking system in many different contextual circumstances.

Second, we include profiles of the central leaders in each case study, providing biographical material to introduce the major players. Many undergraduate students can identify our principal national leaders but know very little about their backgrounds, policy agendas, or institutional positions. The profiles are an important feature because they allow students to better understand why each key player was involved in the policy area and how their career prepared them to play a crucial role. Provided with a better understanding of the key players, students will be better able to follow the cases and will put more effort into learning about the policymaking system and leadership, rather than struggling to follow a narrative populated by anonymous characters.

Confrontation and Compromise: Presidential and Congressional Leadership, 2001–2006 is intended as a supplemental text for courses on American government, Congress, the presidency, political leadership, and public policy. Paired with an introductory-level textbook on American government, this book will bring the policymaking system to life with its case study approach and will provide detailed examples of how the concepts presented in the course are played out in the policymaking system. Paired with an upper-level text on Congress or the presidency, this book will allow for a detailed examination of how the president, administration officials, and members of Congress interact and will provide flesh to the skeletal explanation offered in course texts of how these officials exercise their responsibilities. As an instructional tool, a course might include all six cases or a selection of cases as needed to meet the purpose of the course without losing the larger lessons of the book.

In sum, this book will be useful in most courses on American government and has a number of features that will make the book a valuable selection as a supplemental text. Students will enjoy reading the engaging cases studies, and instructors will find value in the scope and timeliness of the case studies.

Acknowledgments

We thank the editors at Rowman & Littlefield who worked with us on this project, including Renee Legatt, who championed the project in its nascent stage, Niels Aaboe, our executive editor, and Karen Ackermann, our production editor. We also thank Jonathan Olmsted and Samrat Sinha for their excellent research assistance.

We are also grateful to Jeffrey Cohen, David Crockett, Matthew Esbaugh-Soha, Samuel Hoff, Colleen Shogan, Alan Rozzi, and the anonymous reviewers, whose thoughtful comments helped improve our thinking. We are indebted to James Magee and the Department of Political Science and International Relations at the University of Delaware for financial support of this project.

1

The Search for Leadership

National politics during the first decade of the twenty-first century was dominated by the eight-year term of George W. Bush and the Republican Congress that accompanied him for most of his presidency. His election as president in 2000, and reelection in 2004, ensured that the spotlight of political analysis and commentary would focus on his performance in advancing top-priority programs, dealing with the unexpected (for example, terrorist attacks and hurricanes), and working with Congress. Like all his post–World War II predecessors, President Bush entered office with a list of policy goals—an agenda he hoped to accomplish. During the highly contentious election of 2000, education reform, prescription drug benefits for the elderly, and tax reductions stood at the forefront of that agenda. In the 2002 midterm elections, Republicans resecured the Senate majority they had lost midway through 2001 and expanded their majority in the House of Representatives. After the 2004 election, large-scale reform of Social Security and the tax system stood at the top of Bush's list, as well as winning the war on terror. Again, Republicans triumphed in Congress. Thus, national elections produced a *team* of decision-makers, and voters expected President Bush and members of Congress—Republicans and Democrats alike—to provide leadership for the nation. The political system has operated in this way for more than two centuries, and the Bush years are the latest instance of an ongoing search for leadership.

Americans crave strong political leadership. Americans fear powerful leaders. Despite the contradiction, both statements are true and pose a fundamental dilemma for the political system. How does the system provide effective leadership when, in an effort to preclude threats to liberty, its constitutional design fragments and broadly disperses power? This dilemma, based on the ambivalence toward powerful leaders that is deeply ingrained in American political culture, has been visible since the constitutional convention when the Founders debated the appropriate separation of powers and authority between Congress and the president. What emerged was a system that usually requires broad cooperation between the president and Congress to accomplish public purposes—what Mark Peterson has termed a "tandem institutions perspective."[1] In that spirit, this book focuses less on which branch has more power—though we occasionally explore this question—than it does on the possibilities and limitations of leadership in a remarkably fragmented political system further divided by severe partisan conflict and marked by significant crises at the outset of the twenty-first century. We seek to answer a central question: *How do elected policymakers in the legislative and executive branches of national government play leadership roles at different times and under different conditions?*

To make progress, the nation needs to address its collective problems by defining the agenda, developing options, and making choices among possible solutions. Each stage of this problem-solving and policymaking process requires concerted action, and in a democracy we look to elected public officials to provide the skills needed to accomplish that action—the *leadership* essential to producing common effort. In the highly diverse and fragmented American political system, the task of building consensus behind a preferred option is an essential step. In extraordinary times, leadership skills may require the capacity to envision a markedly different future and the skills to mobilize broad support behind a dramatic departure from the status quo.

In this book, we use six case studies to assess how individual political actors lay claim to leadership roles and provide *direction, coherence,* and *energy,* the definition of leadership suggested by Bert Rockman, a political scientist. *Direction* consists of setting the agenda and determining the course public officials follow in addressing those agenda items. Providing direction is a necessary component of leadership in a system as fragmented as that of the United States. This is true nationally but also within the boundaries of legislative-executive relations where the lawmaking process involves hundreds of independent political actors who must be brought to work in concert on common tasks. Rockman argues that "The capacity to generate direction may be produced through elite consensus, public deference, decisive tools for majority rule, or, potentially, entrepreneurial leaders."[2]

Coherence is no less central to leadership. It is critical to have a tangible policy proposal to serve as the starting point for policymaking. Such proposals must address the substantive needs of the problem at hand but also be framed with an eye to the political context so they can attract sufficient support for passage and acceptance. Balancing considerations of substance and politics is an enormous challenge. How does one make bargaining concessions that garner necessary political support without reducing the substantive coherence of a proposal? It is difficult enough to do this within a single chamber of Congress but even more complex when the effort must be coordinated with another chamber and another branch. Thus, providing coherence requires the application of political skills that are essential to leadership.

Finally, Rockman argues that *energy* is necessary to provide the spark that creates interest in a policy area among those responsible for setting the agenda or among enough lawmakers to force political action. Energy also refers to an individual's commitment to an issue, keeping the issue alive until it reaches the agenda for action. The national agenda has limited space and with so many issues and policy proposals competing for attention, some will be dropped from consideration. A critical part of leadership is winning a place on the agenda and taking advantage when opportunity knocks. Leaders dedicated to passing their policy proposals work diligently to gain access to the agenda and win support. In the legislature, because many bills languish in committee for an entire Congress before suffering a quiet death, leaders must revive their proposals by resubmitting legislation in successive Congresses until winning enough support for passage. Presidents similarly build off efforts from the past—the failures must be refashioned in view of changes in the political context and successes serve as the springboard for new efforts.

We argue that presidents, party leaders, congressional committee leaders, rank-and-file members of Congress, bureaucrats, or even organized interests may play significant roles in providing direction, coherence, and energy, something we explore in our six case studies. However, the public, the media, and political actors, themselves, have expectations about who is to lead. While there is a vast literature on political leadership, the concept of leadership has been difficult to operationalize or systematically characterize. In the following chapters we use specific examples to illustrate the operation of leadership concentrating on these three factors—direction, coherence, and energy. In the next section we review features of the institutional design established in the U.S. Constitution.

The Locus of Leadership

Where do Americans look for political leadership? At the national level, the most frequently heard answer is the presidency. This is partly the product of America's constitutional design that makes leadership both problematic and critical. The separation of powers system fragments the tasks of leadership among multiple branches of government at the center, and federalism disperses them broadly through the political system, ensuring that states as well as the national government can serve as separate centers of decision-making. With each branch of government answering to a different constituency and jealously preserving its share of government authority, national elites are often pitted against each other in the battle of checks and balances with each branch exercising some powers over its constitutional competitors. Such fragmentation, largely the product of James Madison's influence, as articulated in Federalist Papers No. 10 and 51, ably reflects the societal pluralism of a continental nation, but it begs the question of how the government achieves *direction* and *coherence of action.*[3] This latter concern was Alexander Hamilton's as he called for "energy in the executive" in Federalist Paper No. 70. Thus, the perpetual search for viable leadership reflects a fundamental dilemma from the design of government in the United States.

> What emerges is not "a government," but many, often competitive and sometimes cooperative, governments; not a decisive point of decision making at the center, but a diffusion of decisional points; and not a state presumably representing a "common and durable interest," but a society whose abundant pluralism finds ready expression through the many conduits available in the polity.[4]

Although political scientists most frequently provide the same answer to this dilemma as did Hamilton—presidents provide direction, coherence, and energy—it is not automatically the case in our constitutional system that leadership arises from presidents rather than Congress. Congress and the president are constitutional equals. This fact is recognized in one of the most apt descriptions of the Constitution, provided by Edward S. Corwin who called it "an invitation to struggle."[5] The recurrent rounds in this centuries-long constitutional wrestling match have been the subject of extensive analysis and commentary. There are many institutional theories on how the president and Congress execute leadership. Some argue that the fulcrum of leadership regularly shifts in the American system, sometimes being exercised principally by the president but then later swinging like a pendulum to the Congress during periods of institutional assertiveness.[6] Others argue that even the potential for congressional leadership will be permanently eclipsed by presidents because of the legislature's institutional incapacity. In this view, even the concept of congressional leadership is an oxymoron given the fragmented nature of the bicameral American legislature that will always experience difficulty speaking with one voice given its collective nature. Nor is it clear that a collectivity can lead; thus, the central challenge of *congressional leadership* is designing a system that empowers a few legislators to impose order and direction on an otherwise disorderly and directionless institution.

But the answer to "Who leads?" is even more complex. Context seems to play a critical role in determining who exercises leadership. Perhaps the leader(s) of one institution will assert primacy in some areas of policy while

those in the other dominate a different set of policies. This is the central con-
tention of the "two presidencies" literature.[7] Aaron Wildavsky's seminal thesis
held that Congress is more deferential to the president in the foreign policy
realm and more independent in domestic policy. He argued that Congress gives
the president more freedom on matters of national security because the Constitution makes the president the commander in chief. On matters of domestic policy, Congress asserts its power and limits presidential freedom in decision-making.
Post–World War II data confirmed that presidents are more successful in attracting congressional support on foreign policy decisions than in the domestic
realm, and subsequent work has confirmed and sharpened this thesis. Richard
Fleisher and Jon Bond found that while the two presidencies theory is valid,
Republican presidents get a larger boost in support for foreign policy decisions
relative to domestic decisions with a Democratically-controlled Congress.[8]
Other work indicated that Congress began to take a stronger position following
the Vietnam War.[9]

Just as leadership may shift depending on the problem being addressed, one
would also expect the locus of leadership to shift as the nation's agenda of problems shifts. For example, I. M. Destler tracked the changing relationship between
the president and Congress on foreign policy, linking it to changes in the world
and shifting domestic influences. Destler divided the post–World War II era into
four periods characterized by increasing congressional involvement in foreign
policy decision-making: Bipartisan Internationalism (1945–1968); Congress
Writes New Rules (1969–1974); Polarized Internationalists (1975–1994);
and Partisan Gridlock (1995–present).[10] Bipartisan internationalism extended
from the end of World War II until 1968, a quarter-century period when Congress and the president coexisted peacefully with the Congress playing a deferential and supportive role to the president's leading role and an activist foreign
policy including international aid, a large standing military, and full participation
in international organizations. Congress spent freely on the military and often
gave the president unwavering support as exemplified in the Gulf of Tonkin
Resolution that gave President Johnson a blank check in escalating war in
Southeast Asia. Upset with the course of events in Vietnam and confronted by
two strong presidents in Johnson and Nixon, the Congress asserted itself in foreign policy from 1969–1974 by enacting several mechanisms designed to force
the president to consult more extensively in making foreign policy. Foremost
among these changes was the War Powers Resolution. The period from 1975 to
1994 saw presidents and their allies in Congress win on most high-profile international issues (for example, the sale of AWACS to Saudi Arabia in 1981 and
NAFTA in 1994), but Congress was able to slow or even defeat the president
on low-profile issues (for example, sidestepping the Boland Amendment in 1983
banning aid to the Contras in Nicaragua). Presidents could still win on the
most important issues but had to use much more political capital than in decades

past to attract majority support in Congress. Finally, 1995 to 2000 was the period of increasing partisan gridlock. Without the galvanizing effect of the Cold War or a consensus on how to approach the world, foreign policy issues during this period suffered through many of the same partisan squabbles as domestic policy. Facing a Republican Congress, bitter partisan battles killed many of Clinton's major initiatives, including fast-track trade negotiation authority and the Nuclear Test Ban Treaty. As Destler makes clear, over time the international and domestic political context changed, and so did the role each institution played.

Institutional perspectives on leadership provide valuable insight into why one branch or the other will take a proactive or reactive role in different policy areas during different historical periods. These institutional parameters constrain the leadership behavior of individuals by limiting the tools available in different circumstances. Although institutional resources and capacities are critical for developing a full understanding of leadership, our interest is not primarily institutional. *This book examines the actions, strategies, and efforts of public officials that determine the outcomes of struggles over policymaking.* Policymaking, in itself, is the effort of government officials to provide direction, energy, and coherence in an all-too-frequently incoherent system of government. In short, we regard leadership as a product of individual action constrained by institutional parameters and political context. In the following sections of this chapter, as a background for the case studies that follow, we review how the presidency and Congress evolved over recent decades and the political context George W. Bush confronted when he entered office.

Presidents and Leadership

For most Americans, leadership is synonymous with the presidency. Constitutional design, socialization, and the nation's agenda of problems ensure that the public will focus on the president's words and deeds far more than on those of any other figure in the political system. This is, however, a relatively new development. For much of American history, Congress, not the president, stood at the center of national government, but institutional primacy shifted dramatically toward the president at the end of the nineteenth century, and the change gained momentum throughout the twentieth century.[11]

As unitary executives, presidents have always had an institutional advantage over a bicameral legislature that faces the challenge of collective decision-making. The contest over who served as president quickly became the centerpiece of the nation's electoral politics. Over time, presidential selection, though officially remaining the province of the Electoral College, increasingly became the focus of popular politics as growing numbers of citizens first gained the franchise and were then mobilized by political parties to vote. The result was a popular selection process that centered on the nation's principal political prize—the presidency—and the widespread belief that presidents, as the only official selected from a national constituency, can legitimately claim to be a "symbol of the nation" and to embody the national interest.

In addition to these important factors, developments in several other areas had to occur before presidents attained their preeminent leadership profile. The rise of a mass media at the end of the nineteenth century made it far easier for the press to spotlight the president's words and deeds than to explain the actions of a complex institution speaking with many voices like Congress. Theodore Roosevelt became the first president to take advantage of the job's newsworthiness, and these trends were heightened with the advent of radio and then television. The emergence of the United States as a world power, even before World War I, substantially raised the stakes of foreign policy for the nation and highlighted the president's constitutional roles as commander in chief and chief diplomat. World War II and the subsequent Cold War raised the president's control of life and death decisions to a far higher level than ever before. Throughout the century, Congress delegated many policy responsibilities to the president (for example, managing the economy, creating a single federal budget, integrating foreign and defense policies) and created new presidential staff units (for example, Council of Economic Advisers, Bureau of the Budget/Office of Management and Budget, National Security Staff) to help them accomplish these tasks.

Presidents stand at the center of American history as taught in most classrooms, and the "great" presidents—Washington and Lincoln, in particular—receive such glorification that they have become virtual icons of American democracy.[12] Americans' outlook on presidential leadership is heavily influenced by what Bruce Buchanan has called *a presidential culture*: "widely held meanings of the presidency, derived from selected episodes in the history of the institution and transmitted from one generation to the next by political socialization."[13] In many respects, Americans have created a mythology that consists of glorious sagas that emphasize presidents' success in the face of enormous odds, lonely decisions on critical issues that emerge from the revered Oval Office, and persistence in the face of adversity. As a result, presidents either become part of this mythology as revered heroes or leave office as disappointments whose efforts fell short of the heroic.[14]

Facing such weighty expectations, presidents have not been reluctant to explain how their own performance places them squarely in this tradition of greatness. As Paul Brace and Barbara Hinckley make clear, presidents consciously take actions to improve their public standing, timing their travel, televised addresses to the nation, and press conferences with an eye to how these actions will affect their public approval ratings.[15] Moreover, a succession of modern presidents use calculated rhetoric and appearances to project the qualities that Americans seek in their leaders, including decisiveness, power, benevolence, altruism, frankness, and vigor.[16]

As Thomas E. Cronin and Michael A. Genovese argue, the public often wants contradictory qualities in the same person: a powerful leader who won't abuse power; a charismatic and visionary leader who also displays the qualities of a common citizen; a compassionate yet cunning and sometimes ruthless figure; a nonpartisan political entrepreneur; a unifier who takes strong stands; someone who will lead the people but at other times will follow their lead; and a self-confident figure who does not succumb to the belief of his or her own infallibility.[17] Overall, then, the public expects presidents to lead in many ways, and presidents work hard to meet those expectations, even though the public's expectations are often contradictory.

Ultimately, presidents stand at the center of American political life. As Hinckley argues, "the president is the initial point of contact [for citizens with government], general symbol of government, and orientation point from which the rest of the government is perceived."[18]

Leadership in the Congress

Several factors distinguish discussions of congressional leadership from those of presidential leadership. The president's leadership role reflects his uniquely central position in both government and national life. In seeking to accomplish their goals, presidents pursue strategies that span institutions, winning support from Congress for legislative proposals, influencing judicial decisions through the indirect process of judicial nominations, or tasking bureaucrats to follow their guidelines in implementing programs. Together with unique access to the public, this centrality enables presidents to function as the nation's principal agenda setter. In striking contrast, discussions of congressional leadership emphasize the roles and activities of leaders *within the congressional system*. In other words, the focus is on *leadership in Congress* rather than *leadership provided by Congress*. In addition, there are multiple leaders in Congress—party leaders for both the majority and minority, in both the House and the Senate, as well as leaders of committees and subcommittees. Unlike in the presidency, where leadership at least appears to be unitary, even if it might not be so simple in operation, the question of leadership in Congress begins from a far more complex starting point.

Nothing in the Constitution precludes Congress from playing a more directive role for the nation similar to the president's, that is, defining the tasks that lie before the nation and the federal government. But both precedent and legislative delegation have assigned this role to presidents rather than Congress. Because the president seems to stand at the center of the American political system and has daily access to the American public through personal appearances and media coverage, the president's agenda-setting activities are more visible and prominent than those of members of Congress. At times, it appears as though the president alone sets the national agenda and leads the public and Congress in addressing the nation's problems even though he routinely consults with members of Congress, particularly with the leaders of his own party on Capitol Hill. No individual member of Congress, not even one with the greatest power, has the same sort of access to or influence over the public, the media, or even other members of Congress as that enjoyed by the president.

But there are exceptions to this pattern, and the exception that proves the rule is Newt Gingrich in the early days of his speakership. In the aftermath of the Republican rise to power in the House during the fall 1994 elections, Gingrich became a unique rival to President Clinton in 1995. Gingrich received presidential-like media coverage and even delivered a prime-time televised speech to the nation similar to those made by presidents. For a short time, Gingrich served as a rival portrayed by the media as nearly equal to President Clinton, but that period of unusual media exposure and agenda-setting power quickly came to an end when President Clinton defeated a Republican effort to assert control over the nation's budget priorities in a dramatic showdown during the winter of 1995–1996 involving multiple government shutdowns.[19] This extraordinary example of Congressional leadership highlights important differences between presidential and congressional leadership. The public and media accept the president's role as the nation's agenda setter and political leader; in this capacity, the president can choose to assert a leading role on nearly any issue with varying levels of success. Members of Congress, even those in formal leadership positions, have far fewer opportunities to lead the nation. When those opportunities arise, members of Congress are often cast in a supporting role, assisting the president or perhaps winning concessions through tough bargaining. Members in the president's party are usually portrayed as helping the president pass his agenda and are thereby seen as playing a subordinate role to the president. Members of the out-party, when in control of a branch of Congress, often provide leadership in articulating opposition to the president and his partisan supporters. Members of Congress are in their weakest leadership position when in the out-party and serving in their chamber's minority. The minority in this case is reduced to waiting for rare opportunities for success when the majority coalition splinters or when the two parties agree on a policy issue.

Therefore, while leadership is commonly seen as a prerogative of the presidency, members of Congress can assert leadership but often on a smaller scale. Instead of leading on an agenda issue of choice like the president, members of Congress, especially those without formal leadership positions, must wait until the opportunity arises to enter the fray and lead the Congress and the nation. In the six cases examined in this book, we will highlight the leadership roles played by individual members of Congress holding formal leadership positions and roles played by rank-and-file members. Within each case, there are examples of how individual members of Congress provided direction, coherence, and energy to lead the Congress, and sometimes the nation, on pressing agenda items. Before turning to those case studies, however, we will review the political context of the Bush years and introduce the individuals occupying the most influential leadership positions.

THE INSTITUTIONAL BALANCE IN 2001

President Bush assumed office on January 20, 2001, and similar to any new president, he faced institutional and substantive policy challenges. He entered a pre-existing political context shaped by a set of ongoing problems both at home and abroad. For example, the most pressing challenge looming on the domestic front was a decelerating economy that followed one of the longest economic expansions in history. The late 1990s were characterized by a booming stock market and rapid job creation. Between 1996 and 2000 the technology-heavy NASDAQ stock index increased in value from 1,000 points to 5,000 points, and in a single year from March 1999 to March 2000 the value of the NASDAQ doubled. This rapid growth was colloquially known as the "dot-com boom" as Internet company start-ups began to drive stock market growth. As growth increased, the dot-com boom transformed into a dot-com bubble that eventually burst starting in March 2000. Over the next year, the NASDAQ began its decline, bottoming out around 1,000 points in 2002. The rise and fall of the NASDAQ accurately reflected the rest of the economy. This precipitous economic decline coincided with the 2000 presidential election and President Bush's arrival in Washington; soon after Bush took office, the economy plunged into recession. While partisans argue over the cause of the recession, and whether President Clinton or President Bush was at fault, it is clear that the economic downturn topped the national agenda and served as the new administration's first challenge.

Bush also faced a peaceful world but an uncertain direction in foreign policy that had yet to take tangible shape in the aftermath of the Cold War. In 2001, the government and public were still grappling with how to define American foreign policy in the absence of a competing superpower. With the collapse of the Soviet Union in 1991, there was no broad consensus on the purpose of American foreign policy. Officials pointed to a number of potential threats as foci for the new foreign policy including unsecured nuclear weapons in the former Soviet Union, international crime, terrorism, and long-standing conflicts in Africa, the Pacific Rim, and the Middle East. The Clinton administration addressed each of these areas and more with varying levels of success. With the Soviet Union's collapse, the U.S. military had begun to scale down in size, and foreign policy issues found less room on an agenda rife with domestic policy issues. In fact, foreign policy issues were largely absent from the 2000 presidential election.

Complicating Bush's ability to deal with these policy challenges was the way he won the 2000 presidential election. Bush won the presidency by collecting a majority of electoral votes, but he received fewer popular votes than his opponent Al Gore.[20] With such a close and controversial outcome, President Bush would be working from a position of weakness because he failed to win either a majority or plurality of popular votes.[21] This failure cast in doubt the victorious candidate's claim to a mandate of public support for his agenda. Most if not all presidents try to parlay their election victory into a winning coalition to implement their campaign agendas.

Relatively few presidents take office as part of an electoral landslide that fundamentally changes the political landscape; Franklin D. Roosevelt's landslide election in 1932 is widely recognized as changing the political landscape, and some argue that Ronald Reagan's surprise victory in 1980 had a similar, yet smaller-scale, effect. The narrow margins of victory registered by Bush in both the 2000 and 2004 elections ensured this was not the case. But, such a landslide victory is not necessary for success. Interestingly, President Bush made the strategic decision to act as if he enjoyed an unqualified mandate from the voters and sought to lead the nation from a position of power rather than weakness. This strategy was largely successful, as evidenced by Bush's ability to pass several high-priority agenda items during his first year in office, including significant tax cuts. No doubt, working with a Republican majority in both chambers of Congress rather than a Congress controlled by the opposition improved the likelihood of success.

The situation Bush inherited had also been shaped by several longer-term developments. In our view, during the last two decades of the twentieth century, presidents sought to meet a set of public expectations that call upon them to dominate national political leadership. Presidents Reagan, Bush, and Clinton surely were more successful in asserting executive power than their immediate three predecessors—Nixon, Ford, and Carter—but their efforts to reestablish presidential preeminence did not unfold without setbacks; there were periods when intense criticism of the president severely hampered their effectiveness in office, for example, the Iran-Contra investigations that occurred under Reagan and the year-long impeachment inquiry of Clinton. Both Presidents George H. W. Bush and Bill Clinton suffered periods when Congress, controlled by the opposition party, sought to construct an agenda totally independent of the president. Nonetheless, we see Presidents Reagan, Bush, and Clinton regaining significant influence that had been severely constrained during their three predecessors' administrations.

After reaching a pinnacle under Nixon, presidential influence hit a modern low during the decade of the 1970s. After the Johnson and Nixon administrations were widely viewed to have overstepped their constitutional boundaries in pursuing the Vietnam War and to have exercised unwarranted unilateral powers such as budget impoundments, Congress dramatically reasserted congressional prerogatives and developed new institutional resources to strengthen legislators' hands in dealing with presidents. These changes included the creation of the Congressional Budget Office (CBO), the establishment of a new budget process, the adoption of the War Powers Resolution, and a new assertiveness in a wide range of policy areas. These efforts and others had varying levels of success in reining in what scholars called "the imperial presidency" of the Johnson and Nixon years.[22]

For instance, the creation of the CBO significantly improved Congress's bargaining position with the president. The CBO provides nonpartisan budget estimates that Congress uses to challenge the president's own estimates produced by the Office of Management and Budget (OMB), the administration's principal budget experts. Since CBO estimates are widely considered more impartial than OMB's, the Congress is often able to win budget battles it might have lost in previous decades. Other efforts, like the adoption of the War Powers Resolution, have improved Congress's position to a lesser extent. Since its adoption, no president has acknowledged the constitutionality of the War Powers Resolution or asked Congress to declare war. Although they have abided by the resolution's explicit procedural requirements, there is no evidence that the resolution has increased congressional influence over presidential decisions to use military force. It is also unclear whether the resolution would be upheld or struck down by the courts if its provisions were ever enforced by Congress and subsequently challenged by an administration. Even the much ballyhooed changes in the budget process may have had the unintended consequence of enabling presidents to run roughshod over Congress. President Clinton used the budget process to make substantive policy changes that he might not have otherwise been able to implement.[23]

These Capitol Hill efforts to regain power were heavily shaped by the Watergate scandal, which ended with President Nixon's resignation from office and multiple felony convictions among his White House and campaign staff members. Two investigative reporters with the *Washington Post*, Bob Woodward and Carl Bernstein, had turned up much of the evidence that documented the Nixon White House conspiracy to cover up the 1972 illegal break-in at the Democratic Party's national headquarters in the Watergate apartment and office complex. A generation of journalists learned that fame and fortune could be won by exercising the press's independent function of skeptical questioning and investigation. The result was a patently more assertive media working in a political environment poisoned by the mutual mistrust built during the Nixon years. Nixon's efforts at strengthening presidential prerogative in dealing with Congress, including reliance on executive operations kept secret from all other centers of political influence, heightened suspicion and ultimately produced increased attention from the media and interest groups acting as watchdogs protecting the public interest. Congress was especially determined to lead rather than follow, and the press took no presidential statement at face value. From their supporters' perspective, Presidents Ford and Carter had the misfortune of serving during this period of mistrust that likely contributed to an inability to successfully pass agenda items.

Both Ford and Carter suffered defeats in their reelection campaigns with Carter defeating Ford in 1976 and Reagan unseating Carter in 1980. Reagan's victory against Carter was widely interpreted as a mandate for change, and during his first year in office, Reagan managed to pass some of the largest tax cuts in U.S. history with substantial support from Democrats. Reagan's electoral and honeymoon successes signified the release of the presidency from the probationary period suffered by Ford and Carter, and the return of a strong presidency with the institutional power to lead the Congress. Politics in Washington and legislative-executive relations since the Reagan administration regained some of the features of the pre-Watergate era while accommodating some new developments.

First, successive White Houses employed new media and public relations techniques designed to magnify the president's effect on the nation's agenda. There were periodic bouts of intense media scrutiny and criticism during this post-Watergate era; at other times, the media were surprisingly compliant in allowing presidents to reassert primacy.[24] So, while the media were poised to pounce on presidents, they also proved susceptible to the administrations' new manipulative techniques.

Second, during periods of unified party control—that is, when both the White House and Congress were controlled by the same party—there was substantial deference from Congress. However, during periods of divided party control, relations frequently disintegrated into total partisan warfare. The latter dominated because during the twenty-year period of 1981–2001, divided party control was the norm, prevailing for eighteen of the twenty years.

Third, although the partisan balance presented an unusual opportunity for congressional assertiveness, this was largely precluded by the institutional fragmentation that Congress was undergoing. With one major exception, there was a broad dispersion of power into the hands of committee and subcommittee chairs in the House of Representatives and into the hands of rank-and-file members in the Senate. Establishing central party leadership became an ongoing task that only met with clear success when Newt Gingrich served as speaker (1995–1998). Gingrich's efforts to provide national leadership from Congress echoed a less-known effort launched by Democratic Speaker Jim Wright during the administration of George H. W. Bush.

Fourth, in the larger political system, interest groups multiplied substantially and began using more sophisticated techniques of influence that involved mobilizing financial and membership resources to levels never previously reached in American politics.[25] This growth of the political class in the nation's capital provided an army of sophisticated operatives ready to be enlisted in the projects set forth by presidents and party strategists and to become engaged in the partisan warfare that was such a distinct feature during this two-decade period.

Finally, Congress continued to be of two minds regarding presidential power. At times, Congress provided presidents with new weapons in the institutional struggle including the line item veto[26] and fast-track authority to secure approval of new free trade agreements that sidestepped many of the delay strategies usually available to members of Congress.[27] However, Congress has agonized over extending some of these powers; for example, it was unwilling to extend fast-track authority on several occasions, and a Republican Congress seemed to regret establishment of the line item veto after it was wielded by Clinton rather than a Republican president.

Vice President Richard B. Cheney

Richard B. Cheney brought extensive Washington and political experience to the new administration, experience that easily eclipsed the president's own. Cheney completed more than two decades of public service that began in 1969 as an aide to Donald Rumsfeld in the Nixon White House and concluded in 1993 as George H. W. Bush's secretary of defense. Before his appointment to the cabinet, Cheney served as Gerald Ford's White House chief of staff and as the sole House member from Wyoming for ten years (1979–1989). During his congressional career, Cheney displayed particular interest in national intelligence issues and served six years as chairman of the Republican Policy Committee, two years as Republican Conference chairman, and two months as the minority whip. During his service as secretary of defense, the United States invaded Panama and conducted Operation Desert Storm, sometimes referred to as the first Persian Gulf War. He also presided over the Department of Defense at the time of the collapse of the Soviet Union (1991) and the subsequent redefinition of America's defense strategy in a dramatically altered world. Thus, Cheney brought to the Bush-Cheney ticket nearly a quarter-century of Washington experience, including service in two White Houses, a decade on Capitol Hill, and nearly four years as a cabinet secretary.

From the outset, President Bush made extensive use of Vice President Cheney's ties and experience. Cheney ran the truncated transition before the administration took office and headed the controversial energy task force formed during the new administration's first year in office whose secret talks with the energy community resulted in heated criticism from the media and environmental groups as well as several lawsuits. Another first-year task force, organized before the attacks on 9/11, focused on security issues, including ways to combat terrorism. Cheney was a leading figure in administration decision-making on Iraq, terrorism, homeland security, and the economy.[28] As presiding officer in the Senate, he was called upon to break seven tie votes through 2005[29] and used his offices in the Capitol building—one in the Senate and, for the first time in history, one off the House floor—as centers of operations for advancing the administration's congressional agenda.[30] During the busy first year of the administration, he met regularly with both the Senate and House Republican caucuses to ease the way for Bush's legislative program.[31]

Speaker of the House Dennis Hastert (R-IL)

Dennis Hastert has served the fourth district in Illinois for ten terms since first winning office in 1986 and enjoys wide support in the district with safe election margins. Hastert quickly rose up the leadership ranks in the Republican Party, serving as the chief deputy whip from 1994 until his election to speaker on January 9, 1999, when he succeeded Newt Gingrich. He has also served the Congress as the chairman of the House Government Reform and Oversight Committee Subcommittee of National Security, International Affairs, and Criminal Justice. While Hastert has held powerful positions for the majority of his tenure in office, he has maintained a low profile, shunning the public limelight that comes with such positions, and has instead focused on leading his party in the cloakrooms and offices of the Capitol. Before winning his House seat, Hastert was a government and history teacher as well as a wrestling coach for sixteen years, and in many ways his leadership style is to coach his colleagues. Hastert also spent six years in the Illinois House of Representatives where he worked on many of the same issues he champions today including tax reform, educational excellence, and economic development.[32]

Since his arrival in Washington, Hastert has dedicated himself to working on health-care policy. His continued efforts to improve health care through his seat on the Commerce Committee led to his appointment by Speaker Gingrich to lead the Speaker's Steering Committee on Health and the Health Resource Group. His efforts led to deep involvement in writing the 1996 health-care reform bill and the 1998 Patient Protection Act.[33]

Speaker Hastert is reserved in manner, a contrast with the dynamic Gingrich who preceded him in office. His reserved manner belies his sharp political acumen and dedication to advancement of his party through partisan warfare. While Speaker Hastert often rules the House with an iron fist, he also recognizes the importance of bipartisanship in finding solutions to national problems. According to Hastert, "Solutions to problems cannot be found in a pool of bitterness. They can be found in an environment in which we trust one another's word; where we generate heat and passion, but where we recognize that each member is equally important to our overall mission of improving the life of the American people."[34] Since 2000, Hastert worked closely with President Bush to move the president's agenda through the House and has served as a reliable and highly skilled ally in the effort. He stepped down as party leader following the elections of 2006 when Republicans lost the majority in the House of Representatives.

House Minority Leader Richard Gephardt (D-MO)

Richard Gephardt was first elected to the House in 1976 and served until retiring after running for president in 2004. As a freshman in the House, Gephardt won a coveted seat on the House Ways and Means Committee, allowing him to work on high-profile issues. His first few years in office were characterized by moderate policy positions, and these views are reflected in his hand in creating the moderate Democratic Leadership Council. In subsequent years, Gephardt's voting record became more liberal. Since his election to the House, Gephardt has always received good support from the voters in Missouri's third district, and his wide support across the Midwest allowed him to do well in Iowa during the 1988 and 2004 presidential election.

Gephardt began his ascension in the Democratic leadership early in his career. First, Gephardt was elected chairman of the Democratic caucus in 1984. After a failed bid for the presidency in 1988, Gephardt moved up to the number two leadership post in 1989 when Speaker Jim Wright and Whip Tony Coelho resigned in scandal and Gephardt was elected majority leader. In 1994, the Democrats lost fifty-two seats, the majority in the House, and Speaker Thomas S. Foley lost reelection.[35]

After the Democrats lost their majority in the House, Gephardt struggled to keep the Democratic caucus together as minority leader and find enough support among Republicans to pass Democratic agenda items. Once George W. Bush was elected president, Gephardt tried to help the party to win seats. The Democrats' regaining of the majority in 2002 put him in a good position to challenge Bush for the presidency in 2004. Gephardt retired from the House after the 2002 election when the Democrats once again lost seats so he could dedicate his full-time effort to running for president. Gephardt was considered a front-runner based on his strong organization in Iowa, and the Midwest, but was quickly eliminated early in the primary season.

Senate Majority Leader Bill Frist (R-TN)

Bill Frist was first elected to the U.S. Senate in 1994 and was the only challenger to defeat an incumbent senator during the election cycle. Frist is a famous name in Tennessee as his family has lived in Tennessee since the settlement of the state. Frist parlayed that notoriety into a Senate seat and an overwhelming reelection in 2000. Frist enjoyed a quick rise to prominence in the Senate. He served as a deputy whip in 1999 before election as chairman of the National Republican Senatorial Committee in 2000 when he directed the successful reelection that saw the Republicans win back majority control from the Democrats. In 2002, Frist replaced Trent Lott as the Senate majority leader, becoming the least tenured senator in history to become floor leader.[36]

Frist gained fame as the first practicing physician elected to the Senate since 1928, having worked as a transplant surgeon for twenty years before going into politics. Frist's interests in health care won him a seat on the Senate Health, Labor, Education, and Pension Committee where he has worked to improve the nation's health-care system. Frist's biggest contribution in health-care policy was sponsoring legislation to combat the global HIV/AIDS pandemic. President Bush proposed the idea in his 2003 State of the Union address, and Frist's legislation funded the HIV/AIDS effort with $15 billion. This legislation is also emblematic of how closely Frist worked with the Bush administration to advance the president's agenda in the Senate; Frist took a personal interest in seeing that Bush's agenda items were passed.[37]

Support for the president and his agenda put Frist in a precarious political position, however. As a front-runner for the 2008 Republican nomination for president, Frist tried to balance his support for the president with his need to define himself for his presidential run. Other conflicts of interest include his intervention in the Terry Schiavo case in Florida. Democratic senators were critical of Frist's diagnosis of Schiavo after seeing only a videotape recording and charged that he was misusing his medical training to improve his image among social conservatives. He chose not to seek reelection to the Senate in 2006.

Senate Minority Leader Tom Daschle (D-SD)

Tom Daschle was elected to the Senate in 1986 after serving four terms in the House and rose through the ranks to become the Democratic leader in the Senate in 1995. Daschle was first elected to the House in 1978 when he won an open seat in the House of Representatives. Throughout his tenure in office, Daschle faced tight elections. He won his House seat in 1978 by a margin of just 139 votes. In 1982, after South Dakota lost one of its two seats in the House due to reapportionment, Daschle narrowly won reelection to the new at-large seat. In 1986, Daschle won his Senate seat with 52 percent of the vote. He was easily reelected in 1992 and 1998, but his luck in close elections came to an end in 2004 when Daschle lost his Senate seat to Republican John Thune in another close election, 51 to 49 percent.

Daschle always had a liberal voting record in Congress. He was a strong supporter of President Clinton's failed health-care proposal and long supported agricultural subsidies that buoyed South Dakota farmers. In January of 1989, Daschle was named the cochairman of the Senate Democratic Policy Committee and became a key ally of Majority Leader George Mitchell in his leadership team. In 1994, Mitchell retired, and Daschle won the minority leader position by one vote over Chris Dodd.[38]

Like his leadership counterpart in the House, Dick Gephardt, Daschle's role in the Senate was largely obstructing the Republican majority during most of his tenure as Democratic leader. Daschle served as the minority leader from 1995–1999, but after the 2000 elections the Senate membership was split with fifty Democrats and fifty Republicans.

Soon Senator Jim Jeffords (I-VT) left the Republican Party and cast his procedural votes with the Democrats, making Daschle the majority leader. Daschle faced a tough situation in the period between Jeffords's split from the Republican Party and the 2002 midterm elections because he was presiding over the narrowest Senate majority in over forty years. As the majority leader, Daschle was the highest-ranking elected Democrat and hence was the de facto leader of the party, making his defeat in 2004 even sweeter for the Republican Party.

The tight seat margin in the Senate meant that everything the Senate did would be more politically charged as both parties tried to position themselves to pick up seats in 2002. Daschle's leadership style in the Senate was highly partisan with a soft-spoken image. He used this image to stave off his opponents' attacks while steadily trying to move the Democratic Party forward. Daschle has never had the reputation of being a great legislator with the power or inclination to move the Senate toward passing his legislation, but he was the epitome of a partisan warrior with a focus on winning elections. As a party leader, Daschle embraced the opportunity to highlight the differences between the Democratic and Republican agendas and used his electoral acumen to improve the party's electoral fortunes.

House Minority Leader Nancy Pelosi (D-CA)

Nancy Pelosi was first elected to public office in 1987 during a special election but had long served the Democratic Party before her arrival in Congress. As the daughter of retired Representative Thomas D'Alessandro (D-MD), Pelosi holds deep roots in Democratic politics. She has been involved in politics for decades and eventually climbed to the top of the ladder in the 1980s, serving as the California Democratic chair in the early 1980s and as the Democratic Senatorial Campaign Committee finance chair in 1985. Since her arrival in the House, she has been a liberal stalwart, which one might expect since she represents a district that includes about 80 percent of liberal hotbed San Francisco. Pelosi's first position in the party leadership came in 2001 when she was elected Democratic whip. Usually, party members serve the party in one or more positions before being elevated to the top of the leadership structure.

Pelosi became the first woman to lead a congressional party when she was elected as Democratic leader in the fall of 2002, when Representative Gephardt retired to run for president in 2004, and she became the first female speaker of the House after Democrats won the majority in 2006.

Since her arrival in Congress, Pelosi has worked on issues with ties to her San Francisco district including trade with and human rights in China and HIV/AIDS. Pelosi is a longtime critic of China's human rights record and lobbied against most-favored-nation status. She used her seat on the Appropriations Committee to fund multiple HIV/AIDS related programs and projects. Pelosi has enjoyed consistently strong support in her district, winning reelection with an excess of 70 or even 80 percent of the vote.[39]

Senate Minority Leader Harry Reid (D-NV)

Harry Reid's political career began in 1968 when he was elected to the State Assembly. He subsequently served as Nevada's lieutenant governor and head of the Nevada Gaming Commission. As gaming commissioner, Reid worked to clean up Las Vegas gambling. These efforts earned him death threats, and his wife reportedly found a bomb attached to their car. He ran for and won a House seat in 1982 in a district centered on Las Vegas before winning a Senate race in 1986.

Reid is a moderate Democrat who has expressed opposition to abortion and supported regulatory reform efforts—both conservative positions—in addition to his support for liberal programs like President Clinton's health-care initiative. According to Senator Orrin Hatch (R-UT), "We all respect Senator Reid. He is one of the moderate voices around here who tries to get things to work."[40] Reid presents himself as the son of a hard rock miner and lives in his boyhood hometown of Searchlight, Nevada. Reid's legislative record is rife with issues important to Nevadans like securing water rights for the state, protecting the interests of the gaming industry, and fighting the Yucca Mountain nuclear waste repository being built in Nevada.

Reid is serving in his fourth term in the Senate. He was elected as the Democratic whip in 1998 and as the Democratic leader in 2004 following the defeat of then Democratic Leader Tom Daschle (D-SD). Reid has won consistently comfortable yet narrow reelection, receiving between 50 and 60 percent of the vote in each of his reelection efforts. Reid's early tenure as Democratic leader has been as the minority leader, so he has spent considerable time raising the profile of Democratic issues, but his most memorable moment occurred away from the cameras. In November of 2005, Reid forced the Senate into closed session to press Republicans and Senate Intelligence Committee Chairman Pat Roberts (R-KS) to speed up the investigation into the possible misuse of Iraq war intelligence.[41] After Democrats won a Senate majority in the 2006 elections, Reid became Senate majority leader.

Tumultuous Twenty-First Century Politics

As the victor in the last presidential election of the twentieth century, George W. Bush confronted several novel features when he assumed office. Partisan conflict, not readily measurable, probably reached a modern high during the election. For the first time in more than a century, the winner of the popular vote plurality did not also win an absolute majority in the Electoral College. The Democratic candidate, Al Gore, won a popular vote plurality of 539,898 over Bush, but Bush narrowly carried the Electoral College 271–266.[42] Moreover, the presidential balloting was not resolved quickly; rather, the close result in Florida gave Bush a slight, 537-vote advantage and Florida's twenty-five electoral votes provided the winning margin for Bush. Gore challenged the close Florida vote, and a series of local recounts and state, as well as federal, court decisions prolonged the drama for thirty-six days after Election Day. The long delay ensured that partisan passions would run high, fanned by the media's minute-by-minute coverage of a complex conflict resolution process. By the time the Supreme Court intervened and issued a decision in *Bush v. Gore* that halted the Florida recounts, partisan tempers had risen to historically high levels.[43]

When the Democrats lost the White House in 2000, they were shut out of national power for the first time in more than four decades. Republicans held onto their majorities in both the House (221–212) and the Senate (50–50 with Vice President Cheney breaking the tie in favor of the Republicans). The last instance of unified Republican control of both houses of Congress and the White House was in 1953–1955, the first two years of the Eisenhower administration.

George W. Bush therefore entered the presidency with an advantage denied to Presidents Nixon, Ford, Reagan, and George H. W. Bush—the support of a Republican-controlled Congress. Republicans had held a majority in both the House and the Senate for the previous six years but had been prevented from achieving their most important policy goals by a Democratic president and his Capitol Hill allies. Clinton had usurped some Republican issues through his famous strategy of "triangulation," adopting modified Republican ideas as his own and adopting positions between Republican and Democratic members of Congress. This was Clinton's strategy in pushing through welfare reform in 1996, a policy change that most Democrats opposed and which was regarded as a "Republican issue." Thus, Republicans enthusiastically welcomed one of their own into the White House.

But Bush entered office at a time when the "venomous atmosphere"[44] created by the impeachment and attempted removal of President Bill Clinton still lingered. The impeachment battle that unfolded during 1998 meant that even before the hotly contested presidential election of 2000, Democrats and Republicans were at each others' throats. Republican members of the House became so frustrated and infuriated with Clinton's ability to block their policy goals and avoid accountability for his personal misconduct that, when given the opportunity, they voted to impeach him on two articles, perjury (228–206) and obstruction of justice (221–212) for lying about his affair with White House intern Monica Lewinsky and then trying to cover it up.[45] Only five House Democrats agreed with the Republican action, though far more would have supported a "censure" of the president that would have attracted bipartisan approval. This lesser action was prevented by the Republican Party leaders. The Republican Senate, however, did not share the same depth of enmity and was unable to muster even a majority vote, let alone the two-thirds vote required for removal, on either count when the charges were presented in the chamber with Chief Justice William Rehnquist presiding over only the second attempted removal of a president in U.S. history.[46] To add insult to injury, Clinton's public approval ratings actually rose during the yearlong impeachment process. As both Democrats and Republicans maneuvered in the lead-up to the high-stakes 2000 election, all communication broke down between the parties' respective leaders in the House who had not spoken for months.[47]

To say, then, that Bush's victory was welcomed by Capitol Hill Republicans is an understatement. Republicans in Congress looked forward to the opportunity to put their agenda into place without the threat of vetoes or battles with an articulate and politically astute opponent. Clinton used the veto thirty-seven times, including fourteen appropriations bill vetoes, and repeatedly threatened to do so. During the 106th Congress, the last with which he worked, Clinton cast five vetoes that blocked Republican-backed legislation including the repeal of the federal estate tax and the "so-called marriage penalty."[48] Bush also inherited a nation enjoying relative peace and prosperity. Budget surpluses, the first in three decades, had been registered during Clinton's final three years in office, and there were no immediate foreign crises to deal with. Nonetheless, there were challenges ahead, including the slowing economy.

During the presidential campaign, Bush kept his distance from Republican candidates for Congress, but after the election he met with party leaders as part of transition planning even before Democrat Al Gore conceded defeat on December 13, 2000. Congressional party leaders had held their positions for four (Hastert) and six years (Lott); they had already mastered their jobs and stood ready to work with a Republican president as the majority party. But the new relationship would require a change. With a Democrat in the White House, the Republicans had been proposing program initiatives. As Jennifer Dunn (R-WA) acknowledged in December 2000, instead of Congressional leaders setting the agenda,

> We all have to remember that now Bush is the leader . . . We've got a president now. A lot of the work that we will be doing in both houses will be the interpretation of the Bush agenda.[49]

Bush also had at his side a Washington-savvy ally; Vice President Cheney quickly became Bush's trusted emissary to Capitol Hill, given the job of bargaining with the party's D.C. chieftains. Cheney's knowledge of the ways of Washington ensured that Bush, yet another outsider president elected to serve in D.C., was less likely to experience the bumps that outsiders Carter and Clinton had suffered during their administration's initial months even while working with a Congress controlled by their own party. More like Reagan, Bush made a point during his first months in office to solicit congressional opinions and worked hard to develop his personal ties to members of Congress, Republicans and Democrats alike.

Cheney's previous experience was relevant in another way. As Ford's White House chief of staff, Cheney had suffered through the erosion of presidential influence that followed the Watergate crisis. When many congressional Republicans lost their seats in the 1974 midterm elections that shortly followed Nixon's resignation, Ford was left with lopsided Democratic majorities in both the House and Senate and resorted to using the veto more heavily than most presidents, his lone weapon in trying to thwart the Democrats' agenda. Cheney believed that the erosion of presidential power had continued during the Carter, Reagan, Bush, and Clinton administrations. He was determined to help President George W. Bush regain a measure of that influence and restore the presidency's prerogatives.

Ignoring much of the advice he received in the media to propose a modest, nonpartisan, middle-of-the-road agenda, Bush quickly established a legislative style: propose bold initiatives in Republican red, not bipartisan proposals in pale pinks. The president put forward a dramatic ten-year tax cut proposal as his first major initiative—a substantial expansion of Republicans' unsuccessful efforts in the previous Congress—arguing that the substantial federal budget surplus, a legacy of the Clinton years, was the people's money and ought to be returned to their pockets. When the economy turned downward, Bush added the argument that tax cuts would encourage consumer spending. Despite speculation that Bush might try to reach out to Democrats by selecting several Democrats to serve in cabinet posts, Bush chose only one, Norman Mineta, a former Congressman who had also served as Clinton's secretary of commerce, to serve as secretary of transportation. The press reported that other overtures to Democrats were rebuffed.[50] During the transition, president-elect Bush conducted two meetings at his ranch that included prominent Democrats, one on defense and one on education. The hope for bipartisanship and becoming a "unifier" in Washington were also prominent in Bush's transition speeches.[51]

But partisanship was deeply entrenched on Capitol Hill. As the House majority whip (later to become the majority leader), Tom DeLay, responded to Democrats' postelection calls for bipartisanship,

> For the first time in 50 years, we have both houses and the White House. The difference now is that they won't have a Democratic president to veto this stuff . . . We will have a president who will be supporting it and who will have worked with Democrats and Republicans to fashion something meaningful . . . Democrats are trying to dictate the Bush agenda by defining bipartisanship . . . They're more or less saying it's [bipartisanship] the goal of a successful Bush administration, and of course Gephardt and Daschle are saying we have to buy into their partisanship—then we'll be "bipartisan" . . . They talked about a bipartisan effort, which we welcome, but bipartisanship doesn't mean they get to pick the agenda.[52]

The president's principal bipartisan effort was education reform (see chapter 2) for which he actively solicited the support of Mr. Democrat—Ted Kennedy, the longtime senator from Massachusetts who had publicly ridiculed Bush's father at the 1988 Democratic nominating convention. In general, the president leaned more to "party building" than "coalition building." The former stresses appeals to his own partisans on the Hill and their priorities rather than trying to find common ground with opposition party members. In making this choice, Bush opted not to embrace "compassionate triangulation," the strategy encouraged by two former White House legislative liaison aides, one a Republican and one a Democrat, who suggested the president keep "the proper distance from the extremes of both parties on the Hill" while "maintaining charm and compassion when distancing oneself from lawmakers."[53]

But by the end of his first year in office, even Republicans chafed at the president's expansive interpretation of presidential prerogatives vis-à-vis the Congress. As one close observer of the White House noted, "Bush's habit of acting first and asking later has set some [Republican] teeth on edge."[54] The administration refused to provide a Republican-controlled congressional committee with information they sought as part of investigations, an act justified under the doctrine of executive privilege; the president also made aggressive use of executive orders rather than legislation to accomplish some policy goals; and the administration unilaterally announced its intention to withdraw from several major international treaties. As White House Press Secretary Ari Fleischer explained, withholding information was part of a larger interpretation of presidential power:

> The pendulum probably shifted too far toward the Congress, in terms of probing the Administration, during the Clinton years . . . I think there's been a healthy rebalancing so the executive can have the authority to get the job done . . . Is it because we have something to hide? No. It's because it's the best way to have a healthy discussion inside an Administration. And that serves the President.[55]

And the administration offered an elaborate legal justification for its exercise of power after the attacks on September 11, 2001. Alberto R. Gonzales, then White House counsel and later attorney general in the second Bush administration, defended these actions with an expansive reading of the president's constitutional powers:

> The President, as the head of the executive branch and the commander in chief of our armed forces and the only political leader directly accountable to all Americans, has the unique personal responsibility to ensure the safety and security of our citizens . . . The Framers, in The Federalist Papers, spoke explicitly about the need for a unitary executive presidency, precisely to allow for bigger effectiveness and accountability in the conduct of our foreign and military affairs.[56]

In short, George Bush was reasserting the power of the presidency to shape national affairs and serve as the nation's principal leader. As the case studies that follow will demonstrate, Congress would have much to say about national problems, and Republican members of Congress sometimes broke with the president even during his first term in office.

Unified-party control and the prospect for Republican domination, however, were short-lived. Starting with a 50–50 split in the Senate that could only be broken by Vice President Richard Cheney casting a tiebreaking vote, the Republican majority disappeared when Senator Jim Jeffords of Vermont changed his party affiliation from Republican to Independent in June 2001. Thus, for the next eighteen months, Democrats controlled the Senate with a bare majority 50–49 with Independent Jeffords voting with the Democrats, and Republicans held a small majority in the House. Divided government ended with the 2002 midterm elections when the Republicans won handily by gaining a majority in the Senate (51–48 and Jeffords the lone Independent) and expanding their majority in the House (229–205).

The controversial 2000 presidential election and narrow majorities in the Congress galvanized partisan warriors on each side of the aisle in Congress and in the national party leadership. The closeness of the 2000 election convinced both sides they could win in 2002. With narrow Republican majorities in both the House and Senate, the Democrats had a chance to recapture both in a single election while the Republicans were at risk of losing both and wanted to use the 2002 election to expand their majorities to a more comfortable margin. Thus, much of 2001 was consumed by partisan strategizing and confrontation.

Partisanship was suddenly cast aside in the wake of the terrorist attacks of September 11, 2001, at least on the surface. On September 20, 2001, exactly eight months from the time he was sworn in as president, George W. Bush returned to Capitol Hill to deliver a speech to a joint session of Congress. The public support from Republicans and Democrats alike was no doubt reassuring to a national television audience. Bush struck a unifying theme: "Ladies and gentlemen of the Congress, I thank you," the president said, "for what you have already done and for what we will do together."[57] Congressional leaders who had often behaved as sworn enemies strove to define new, cooperative work relationships. Senators Lott and Daschle, their parties' leaders in the Senate, delivered a joint response to the president's address rather than the Democrats' customary one-party response. House Speaker Dennis Hastert and Minority Leader Richard Gephardt who had barely spoken to one another for two years began to coordinate their activities daily after spending much of a day together in a bomb shelter. An eerie reminder of the recent tragedy was Vice President Cheney's absence from the president's speech, during which he ordinarily presides in conjunction with the House speaker; Cheney remained at an undisclosed location to ensure that a repeat attack would not wipe out both of the nation's elected executive leaders. More subtly, the congressional campaign committees that were busily raising money for the next round of elections suspended fund-raising operations.

Beneath the surface, there were still disagreements. The Democrats objected to allowing the administration to decide unilaterally how to spend a $40 billion relief package. Behind the scenes, negotiations were needed to establish terms acceptable to both sides, and the package passed Congress unanimously. Again, negotiations resolved differences over authorizing the president to respond to the attack with military force; only a single vote was cast against this resolution. Everyone on Capitol Hill tiptoed around the deep differences that lingered over the administration's agenda that had been at the center of their attention before the attacks took place; for a while, the United States seemed to enjoy a "unity government" of the sort more commonly found in parliamentary systems during times of national emergency. But Karen Foerstel and David Nather of *CQ Weekly* forecast growing disputes in the future:

> Few in this War Congress, of either party, will be content for long to serve only as an applauding chorus for the president. Their disputes with one another and with the White House have not disappeared. They have simply been taken out of public earshot. The strains of a 535-member legislative body trying to speak with one voice may have been muffled, but they have not been silenced. In the weeks ahead, they will undoubtedly grow louder.[58]

Thus, the new millennium began in a truly tumultuous political setting. From remarkably high levels of partisanship at the year's outset, political conflict had receded to unusually low levels by the year's end; but partisan struggle was rekindled as the election approached in 2002 and the president campaigned aggressively for his own party's candidates. Mobilization for the Iraq war and the long shadow of the September 11 attacks created a political environment in which those who criticized the administration's position on the war on terror, like Senator Daschle, were labeled as unpatriotic or soft on terror. The 2004 election again triggered partisan warfare followed by a government adrift with a politically wounded president trying to recover popular support just months after winning reelection. The Bush-Kerry contest was the most expensive in history with both candidates raising more than $250 million to win the nomination.[59] (President Bush, of course, ran unopposed so the money was used to begin campaigning against the Democratic nominee whose identity was known by mid-March.) Negative campaigning thrived, mostly conducted by groups supporting the candidates but not officially associated with the campaigns. Kerry's war record was questioned, and he was branded a "flip-flopper," someone who changed positions on the issues and therefore was not trustworthy as commander in chief. Bush's lack of military service was questioned, and Kerry criticized Bush for knowingly misleading the nation and Congress on weapons of mass destruction in Iraq. Both parties did a better job at getting their voters to the polls; nationally, turnout rose to 55.3 percent of the voting age population and 60.9 percent of the voting eligible population.[60] The Democrats' ticket of Kerry-Edwards won nearly eight million more votes than Gore-Lieberman had in 2000, but Bush-Cheney increased their total by eleven and a half million, thereby securing a comfortable popular vote victory margin of three million votes. The Bush-Cheney ticket also increased its margin in the Electoral College, 286–251, whereas the 2000 election had seen a narrower margin of 271–266. In 2004, the election's outcome hinged on returns in Ohio rather than

Florida, but Bush's margin of victory in the buckeye state exceeded 118,000, far more robust than his 2000 margin of victory in Florida, a mere 537 votes.[61] Moreover, Bush was the first victorious candidate since 1988 to win a majority (rather than a plurality) of the popular vote. As he basked in the glow of a clear-cut victory without questions about the legitimacy of his power, Bush promised to use the "political capital" earned in the campaign to pursue a number of prominent policy initiatives, including Social Security and tax reform.[62] Soon afterward, however, as news from Iraq worsened, gas prices soared, and Hurricane Katrina ravaged the Gulf Coast, Bush's public approval ratings began a nosedive that took him to the mid-30s level in the Gallup Poll (and even lower in some other polls) by the end of 2005.[63]

The six case studies that follow examine how Bush and Congress used their leadership skills to negotiate this perilous political landscape of bitter partisanship, narrow congressional margins, and war in Afghanistan and then Iraq. With a minefield of contextual obstacles blocking the way, Bush and Congress were able to find successful resolution to some national problems (education reform, campaign finance reform, intelligence reform, creating the Department of Homeland Security), failed to find successful solutions (Social Security), and came to solutions that have yet to be fully implemented (Hurricane Katrina). In each case, however, the strategies and actions of policymakers proved critical to the outcomes.

NOTES

1. Mark A. Peterson, *Legislating Together: The White House and Capitol Hill from Eisenhower to Reagan* (Cambridge, MA: Harvard University Press, 1990), 2.

2. See Bert A. Rockman, *The Leadership Question: The Presidency and the American Political System* (New York: Praeger, 1984), xv–xvi and chapter 1.

3. See Rockman, *The Leadership Question*, xv–xvi and chapter 1.

4. See Rockman, *The Leadership Question,* 41.

5. Edward S. Corwin, *The President: Office and Powers, 1787–1984,* 5th ed. (New York: New York University Press, 1984), 201. Corwin used the phrase in reference to foreign policy, but it is equally appropriate to other areas, as well.

6. Arthur M. Schlesinger Jr., *The Imperial Presidency* (Boston: Houghton-Mifflin, 1973).

7. Aaron Wildavsky, "The Two Presidencies," in *The Presidency,* ed. Aaron Wildavsky (Boston: Little Brown, 1969), 230–43. This is a reprint of Wildavsky's original essay that appeared in *Transaction* (December 1966).

8. Richard Fleisher and Jon R. Bond, "Are There Two Presidencies?" *Journal of Politics* 50 (1988): 747–67.

9. James M. Lindsay and Randall B. Ripley, "Foreign and Defense Policy in Congress: A Research Agenda for the 1990s" *Legislative Studies Quarterly* 17 (1992): 417–49.

10. I. M. Destler, "Congress and Foreign Policy at the Century's End," in *Congress Reconsidered*, ed. Lawrence C. Dodd and Bruce I. Oppenheimer (Washington, DC: CQ Press, 2001).

11. Theodore Lowi, *The End of Liberalism: The Second Republic of the United States* (New York: Norton, 1979).

12. Barry Schwartz, *George Washington: The Making of an American Symbol* (Ithaca, NY: Cornell University Press, 1987). Also see George C. Edwards III, *On Deaf Ears: The Limits of the Bully Pulpit* (New Haven: Yale University Press, 2003), chapter 5.

13. Bruce Buchanan, *The Citizen's Presidency: Standards of Choice and Judgment* (Washington, DC: CQ Press, 1987), 25.

14. John Kessel argues that presidency-watchers are too eager to stress "failures" and that "every administration has successes, failures, and mixed outcomes." There is too little appreciation for this mixed record. Kessel, *Presidents, the Presidency, and the Political Environment* (Washington, DC: CQ Press, 2001), x.

15. Paul Brace and Barbara Hinckley, *Follow the Leader: Opinion Polls and Modern Presidents* (New York: Basic Books, 1992).

16. Barbara Hinckley, *The Symbolic Presidency: How Presidents Portray Themselves* (New York: Routledge, 1990).

17. Thomas E. Cronin and Michael A. Genovese, *The Paradoxes of the American Presidency* (Oxford: Oxford University Press, 2004), 1–26. Others have also pointed out the incompatibility of public expectations; see George C. Edwards III, *At the Margins: Presidential Leadership of Congress* (New Haven: Yale University Press, 1989), 13.

18. Hinckley, *The Symbolic Presidency,* 10.

19. Barbara Sinclair, *Unorthodox Lawmaking: New Legislative Processes in the U.S. Congress,* 2nd edition (Washington, DC: CQ Press, 2000).

20. See our more detailed discussion of the 2000 election below for more detail.

21. While winning the presidency without a plurality of popular votes is quite uncommon, failing to win a majority of the popular vote had become the norm. Until the election of 2004, Bush's father was the last presidential candidate to win a majority of popular votes, doing so in 1988.

22. Schlesinger, *The Imperial Presidency.*

23. Sinclair, *Unorthodox Lawmaking.*

24. Mark Hertsgaard, *On Bended Knee: The Press and the Reagan Presidency* (New York: Farrar Straus & Giroux, 1988).

25. Jack L. Walker, "Origins and Maintenance of Interest Groups in America," *American Political Science Review* 77, no. 2 (June 1983): 390–406.

26. Line item veto power was short-lived, going into effect during 1997 but becoming inoperative in June 1998 when it was declared unconstitutional by the Supreme Court. It was used by President Bill Clinton to delete items in eleven bills. Victoria Allred, "Versatility with the Veto," *CQ Weekly,* 20 January 2001, 175.

27. Under fast-track authority, presidents exercise greater control over negotiating complex trade agreements, and the Congressional approval process provides for mandatory deadlines, no amendments of legislation, and limited debate. The authority was extended to presidents from 1974 to 1994 but lapsed until August 2002 after an eighteen-month effort by the Bush administration to have it restored. For a general discussion, see Lenore Sek, "IB10084: Fast-Track Authority for Trade Agreements," *CRS Issue Brief for Congress,* 4 May 2001.

28. Elisabeth Bumiller and Eric Schmitt, "Threats and Responses; The Vice President," *New York Times,* 31 January 2003, A1.

29. Secretary of the U.S. Senate, "Votes by Vice Presidents to Break Tie Votes in the Senate," <http://www.senate.gov/pagelayout/reference/four_column_table/Tie_Votes .htm> (8 July 2006).

30. <http://archives.cnn.com/2001/ALLPOLITICS/stories/01/05/cheney.hill/> (8 July 2006).

31. Nicholas Lemann, "The Quiet Man: Dick Cheney's Discreet Rise to Unprecedented Power," *New Yorker,* 7 May 2001, 56.

32. Michael Barone and Grant Ujifusa, *The Almanac of American Politics* (Washington, DC: National Journal, 1997), 505–6.

33. Dennis Hastert's House webpage, <http://www.house.gov/hastert/bio.shtml> (10 July 2006).

34. Dennis Hastert's House webpage.

35. Barone and Ujifusa, *The Almanac of American Politics*, 1997, 832–36.

36. Bill Frist's Senate webpage, < http://frist.senate.gov/> (5 June 2006); Barone and Ujifusa, *The Almanac of American Politics*, 1997, 1309.

37. Bill Frist's Senate webpage.

38. Barone and Ujifusa, *The Almanac of American Politics*, 1997, 1298.

39. Nancy Pelosi's House website, <http://www.house.gov/pelosi/> (4 June 2006); Barone and Ujifusa, *The Almanac of American Politics*, 1997, 164.

40. Harry Reid's Senate webpage, < http://reid.senate.gov/> (2 June 2006).

41. Harry Reid's Senate webpage; Barone and Ujifusa, *The Almanac of American Politics*, 1997, 882.

42. To win in the Electoral College, a candidate must receive an absolute majority of the ballots cast, 270 of the 538 votes. One elector from the District of Columbia, Barbara Lett-Simmons, cast a blank ballot instead of voting for Gore in order to protest the absence of home rule in the District. This accounts for the total number of ballots being less than 538. In all states except Maine and Nebraska, the winner of a plurality of popular votes in a state receives all of the states electoral votes. Hence, Bush's plurality of 537 votes of 5,963,110 cast in Florida resulted in his receiving all 25 of Florida's electoral votes.

43. For an extensive discussion of the Florida results in 2000 see Political Staff of the Washington Post, *Deadlock: The Inside Story of America's Closest Election* (New York: Public Affairs, 2001).

44. Sue Kirchoff, "A Conservative Juggernaut," *CQ Weekly,* 19 December 1998, 3340.

45. Jeffrey L. Katz and Andrew Taylor, "House Accuses Clinton of Perjury, Obstruction," *CQ Weekly*, 19 December 1998, 3220. Two other articles of impeachment failed. House Republican Party leaders had refused to allow a vote to censure Clinton, an action that would have attracted more bipartisan support.

46. On the charge of perjury by lying to a grand jury, the vote was 45–55. On the charge of obstructing justice, the vote was 50–50 with five Republicans voting with a unified Democratic delegation. Carol J. Doherty, "Senate Acquits Clinton," *CQ Weekly,* 13 February 1999, 361.

47. Karen Foerstel, "House: The Limits of Outreach," *CQ Weekly,* 11 November 2000, 2649.

48. Mary Agnes Carey, "Parties' Ambitious Agendas Made Little Headway in 106th," *CQ Weekly,* 16 December 2000, 2883.

49. Quoted in Lori Nitschke, "Bush's Capitol Course Relies on Cheney's Steadying Hand," *CQ Weekly,* 16 December 2000, 2842.

50. Mark Murray, "An Outsider Moves In," *National Journal,* 26 January 2001. Reportedly, former Senator Sam Nunn had been approached about becoming secretary of defense and Senator John Breaux (D-LA) about becoming secretary of energy.

51. Dana Milbank, "Bipartisanship's Lesson: It's Easy Come, Easy Go," *Washington Post,* 9 January 2001, A2.

52. As quoted in Ralph Z. Hallow and John Godfrey, "Bipartisan Is Two-Way Street, DeLay Cautions Democrats," *Washington Times*, 15 December 2000, A1.

53. Gary Andres and Patrick Griffin, "Will 'Compassionate Triangulation' Work for Bush, Congress?" *Roll Call*, 15 January 2001.

54. Alexis Simendinger, "Power of One," *National Journal*, 25 January 2002.

55. Simendinger, "Power of One."

56. Simendinger, "Power of One." Drawn from a November 30, 2001 speech to the American Bar Association.

57. Karen Foerstel and David Nather, "Beneath Capitol's Harmony, Debate Simmers Patiently," *CQ Weekly,* 22 September 2001, 2186.

58. Foerstel and Nather, "Beneath Capitol's Harmony," 2186.

59. Bush raised nearly $275 million and Kerry more than $250 million. See Political Money Line, <http://www.tray.com/cgiwin/pml1_sql_PRESIDENTIAL.exe?DoFn=2004> (12 July 2006).

60. There is a controversy about whether voter turnout should be measured based on all the age-eligible residents (the traditional measure) or be adjusted for only those who meet other eligibility requirements, that is, legal citizenship and absence of criminal record. See the United States Elections Project, <http://elections.gmu.edu/VOTER_TURNOUT_2004.HTM> (12 July 2006).

61. An excellent source for presidential election returns is Dave Leip's Atlas of U.S. Presidential Elections, <http://uselectionatlas.org/> (15 July 2006).

62. George W. Bush Press Conference November 4, 2004, <http://www.whitehouse.gov/news/releases/2004/11/20041104-5.html> (12 July 2006).

63. See the Gallup Poll data at The American Presidency Project, <http://www.presidency.ucsb.edu/data/popularity.php> (12 July 2006).

2

No Child Left Behind

President George W. Bush confronted a highly unfavorable set of conditions as he took office on January 20, 2001, and sought to deliver on his campaign's top priority—education reform—popularly known as No Child Left Behind (NCLB). The odds were stacked against winning reauthorization of the Elementary and Secondary Education Act (ESEA), first passed in 1965 and most recently rewritten in 1994. Bush faced significant obstacles including a tenuous mandate, partisan conflict in the Congress, and failed education reform in the previous Congress due to intense partisan disagreement.

First, Bush had just won the most divisive presidential election in more than a century that was not concluded until December 12, 2000, when a Supreme Court ruling halted a vote recount in Florida. Bush's administration began with modest public support, a mere 55 percent rather than the higher levels normally enjoyed by a new president.[1] Despite a small margin of victory and lower-than-normal public support for a new president, Bush was determined to launch his administration as though it had received a mandate.

Second, the partisan conflict was exacerbated by razor-thin Republican majorities in the House and Senate. Republicans held a margin of 222 to 213 in the House, and the Senate faced a 50–50 tie that could be broken by the vice president. During the Clinton years, Republicans had chafed under their inability to enact their own program; they were repeatedly frustrated by Clinton's strategies. Thus, there was a strong desire to move forward on a broad range of issues that had been bottled up over the previous six years.

Finally, one of the areas where partisan conflict had been especially intense in the previous (106th) Congress was education policy. Despite efforts in both the House and the Senate, Congress allowed authorization for ESEA to lapse; Congress continued funding for existing programs into the next fiscal year, but everyone expected intense conflict to resume. Battle lines had hardened around a number of highly controversial policy issues: Republicans pushed school vouchers that would provide public funding for students to attend private schools, anathema to Democrats and their allies in the major teachers unions; some legislators called for a national test to gauge state performance in advancing students, a reform that conservative Republicans regarded as hiding a liberal agenda and invading local control of education; and school safety, a concern raised by the 1999 shooting deaths of students at Columbine High School in Colorado, led Democrats to calls for expanded federal gun control, aggressively opposed by most Republicans and the National Rifle Association.

On top of these initial difficulties, Bush encountered additional problems during his first year in office that threatened to derail passage of landmark education legislation:

1. Republicans lost control of the Senate in May 2001 when Senator Jim Jeffords of Vermont bolted from the Republican Party and became an Independent who caucused with the Democrats. At the time of this defection, Jeffords served as chair of the Health, Education, Labor, and Pensions Committee that had jurisdiction over ESEA.
2. In the midst of negotiations to reconcile differences between House and Senate versions of ESEA, terrorists attacked the World Trade Center in New York City and the Pentagon just outside Washington, D.C., and crashed another plane in Pennsylvania.[2] These attacks on September 11, 2001, triggered a national crisis that redirected presidential and congressional attention to national security and homeland security, concerns that were a long way from the domestic issues that had dominated the nation's agenda to that point.
3. Even as the nation prepared to take action against terrorists overseas, additional scares disrupted work in the nation's capital as letters containing deadly anthrax spores were received by Democratic Senators Tom Daschle (SD), Patrick Leahy (VT), Ted Kennedy (MA), and Chris Dodd (CT) as well as four House members' offices in October and November.[3] Capitol Hill was thrown into turmoil as whole buildings were abandoned for decontamination, and the disruption rippled throughout the rest of the city.

Given this list of problems, it seems nothing short of miraculous that President Bush won passage of Public Law 107-10, the No Child Left Behind Act—reauthorizing ESEA but also dramatically altering the terms of federal involvement in education policy. Along the way, numerous leaders other than the president contributed to the success of this effort, a fact the president acknowledged by signing the legislation on January 8, 2002 during trips to Ohio, New Hampshire, and Massachusetts. The president's first stop on January 8 was at the high school in Hamilton, Ohio, in the congressional district of the chair of the House Committee on Education and Labor, John Boehner (R-OH). In a setting described as "a heartland pep rally," President Bush signed the bill into law even though an elementary school would have been a more appropriate setting.[4] He later flew to New Hampshire and Massachusetts for similar stops that honored the contributions of Senators Judd Gregg (R-NH) and Ted Kennedy (D-MA) to the legislation. During the previous week, President Bush visited the district of George Miller (D-CA), the ranking member of the House Education and Labor Committee, who was critical to the bill's passage.

The law established dramatic new pressures on school districts and states. The three most important were state testing, the specification of students' "adequate yearly progress" in academic improvement, and teacher quality. By 2005–2006, all states were to establish annual, statewide assessments in reading and mathematics for grades 3–8 aligned with state academic standards. Science assessments would be added in 2007–2008. In addition, high school students would have to be assessed once in grades 9–12. Test results were to be reported in disaggregated form so that the performance of population subgroups would be clear. Within twelve years, all students in all subgroups were to have attained proficiency in reading and math. And by 2005–2006, all teachers were to be "highly qualified," meaning that they would meet the state's certification requirements and demonstrate competence in the subject they teach.[5] These ambitious goals were presented in the context of striking failure to reach the goals of the last reauthorization of ESEA when states receiving money under the Title I program for disadvantaged students were to "develop challenging academic content and performance standards, student assessments aligned with those standards, and accountability systems to help ensure the standards are met."[6] In other words, many of the goals set forth by No Child Left Behind were already to have been accomplished on a voluntary basis. After seven years had passed, only sixteen states had fully complied with the standards and assessment requirements from the last round of reauthorization. Skepticism about the new round was understandable.

But the legislation also had some carrots as well as sticks. It authorized substantial increases in federal spending on education and greater flexibility in how local districts would be allowed to use those funds. It also provided new opportunities for students to escape low-performing schools. This combination of carrots and sticks had been fashioned over the previous year by a bipartisan coalition of leaders, urged on by the president who intervened at critical moments in the process to encourage negotiators. The president also sweetened the pot by approving additional education spending, the Democrats' principal goal. Bush and his White House aides guided the process to completion, and these efforts energized and maintained the legislative process. There was also some urgency about education reform because the president had placed it at the forefront of his domestic program, authorization for ESEA had expired, and education was the top domestic issue in public opinion polls.

In this chapter we address how Bush and Congress reached consensus on education reform after the effort was abandoned due to partisan gridlock in the previous Congress. First we provide a brief history of federal education policy, from President Lyndon Johnson's "War on Poverty" to reform efforts of Presidents George H. W. Bush and Bill Clinton followed by a discussion of failed reauthorization of ESEA in 2000. We then discuss President Bush's NCLB education reform plan and analyze his efforts at building a supporting coalition early in his presidency. We also follow the legislative history through House and Senate consideration, a conference committee, and bill signing with special emphasis on the role of committee chairs in negotiation and building consensus. We conclude by exploring themes of leadership demonstrated by this case.

BACKGROUND: PREVIOUS EDUCATION REFORM EFFORTS

The Elementary and Secondary Education Act of 1965 was a central part of President Lyndon Johnson's "War on Poverty." By providing targeted funding for children from low-income families, the federal government hoped to help local school districts meet the extra needs of such students. This represented a major policy departure—an aggressive extension of federal involvement through the first comprehensive federal program for education, an area traditionally reserved for state control. As Johnson explained in his remarks after passage of the legislation:

> Congress has taken the most significant step of this century to provide widespread help to all of America's schoolchildren. I predict that this is just the beginning, the first giant stride toward full educational opportunity for all of our schoolchildren . . . It will offer new hope to tens of thousands of youngsters who need attention before they ever enroll in the first grade. It will help five million children of poor families overcome their greatest barrier to progress—poverty. It will put textbooks in now empty hands. It will establish new centers of learning throughout our entire land, and it will do all of this while leaving the control of education in the hands of local citizens.[7]

Title I was the centerpiece of the act, a set of special programs whose funding would flow to schools with high concentrations of high-poverty students especially in urban areas. State departments of education would convey the funding that would hopefully help the poor escape poverty. Head Start (a preschool program for disadvantaged students) and special programs for bilingual education were singular federal efforts launched in the 1960s and continued thereafter. ESEA also included aid for libraries and textbooks as well as support for education research. Because assistance was targeted at low-income students, the administration was able to sidestep opposition from two groups, those who feared federal encroachments on local control through more general federal assistance to education and those from church-related schools, especially parochial, who were also eligible to receive federal assistance for low-income students.

George H. W. Bush, Bill Clinton, and Education Reform

Congress regularly renewed this federal commitment at five-year intervals, making adjustments to the programs along the way. The Clinton administration won congressional reauthorization in 1994 and renamed the bill the "Improving America's Schools Act." At the signing ceremony at a high school in Framingham, Massachusetts, President Bill Clinton stressed a philosophical departure from the past:

> The important thing about this bill is that it represents a fundamental change in the way the Federal Government looks at how we should do our job in helping you students achieve those [education] goals. For 30 years, the Federal Government has shipped money to the States and the local school districts to try to help with problems that needed the money. But mostly, they have done it in ways that prescribed in very detailed manner the rules and regulations your schools had to follow, the rules and regulations your States had to follow in applying for the money and in complying with it. And very often, we had teachers at the grassroots level who said, "This doesn't make any sense."
> This bill changes all that. This bill says the National Government will set the goals. We will help develop measurements to see whether Framingham School District is meeting the goals. But you will get to determine how you're going to meet the goals, because the magic of education occurs between the teacher and the students in the classroom, with the parents, with the principals, with the schools supporting it.[8]

Clinton also stressed the bipartisan support for the legislation including Sen. Jim Jeffords (R-VT) who was part of the group of dignitaries in attendance.

By the time of this 1994 reauthorization, the nation's education agenda had changed dramatically. President George H. W. Bush met with the nation's governors at a September 1989 summit in Charlottesville, Virginia, where a process was launched to establish a set of national performance goals in education. Bush adopted six goals to serve as the foundation for his ultimately unsuccessful

"America 2000" plan, and Bill Clinton played a central role in articulating those goals. As governor of Arkansas, Clinton had embraced the education reform movement that called for national standards and a way to measure student performance ("accountability") as did Clinton's education secretary and deputy secretary, Richard Riley and Madeline Kunin, who had served as governors of South Carolina and Vermont, respectively. Clinton restated the goals at the 1994 signing event:

> We will make sure every child shows up for school ready to learn; that we will raise the high school graduation rate to at least 90 percent of all students, which is the international standard, all over the country; that we will make sure our young people learn and are proficient in, by international standards of excellence, basic subjects in English and mathematics and history and geography and languages, and we will learn how to measure whether we are doing that or not at least three times during the course of a student's career; that we will lead the world in math and science achievement, not bring up the rear; that our schools will become safe, disciplined, and free of drugs; and that we will develop a system of lifetime learning so that people, no matter how old they are, will always be able to develop new skills, acquire new knowledge, know what they need to know to move forward with confidence.[9]

Clinton established voluntary national education standards in a companion piece of legislation, "Goals 2000: Educate America Act," which passed in March 1994. On this basis, states moved forward with the establishment of education standards that specified what students needed to master in school. The "Improving America's Schools Act" then required that disadvantaged students be held to the same standards as all other students and required that states improve the performance of schools that fell short of this goal.

Bipartisan agreement on education policy, to the extent it had resulted from the Bush-Clinton initiatives, soon disappeared. The year 1995 opened with a new political configuration in Washington and new elements on the education agenda. For the first time in four decades, Republicans constituted a majority in the House of Representatives, and they also controlled the Senate. One of their first steps was to invite two former secretaries of education from Republican administrations, Lamar Alexander and William Bennett from the Bush and Reagan administrations, respectively, to testify on the desirability of abolishing the U.S. Department of Education, a proposal first advanced by Ronald Reagan in 1980. Later in 1995, Republicans sought $30 billion of cuts in federal education spending as part of the deficit-reduction package that produced intense conflict with the Clinton administration and resulted in the dramatic budget showdown that twice shut down the federal government. The final agreement between Clinton and the congressional Republicans, concluded in spring 1996, preserved the principal federal education programs that had been fashioned by Democratic congressional majorities over the previous forty years.

President Clinton won reelection in 1996, and most of his 1997 State of the Union address, the first of his final term in office, was devoted to education. In this speech, he presented a ten-part "call to action for American education" as a way to prepare the nation for global competition in the twenty-first century. Clinton called upon the members of Congress, "all our Nation's Governors . . . parents, teachers, and citizens all across America for a new nonpartisan commitment to education because education is a critical national security issue for our future, and politics must stop at the schoolhouse door." We summarize the ten steps below.

1. Raising education standards and improving the quality of teachers
2. Launching a major reading initiative
3. Expanding Head Start
4. Expanding parental choice by encouraging the creation of charter schools
5. Teaching character education
6. Renovating old schools
7. Building new schools
8. Making completion of junior college rather than high school the universal standard
9. Encouraging lifetime learning
10. Connecting all schools to the Internet[10]

To a remarkable degree, this speech defined the nation's education agenda for the next decade, but politics persisted and new areas of disagreement arose. Many Republicans were suspicious of national testing; advocates saw testing as a national yardstick against which states' progress could be measured, but opponents viewed it as a way to reduce local control over curriculum and impose liberal values. Several communities and states experimented with school vouchers, defended as a way to help students escape low-performing public schools (especially in urban areas), but criticized as a way to shift public funding to private schools. School violence rose to the top of the national agenda with the student shootings in Columbine, but while Democrats saw the need for expanded gun controls, Republicans objected to an infringement on civil liberties. Faith-based organizations other than parochial schools also became more active in seeking eligibility to receive federal education grants, triggering Republican support but Democratic opposition. Finally, Republicans believed that Clinton's 1994 rhetoric about reducing federal control over education dollars was overblown and instead sought to dramatically expand local flexibility in the use of federal education funds. Because of divided party control—a Democrat in the White House confronting Republican majorities in both the House and Senate—the potential for conflict was great.[11]

Failed ESEA Reauthorization (1999–2000)

One casualty of this heightened partisanship in Washington was reauthorization of ESEA that normally would have occurred during the 106th Congress (1999–2000). Although moderates on both sides explored ways to establish school accountability through student testing, as a way to demonstrate that federal spending on education was making a difference, party disagreements on funding levels and school vouchers—issues that could be used in the fall elections—doomed the compromise effort.[12]

In the House, the Committee on Education and the Work Force was notoriously conflictual and lived up to its reputation in the 106th Congress. The Republicans introduced a series of seven proposals to collapse many existing federal programs into five-year block grants, but only three of the seven proposals made it out of committee and all failed to become law. Republicans on the committee were divided over several of the remaining provisions that made committee approval impossible. Likewise, the Senate committee voted out a reauthorization plan in 2000 that fell victim to partisan bickering on the Senate floor. When the acrimony threatened to bog down the Senate indefinitely, Majority Leader Trent Lott pulled the legislation from consideration. With legislative failure in both chambers, appropriations committees in the House and Senate continued federal education programs without authorizations for an additional year as part of the omnibus spending bill that lumped together funding for many federal programs.

A good part of the inaction on education reform can be attributed to the 2000 congressional and presidential elections. Both parties calculated whether it was more advantageous for their electoral prospects to reach a compromise accomplishment in education or to draw sharp battle lines. As polls indicated that education was the number one domestic issue on the minds of Americans, competition won out over compromise.[13]

BUSH'S EDUCATION PROPOSAL—TAKING THE INITIATIVE

The Bush Plan

During the 2000 presidential campaign, Republican candidate George W. Bush stated, "I'm not running for federal superintendent of schools, and I don't want to be the federal principal. I want to pass power back from Washington, D.C., to states."[14] The administration's top priority was to reform education policy much like Bush had in Texas by relying on accountability.

On January 23, 2001, just three days after his inauguration, the new president released a twenty-eight page "blueprint" of his education proposal. Congressional Republicans had reserved the legislative designations of S.1 and H.R.1 for the proposal, further evidence of its top billing. Bush's strategy was different from that adopted by many other administrations. Rather than starting with a highly specific, detailed proposal, the administration presented an outline of ideas with the clear implication that future negotiations with Congress would provide meat on the skeleton. As observers quickly learned, however, this blueprint strategy did not mean the White House would be a passive observer in the legislative process; rather, presidential aides were actively involved in sessions that drafted specific language and negotiated major disagreements. Starting with a blueprint gave these emissaries flexibility on many issues but also allowed them to defend the administration's fundamental, nonnegotiable positions.[15]

There were several central features of the Bush plan:

- Fifty programs would be collapsed into five block grants that would address aid to disadvantaged children, improving teacher quality, developing English proficiency, expanding school choice, and advancing school safety.
- The accountability system would be substantially beefed-up through annual testing in grades 3–8 in reading and math (a more demanding regimen than the three tests previously demanded by Clinton), and tests were to be added in history and science.
- There would be school report cards recording how their students performed on these student assessments, and schools would receive rewards or sanctions depending on whether they were successful or underperforming (that is, "failing").
- States were required to participate in the National Assessment of Educational Progress (NAEP) tests for 4th and 8th grade students, a way to gauge whether states' efforts measured up to national standards.
- Student progress would be calculated by disaggregated groups (African-American, Hispanic, special education, English as second language, etc.) and their targets for growth would be expressed as "adequate yearly progress" (AYP).
- A modest voucher proposal would allow students attending public schools that performed poorly for three consecutive years to use their share of federal funds (approximately $1500) to pay for private school services.

Developing the proposal involved a whirlwind of meetings and discussions during a necessarily abbreviated transition period. There was only one month between the Supreme Court decision that ultimately determined the 2000 election's winner and the inauguration. Five people were primarily responsible for developing the proposal, and they barely had time to access the Department of

Education's permanent bureaucracy after the inauguration.[16] The administration's point man in this effort was Alexander (Sandy) Kress, a moderate Democrat who had worked on education policy with Bush in Texas. He worked closely with Margaret La Montagne, Bush's de facto education advisor in Texas, who became the White House director of the Domestic Policy Council in the first Bush administration and, after adopting her married name of Margaret Spellings, secretary of education in the second.[17] The secretary of education–designate in the first Bush administration, Rodney Paige, played an almost embarrassingly minor role in the proposal's development.[18] Paige had served as superintendent of the Houston schools and pointed to dramatic gains made by his disadvantaged students under a Texas accountability system very similar to the one being proposed by President Bush for the nation. Thus, Paige could credibly claim that he had been on the front lines of education reform, understood the challenges faced by educators, and could provide personal testimony to the effectiveness of the new strategy.

Not only was Sandy Kress important at the outset, but he also played a key role throughout the entire process, serving as Bush's representative in countless negotiating sessions that required his mastery of the arcane details of education policy as well as the politics of bargaining. Bush's lieutenant governor in Texas, Bob Bullock, a powerful Democrat who helped fashion bipartisan support for education reform, had appointed Kress to a variety of education-related committees, including the one that designed the Texas accountability system.[19] Kress, a lawyer who had chaired the Dallas County Democratic Party and was later elected to the Dallas School Board, also grew close to Governor Bush and advised him on education policy during both the 2000 and 2004 elections.[20] Given these advisors, it should be no surprise that, once elected, President Bush would push the "Texas education model."[21]

Building a Coalition of Support

While a small number of Bush advisors were responsible for crafting Bush's proposal, the proposal was not developed in isolation. A series of critical meetings were held with the president-elect in Texas during the transition, evidence that Bush was following the conventional advice given to newly elected presidents to "hit the ground running" in order to take maximum advantage of a brief window of policy opportunity. Approximately twenty members of Congress met with Bush in the governor's mansion on December 21, 2000. Included were the Republican chairs of both committees that would have jurisdiction over the legislation; John Boehner (R-OH) was the incoming chair of the House Education and Workforce Committee, and Jim Jeffords was the returning chair of the Senate's Health, Education, Labor, and Pensions (HELP) Committee. The group included several "New Democrats" associated with the DLC and one traditional

Democrat. Senators Evan Bayh (D-IN) and Zell Miller (D-GA) as well as Representative Tim Roemer (D-IN) were considered moderates who were potential supporters of a Bush proposal. (So was Joseph Lieberman, the Connecticut senator, but as the defeated Democratic candidate for vice president in 2000, his absence was understandable.) There was less optimism about the support of George Miller's (D-CA), a notoriously liberal House member, but Boehner insisted on Miller's inclusion in the meeting, arguing that the support of the incoming ranking minority member on the committee would be critical to winning passage of the legislation.[22] As Nicholas Lemann reported, Miller was actually seated next to President Bush during the lunch, and a cordial relationship was established. As Miller recalled,

> "We hit it off. We hit it off very well. We sat next to each other. He has"— Miller chuckled helplessly—"a *very* relaxed manner. I was sitting next to him, and he was giving me a running commentary on what people were saying." By the end of the meeting, Miller had acquired his official George W. Bush nickname, Big George, and Bush had acquired an important ally.[23]

Nor was that seating arrangement an accident. Judd Gregg, who knew Bush well, intervened before the lunch to switch his own name tag with Miller's, enabling the president to give the representative the Bush treatment.[24]

A later meeting, held with nineteen Republican governors at Bush's Texas ranch, was also designed to win necessary support. Bush again met with Republican and Democratic governors after the inauguration with a similar purpose. Finally, education was one of the topics discussed with business groups who met with the president-elect during the transition period, a meeting that triggered the formation of a supportive business coalition.[25]

Thus, President Bush made several strategic moves at the very outset of the process. Education reform was identified as his top legislative priority during the honeymoon period that typically prevails in an administration's initial three to six months. He sought to build support among the key constituencies that would determine the outcome of the effort, even reaching out to possible opponents. In this last category, one would have to place his meeting with Senator Edward M. Kennedy (D-MA), ranking member on the HELP Committee, on the day before Bush's education blueprint was released. Kennedy was included in a briefing for congressional committee leaders and had the opportunity to size up Bush and his proposals. When Kennedy did not take the opportunity to blast the president's proposal for including vouchers, Bush reportedly knew there was room for negotiation.[26] This initial meeting was followed by a series of relationship-building interactions with this lion of liberalism. Bush had also fashioned a plan with considerable flexibility, signaling his willingness to negotiate many details, and those negotiations would reveal which issues were most important to the administration. Bush was searching for partners and was willing to make the effort bipartisan.

THE EARLY LEGISLATIVE PROCESS—
ACTION IN COMMITTEES

The key to passage of the No Child Left Behind Act was teamwork: President Bush enlisted the efforts of four legislators, the chairs and ranking members of the House and Senate committees with jurisdiction, who worked long hours behind the scenes to steer a delicate compromise through committee, floor, and conference committee stages of action. On numerous occasions, they had to resist the demands of their own partisans for more strident provisions that harkened back to the party warfare of the 106th Congress.

House Committee Passage

As in the previous Congress, committee action in the House was more difficult than that in the Senate where many of the most contentious issues were left for consideration by the full chamber. In fact, the Senate Health, Education, Labor, and Pensions Committee completed work on S. 1 on March 8, 2001, fully two months before the House Education and Workforce Committee completed action on May 8. Yet the House completed floor action on H.R. 1 on May 23 while the Senate did not approve H.R. 1 (the amended version of its own bill) until June 14, following six weeks of floor debate.

Representative John Boehner (R-OH)

John Boehner became chairman of the House Committee on Education and the Workforce at the outset of the 107th Congress, the beginning of his sixth term in the House. After winning a three-way Republican primary in 1990 and going on to a safe victory in the general election, Boehner won his subsequent campaigns by comfortable margins of 70 percent and better. Not content to play the quiet role ordinarily expected of freshman members, Boehner was one of seven new House members who triggered the House banking scandal in 1991 in which it was revealed that 355 members had overdrafts at the House bank. Congressional perks and pay were Boehner's principal targets at the outset of his service. In subsequent years, his ambition became still clearer. He ran Newt Gingrich's campaign to become leader of House Republicans, and he played a prominent role in the 1994 campaign constructed around the

"Contract with America" that helped secure a House Republican major-ity for the first time in forty years. For his loyalty and efforts, Gingrich supported Boehner for the party's number four job, chairman of the Republican Conference, a position Boehner held until fall 1998 when he was ousted from the chairmanship at the same time Gingrich resigned, following a second consecutive loss of Republican House seats.

Boehner played an important legislative role in 1999–2000 in crafting the Republicans' health-care agenda as chair of the subcommittee on Employer-Employee Relations and when he sought the chairmanship of Education and Workforce (rather than House Administration where he was ranking member). In late 2000, both Speaker Hastert and Majority Leader Armey backed his campaign for committee chair, which propelled him past two other committee members, including one more senior. Boehner's performance as committee chair completed a significant trans-formation "from conservative ideologue to bipartisan coalition builder." As David Nather of *CQ Weekly* pointed out, "As chairman of the House Republican Conference during the 104th and 105th Congresses, Boehner churned out a steady stream of Democrat-bashing statements."[27] But as the person charged with advancing the president's top-priority legislation, Boehner became a pragmatist who reversed previous positions and angered former conservative allies. When the House Republican leader-ship was shaken in 2005 by the indictment of Majority Leader Tom DeLay (R-TX), Boehner became one of three candidates who vied for the position, which he ultimately won in a tight election. He became House minority leader after the 2006 elections.

Boehner was a plastics and packaging executive before serving six years in the Ohio House and then running for Congress. Consistent with his professional background, he worked closely with the business com-munity on health-care issues before moving up to chair the committee.

Action in the House Committee adhered to the delicate compromise worked out by Representatives Boehner and Miller. Even though there was an over-whelming 41–7 final vote, six Republicans voted against the proposal, which they saw as leaning too heavily Democratic.[28] In particular, Democrats got a substan-tial increase in authorized funding for education, including a doubling of federal aid to poor schools over five years without the greater flexibility Republicans had wanted to give school districts in how the funds could be used. More critically to some, vouchers were removed from the bill by a 27–20 vote when five Republi-cans voted with a united twenty-two Democrats against the provision. Boehner had to convince his colleagues not to insist on a more muscular "Straight A's" (funding flexibility) proposal that Democrats said would destroy the compromise; similarly, Miller had to convince a colleague to accept a voice vote in commit- tee on a proposal to strip annual testing out of the legislation (a White House priority) because he and Boehner feared a roll call vote would win.[29]

Representative George Miller (D-CA)

George Miller of California entered Congress as part of the class of 1974, the large group of seventy-five Democrats elected in the wake of public disenchantment with Watergate and sometimes dubbed the "Watergate babies."[30] By 2000, that group had dwindled in size, and Miller was among the most liberal members of the House. As described by National Journal's *Almanac of American Politics*, "To his work Miller brings an aggressiveness and zest for political combat reminiscent of [Phil] Bur- ton," his political mentor and a stalwart advocate of liberal Democratic thinking in the 1970s. Such an approach was perfect for service on the House Education and Workforce Committee, long known as a partisan battlefield. Miller had served as chair of the Natural Resources Commit- tee (previously named Interior and Insular Affairs and later renamed Resources) from 1991–1994 where he made a legislative mark as a "com- bative environmentalist."[31]

At first glance, Miller appears an unlikely ally for either George W. Bush or John Boehner, but he had the record of being a maverick on edu- cation policy, having broken with the Democrats' party positions on the issue in 1994 and 1999. Miller's official website describes him as "a lead- ing spokesman in Congress on education, labor, the environment, and Native Americans."[32] Job creation and pension protection have been important economic concerns as he has advanced a traditional Democra- tic domestic agenda. He pushed hard for investigating the Exxon Valdez oil spill in 1989 and was a major critic of U.S. foreign policy in Central America during the 1980s and 1990s. His voting record is rated high by abortion-rights groups, labor unions, and liberal organizations and low by right-to-life, business-related, and conservative groups.

Miller was appointed cochair of the House Democratic Policy Com- mittee, an important strategy-developing group, by Minority Leader Nancy Pelosi in 2003 and had previously served in that capacity in 1995–1996. He also served on the Budget Committee and was the founding chairman of the Select Committee on Children, Youth and Families (1983 to 1990).

In the end, none of the hot-button party priorities that had made progress impossible in 2000 made it out of committee in 2001: Republicans got neither vouchers nor block grants; Democrats got additional funding for neither class-size reduction nor school construction. Boehner and Miller were considered a true political odd couple and had weathered forty-six amendments and eight roll call votes in committee, many of which could have fractured their carefully constructed compromise. Both had been partisan firebrands in the past but found ways to get things done in 2001. Recognizing that he had once been a leader in shaping the Republicans' partisan message, Boehner acknowledged that as chair of the committee, "My job now is to move legislation." In that new role, he recognized that "there was a certain number of Republicans who could never jump over the divide between where we had been and where the president wanted to go."[33] Republican conservatives had just a short time earlier called for the Department of Education's elimination; now Bush was calling for a more active federal role and annual student testing that was opposed by thirty to forty Republicans. He needed Democratic votes but could not afford to lose too many Republicans. To help manage this tightrope act, Boehner formed a working subgroup of five Republicans and four Democrats to help him draft H.R. 1 and steer it through the committee stage. They met two to three times per week and were usually joined by Sandy Kress and staff from the Department of Education. Miller was a full participant in these meetings. For some years, he had been openly critical of educators' performance and the large number of low-income students left behind; he had broken with his party's orthodoxy on several occasions to support stronger demands on teachers. Throughout the process, he was one of the most insistent voices on the urgency of stressing rapid and steady progress for all groups of students.[34]

Senate Committee Passage

At the time of the Senate committee's action, Jim Jeffords served as chair and Ted Kennedy as the ranking member. Because of the overall 50–50 balance in the Senate, the committee's party balance was 10–10, so partisan deadlocks blocked action altogether. Jeffords, however, was not the administration's principal ally on the committee. That role fell to Judd Gregg (R-NH), who was regarded as casting a more predictably conservative vote. Ultimately, the committee voted 20–0 in favor of the bipartisan compromise, but defeated partisans knew they would fight another day when the same issues were raised on the Senate floor. Thus, Democrats lost at the committee stage in their effort to raise federal education spending even higher, and Republicans failed to get greater local flexibility in the use of funds. Party-line votes were registered on proposals to hire more teachers and spend more on building renovation, and these proposals therefore failed. Gregg proposed and then withdrew a voucher proposal. In short, most of the critical battles were delayed until later in the process when the leadership of Kennedy and Gregg would also become more critical.

Senator Judd Gregg (R-NH)

After eight years of service in the U.S. House of Representatives and two consecutive two-year terms as governor of New Hampshire (a position his father had held before him), Judd Gregg won a Senate seat in 1992 by a narrow 3 percent margin. Reelections in 1998 and 2004 were by far more comfortable margins of 40 percent and 32 percent. Though not regarded as a right-wing ideologue, Gregg is a solidly conservative senator with a strong record of voting support for President Bush. During President Bush's preparation for the 2004 televised presidential debates, Gregg reportedly was a stand-in for Senator John Kerry, the Democratic nominee.

Gregg became chair of the Senate Budget Committee in 2005, a more powerful position than chair of Health, Education, Labor, and Pensions, which he held from 2003–2005. Service on the Senate Appropriations Committee extends his reach into many policy areas. He is chair of the Homeland Security Appropriations Subcommittee and was previously chair of the Subcommittee on Commerce, Justice and Science. He has been chief deputy whip since 1995. Gregg has championed several issues during his congressional career, including expanding access to health care and generic drugs, identity protection, tax-free Internet purchasing, and enhancing local control of resources. He has been a staunch supporter of right-to-life legislation and small businesses. Social Security reform has been a particular area of emphasis, and Gregg served as bipartisan cochair of the National Commission on Retirement Policy, cochair of the Senate Republican Task Force on Social Security, and chair of the Senate Budget Committee Task Force on Social Security. He favors mandatory personal investment accounts as well as means-tested benefits. As chair of the Budget Committee, he was in a key position to influence policy on managing the budget deficits that have grown dramatically since 2001. Gregg became ranking member of the HELP Committee when Jim Jeffords defected from the Republican Party in May 2001. He then took over the chairmanship in 2003 when Republicans regained their majority in the Senate.

Though it is not precisely clear when Kennedy was admitted into the small group guiding the fate of NCLB, it has been suggested that this happened before the June 2001 change in party control. Kennedy's price for becoming part of the guiding bipartisan coalition was clear: minimum block grants and no vouchers. When the administration accepted only a small consolidation of education programs and substituted supplemental services to students for vouchers, Kennedy joined the effort.[35] Andrew Rudalevige suggests that Kennedy did not want to be excluded from helping to shape a major educational initiative and that the New Democrats working with the bipartisan coalition insisted that Kennedy become part of the process.[36] This group of moderate to conservative Democrats played a pivotal role in the Senate; with an overall party balance of either 50–50 or 50–49–1 after Jeffords's party shift, this group had the potential to swing the votes needed to determine outcomes and even to invoke cloture—the parliamentary vote needed to halt a Senate filibuster that requires sixty votes. The group had proposed a compromise solution for ESEA reauthorization in 2000 that had received only thirteen votes on the Senate floor, but close observers noted that Bush's NCLB proposal resembled the DLC proposal in several respects.[37] Kennedy, as a veteran legislator, was well aware of how important this group's views would prove to be on the outcome of Bush's initiative.

Senator Edward M. (Ted) Kennedy (D-MA)

Now in his eighth term in the Senate, Edward (Ted) Kennedy is a liberal icon. First elected to the Senate in 1962 when his brother was president (he was elected to serve out the final two years of his brother's term in the Senate), Kennedy was used repeatedly by President Bush in 2004 as the foil to establish just how liberal his opponent, John Kerry, really was—so liberal that Kerry made Kennedy the conservative senator from Massachusetts despite his "longstanding practice of defining liberalism's outer edge in the Senate."[38] Having completed forty-two years in the Senate, Kennedy has served "longer than all but four other senators in American history—and he is still going strong."[39] During this long career, he was once a presidential candidate (1980) and a potential candidate on several other occasions; he served for two years as Democratic Senate whip; he chaired the Labor and Human Resources Committee (1987–1994) and earlier the Judiciary Committee (1979–1980). His rousing speeches at Democratic presidential nominating conventions have repeatedly brought the faithful to their feet.

An old congressional adage suggests that legislators can be "show horses" or "workhorses." The former stress primping and posing for the cameras while the latter focus on policy and legislative details. Looking at Kennedy's long career, one might conclude he has been both, though there have been far more workhorse years as he evolved into an effective, energetic legislator. Among his many causes in the Senate have been civil rights, programs to assist the poor (for example, the Women, Infants, and Children's Nutrition Program, Low-Income Energy Assistance Programs, Head Start), health care (Medicare), family and medical leave, abortion rights, rights of the disabled, raising the minimum wage, immigration liberalization and amnesty, and opposition to foreign military involvement. As the 1990s dawned, one journalist argued that "Even Kennedy's political adversaries acknowledge that as he nears the end of his third decade in the Senate his fingerprints may be found on much of the significant social legislation of the past quarter-century: voting rights, immigration reform, occupational safety, fair housing, consumer protection, and on and on."[40]

Yet Kennedy's career has been dogged by controversy, much of it associated with his personal behavior. An accident in 1969 in which a young woman on his staff drowned when the car driven by the senator plunged into the water resulted in a conviction for leaving the scene of an accident and enormous controversy about his relationship with the young woman. Similarly, frequent bouts of excessive drinking and rumors of womanizing damaged his image. Nearly fifteen years have passed since a political profile described him as "a peculiarly American archetype—the Good Bad Boy—who perseveres, with charm, despite life's vicissitudes and his own defects."[41] With one brother an assassinated president and another assassinated on the presidential campaign trail, Kennedy is "the sole male survivor in a family obsessed with public achievement . . . constantly confronted with the unfinished agenda—and legendary stature—of his brothers; by nature and upbringing, his private happiness is predicated on public accomplishment."[42]

These political fault lines were probably still forming in early March when the Senate HELP Committee passed S. 1. As in the House, an informal negotiating group formed to craft a substitute bill that would be debated on the Senate floor. Four factions were represented: conservative Republicans (three senators), New Democrats (two), liberal Democrats (three), and moderate Republicans (two). Although Jeffords was a member of the group, Gregg and Kennedy were the key players with Sandy Kress playing an active role. When a number of governors suddenly raised concerns about the language that was being crafted around "adequate yearly progress" that all students would be expected to make, the group worked to develop compromise language that would be less draconian in its consequences. This crisis that arose late in the process substantially delayed Senate action.[43]

PASSAGE ON THE HOUSE AND SENATE FLOOR

Although the version of H.R. 1 approved by the House gave both Republican conservatives and Democratic liberals reasons to be unhappy, only thirty-four Republicans, ten Democrats, and one Independent cast negative votes on the final product. Both extremes proposed a series of amendments to the committee's work that favored their own preferred solutions, though the Rules Committee limited the total to twenty-eight amendments and structured their consideration in a way likely to produce the amendments' defeat. In one instance, Republican conservatives and Democratic liberals (including the Democrats' leader, Richard Gephardt, and his top lieutenant) allied in an effort to scuttle annual testing, a centerpiece of the Bush plan; the effort failed following vigorous White House lobbying by Chief of Staff Andrew Card and top political advisor Karl Rove.[44] The Republicans' majority leader, Dick Armey (R-TX), proposed two failed amendments to restore vouchers. Jim DeMint (R-SC) voted against the bill in committee and on the floor largely because it lacked a strong block grant to enhance local flexibility. When he threatened a fight on the floor, Boehner enlisted President Bush in a successful effort to dissuade him.[45] Similarly, when the House Republican Party leaders wanted to propose a similar block grant, Boehner advised against it, and in a meeting with Bush the president sided with Boehner.[46] Most of these floor efforts were fended off by the core alliance of moderates in the two parties. As David Nather reported in *CQ Weekly*, "there was nothing easy about steering through a House full of unhappy conservative Republicans and skeptical liberal Democrats looking for a good reason to bolt."[47]

The White House and President Bush, far from keeping a hands-off approach to the nitty-gritty of floor politics in the House, were heavily involved. Either Bush personally intervened at critical times to convince unhappy Republicans not to take actions that would endanger the bipartisan coalition or he designated his top political aides to do so in his stead. Bush thus demonstrated a more sure-handed mastery of Washington politics than outsiders are usually credited with possessing. At this point, as a first-year president advancing his top legislative priority, Republican legislators were more likely to defer to his preferences.

Senate floor action offered the greater challenge. Many interparty disagreements had been sidestepped, delaying them for action on the Senate floor. Kennedy became the bill's manager after Jeffords defected from the Republican

Party in late May. As chair of the committee, Kennedy's astute floor management and encouragement of Democratic amendments put a more Democratic cast on the final product in several ways: higher spending levels were authorized but were unlikely to be realized because they were inconsistent with the previously passed budget resolution; spending for IDEA, the federal program for disabled students, for which a promise of 40 percent federal funding had never been met, was made mandatory;[48] Gregg lost his attempt to get a block-grant demonstration project approved but was successful in an effort to allow students in low-performing schools to attend better public schools; liberal Democrats' attempts to delay annual testing failed. Throughout the seven-week debate, Gregg and Kennedy regularly communicated with each other and with the White House about which proposals were "deal breakers" and which were acceptable. With more than one hundred fifty amendments offered on the floor, such communication was critical, and the core group had to abide by their pledge to reject killer amendments (most of which were raised by Democrats) that would challenge the compromise package by splintering the supporting coalition. Ultimately, only six Republicans and two Democrats voted against the final version.

INACTION, CRISIS, AND NEGOTIATION:
THE CONFERENCE COMMITTEE

By early summer, both the House and Senate had completed action on the ESEA reauthorization, but the two chambers passed different versions of NCLB and faced negotiation in a conference committee to settle their differences. Expectations were widespread that Bush's first policy accomplishment was close at hand, but delay was the enemy of success. Interest groups on the left and right, looking to prevent change on select NCLB provisions, began to mobilize their members to pressure Congress. Multiple groups expressed concern: state legislators and local school officials worried about annual student testing for grades 3–8, the possibility of reduced federal spending, and reduced local control; teachers worried about their ability to raise the performance of all student groups and the problems likely to be experienced by disabled students in meeting the standards; conservative groups were distressed by the absence of vouchers and the potential for a national test to be established. Partisans began to recalculate whether the concessions that had been made were really necessary and whether compromise was really the best policy. Conservative Republicans in the House feared that additional concessions that would have to be made to the more liberal Senate version in the conference committee would further water down a bill that they found barely acceptable.[49]

Slow Progress: The Early Stages of Conference Committee Consideration

Before the conference committee members were named, Nicholas Lemann wrote in the *New Yorker* that "The next month will be a pure test of Bush's level of energy, commitment, attention to detail, political skill, and courage on the issue that took him to the White House and that he cares about most."[50] In early July the congressional leadership named twenty-five senators (including Lieberman and Bayh, noncommittee members) and fourteen representatives to represent their chambers in the conference. The conference committee was charged with finding common ground on approximately 2,750 differences between the House and Senate bills, and this was even after the most contentious issues such as vouchers and federal funding for school renovations had been removed.[51] By early August, before the annual summer recess, progress had been made in resolving very few issues. Ultimately, it took five times longer than Lemann projected to achieve success.[52]

In part, the delay flowed from uncontrollable events: the September 11 terrorist attacks; a reshuffled congressional agenda; a slowing U.S. economy; and an anthrax attack on the capital. First, the national agenda was dramatically restructured on September 11, 2001, when terrorists struck New York City and Washington, D.C. On that morning, President Bush was visiting Emma E. Booker Elementary School in Sarasota, Florida, at an event designed to put pressure on the conferees to make progress, because after great optimism, little progress had been made. Sandy Kress later remembered, "On September 10th, I was the most discouraged I had ever been. Inertia had taken hold. Another school year had begun without any change in federal policy. The partisan atmosphere on Capitol Hill was awful."[53] On the 11th, education was knocked from its high-priority status by homeland security and national intelligence.

Congressional party leaders suggested that education reform be delayed while attention focused on more pressing matters. Education, though important, had suddenly slipped several notches on the long list of pressing issues including the thirteen unfinished appropriations bills that finance the government, "military and intelligence matters, aid for survivors and families of victims, help for the hard-hit airline industry, and a possible economic recovery package."[54] There was also a strong desire to avoid issues likely to produce partisan divisiveness; but this desire also helped keep the push for education reform alive since the legislation had been crafted through a bipartisan effort, and the president continued to provide public support.[55]

Boehner insisted that reform was too important for Congress to allow it to drift without action; after canceling the conference meeting originally scheduled for September 13, he reconvened the full conference again on September 25 to underline his point, and progress was made on several minor provisions. The Big Four issued a joint statement on September 12 that stated "despite yesterday's tragedies, final work on the education bill will continue" and "there are no plans at this time to suspend the conference process."[56] Boehner made sure that promise was kept and in the first post-9/11 conference meeting announced that "We're sending a message to the nation and the world that America's domestic-policy agenda is moving forward."[57] So despite a tremendous setback in losing priority status on the agenda, education reform continued to move forward—slowly.

Second, an interview with George Miller that aired the morning of September 11 on National Public Radio highlighted the principal sticking point for Democrats. As Miller explained, Democrats believed the administration needed to make a greater financial commitment.

> Either education is a national priority or it isn't. If the federal government's going to demand these very, very substantial reforms, annual testing and all the rest of it that are on this bill, then we are going to have to pay for it. The president knew that at the outset. He assured Senator Kennedy, Senator Jeffords, Congressman Boehner and myself that the resources would be there to implement this bill.
>
> This president came to office saying this was his number-one priority. You cannot close the gap between rich and poor children, majority and minority children, without putting additional resources into the schools. It's very clear that, unfortunately, the states, you know, have not provided the kind of resources for poor-performing schools that they should so they can have the best teachers, the best curriculum and decent facilities for these kids to go to.[58]

The math was pretty straightforward. In fiscal year 2001, the federal government was spending $18.6 billion on education, and the administration was proposing to increase that to $20 billion. The House bill called for $23.6 billion and the Senate version $33 billion. Sandy Kress was quoted as saying the administration figure was enough, but the Democrats made it clear they wanted more and that would be their price for agreeing to other provisions. Part of this concern arose from the traditional Democratic strategy of providing more resources but part also arose from the dire forecasts that state revenues were in trouble as the economy slowed. With a majority in the Senate, Democrats had much more bargaining leverage behind their demands than they had possessed when the legislative process began earlier in the year, and they were taking advantage of that leverage.

Finally, another disruption emerged when anthrax spores were detected in congressional offices on October 15. Congresspersons and their staffs, as well as committee staffs, were suddenly scrambling to find meeting space in unfamiliar locations because their own office buildings were shut down. Even after space was found, communication was difficult with different computer systems and phone numbers. Hill staffers were also contending with new procedures established for handling mail. Nonetheless, the committee's principals continued to meet—a far easier task than scheduling a meeting for the thirty-nine-member conference committee—and met with President Bush on October 12 to discuss some thorny issues. After its meeting on September 25, the full conference did not meet again until October 30; two scheduled meetings were canceled because of anthrax-related problems.[59]

Negotiation and Compromise Leads to Final Passage

Through the dedication and tenacity of the Big Four of Boehner, Miller, Gregg, and Kennedy, education reform continued to edge closer to success as the conferees and their staffs closed the gap on differences between the House and Senate bills systematically through the fall. Progress was made step-by-step, issue-by-issue, but the critical questions had to be resolved by the Big Four rather than by the unwieldy full committee. During this period, the president's attention was understandably diverted by national security matters, but Kress remained the administration's representative in discussions.

Compromise on Social Issues

On October 30, the Big Four met and focused on differences over "social issues." Boehner proposed a Republican-backed provision that would have ended funding for "hate-crimes prevention programs that 'discriminate against, denigrate, or otherwise undermine' the religious or moral beliefs of participating students."[60] Reportedly, the leaders of some education programs had suggested that Christian beliefs were intolerant, particularly toward homosexuals, and less than supportive of equal rights for women. Democrats complained that the vague language was really an effort to end all such programs. The result was a straight party-line vote that killed the proposal since both House and Senate conferees had to agree to make it part of the final product and Democrats controlled the Senate group. All other votes were unanimous even though they included the difficult issues of constitutionally-protected school prayer and providing meeting space in schools for groups that might discriminate in their membership (for example, Boy Scouts' exclusion of homosexuals). The Big Four, and their staffs, found acceptable solutions to hot-button issues that reflected significant partisan differences, and as *Education Week* noted, "The formal conference meeting, like two previous ones, . . . [served] as a rubber stamp for behind-the-scenes negotiations involving staff members and key lawmakers."[61]

Compromise on Testing Issues

It took most of November to fashion a compromise on testing issues. The conference meeting on November 30 established that NAEP, the national assessment, would be required of states, but results would not be tied to consequences and federal funds would pay for the testing. House Republicans had insisted upon both points. New Democrats and George Miller argued for ambitious targets for all students, or "adequate yearly progress," that would be calculated and reported by key social groups; but a "safe harbor" provision was established to protect against too many schools and states being labeled as "failing," a concern of the president and most traditional Democrats. Schools would be required to produce student proficiency after a twelve-year period rather than the originally proposed ten years. Sanctions against schools that fell short of targets would be delayed for three years instead of one year as the House had insisted. Bush's top priority—annual reading assessments in math and reading for grades 3–8—was included in the package.[62]

But the November 30 meeting had nearly been canceled. It was delayed an hour in order to provide enough time for the Big Four to negotiate a solution to a problem that their staffs had been unable to resolve during all-night negotiations. These four had met nine times over the previous three months to work on critical issues; Sandy Kress and Margaret Spellings usually joined them. Boehner conducted a form of shuttle diplomacy as he moved between Kennedy and Miller in one room and himself and Gregg in another as they tried to work out language to resolve "whether religious and community groups should have to follow civil rights laws when hiring employees for after-school and summer educational programs."[63]

Compromise on Funding

The final provision at issue was the cost of the legislation. Democrats, joined by a few Senate Republicans, insisted on linking ESEA reauthorization to mandatory funding for students with disabilities instead of the discretionary funding that continued to fall short of the promised level of federal resources. House Republicans were united in opposition, as was President Bush, and this had been a consistent point of disagreement since the spring. Thus, Democrats confronted the dilemma of deciding whether the issue was sufficiently important to block action on ESEA. While the ESEA conference committee was meeting, the House-Senate conference committee on appropriations continued to tread water regarding the next year's spending levels for education even though the new budget year began on October 1, 2001.[64] Bush and House Republicans had already given way on vouchers and demands for a major restructuring of federal funding, settling for weaker alternatives. Instead of vouchers, students would have the opportunity to escape poor-performing schools after two years of missing their targets, and students would be able to receive private tutoring after schools performed poorly in three consecutive years. There would also be a demonstration project to provide for greater flexibility in using federal funds, another Republican priority. The total number of education programs was whittled down modestly from fifty-five to forty-five rather than the thirty-two that President Bush had originally proposed. In return, Bush expected the Democrats to settle for less than their desired goal on funding; they finally did so, accepting the $4 billion increase Bush had agreed to earlier.

Final Approval: NCLB Becomes Law

The final deal was approved by voice vote in the conference committee on December 11. During this final conference committee meeting, Senator Tom Harkin (D-IA) revisited the special education issue and proposed a revised version of mandatory funding for special education programs that had been voted down in the November 30 meeting; once again, it lost among House conferees despite bipartisan support among Senate conferees. The president also opposed the revised proposal. Because of this, Senators Jeffords (I-VT) and Wellstone (D-MN) adamantly refused to support the final compromise in either the conference committee or on the Senate floor. (Jeffords, of course, had been committee chair back in March when the HELP Committee had approved the first version of the reauthorization bill.) Senator Kennedy, Jeffords's successor as chair, argued that the numerous program improvements that had been attained justified agreement, though he regretted "that we are not going to be able to reach all of the children that could benefit from these kinds of programs . . . We will see a significant increase in the resources," and he promised his colleagues and educator groups that he would keep fighting for more money in the future.[65]

Many Republicans believed the bill reflected Kennedy's imprint more than Bush's, particularly since so many of the Republicans' major policy departures were missing from the final law. Democrats viewed the final product as having too many Republican features. In short, it was a true compromise.

THEMES OF INDIVIDUAL LEADERSHIP ON EDUCATION REFORM

The saga of No Child Left Behind illustrates the possibilities of collective leadership, something that Americans are less familiar with than citizens of parliamentary systems. Whereas Americans, familiar with a single-executive form of government, are more likely to think of leadership as an individual trait, parliamentary systems place responsibility in the cabinet, a collective entity, rather than in the prime minister alone. In the case of NCLB, the congressional quartet of Boehner-Miller-Kennedy-Gregg worked in tandem with President Bush to produce a truly bipartisan piece of legislation. Few, if any, were fully satisfied with the final product, but an overwhelming majority could be partially satisfied.

What were the acts of leadership that made this possible? Paul Manna attributes much success to the "savvy leadership of the 'Big Four.'"[66] As our case study makes clear, President Bush must be included as a key player, as well. Thus, we concentrate on how the efforts of the Big Five, when Bush is included, ultimately proved successful. Collectively, they provided the *direction, coherence,* and *energy* that were essential to success.

Individually, each of the five central figures had to be willing to settle for less than the full loaf they sought. In other words, to accomplish part of their education goals, they needed to concede something to others' goals or redefine their own preferences to recognize how other strategies might also be worthwhile. It is not clear who gave the most. There were critics from both ends of the spectrum. As one disappointed Bush supporter commented on the compromise package, "the legislation being debated in Congress is about as close to his [the president's] original proposal as a first-grade book report is to a doctoral dissertation."[67]

But the president's willingness to compromise, as well as his willingness to give education reform enormous impetus by putting it at the top of his domestic agenda, was lauded by more balanced assessments:

> Like so many domestic issues, education had been one that was impossible to take on without ideological fights over nearly everything, including federal versus state and local control, school vouchers, and guns in schools. The political environment had been so toxic that the 106th Congress failed to reauthorize ESEA, leaving its programs to run on autopilot as they received an extra year of appropriations under the old rules.
>
> Bush, however, put education at the top of his agenda, and he laid out his plan to Congress shortly after taking office in January 2001. It included provisions no one expected would survive, such as private school vouchers, and Bush did not fight very hard for them. But its centerpiece—annual testing in reading and math for students in grades 3 through 8, with rewards for the best-performing schools and penalties for the worst—was important enough to him that his White House team tried to work out bipartisan agreements early on.[68]

As each member of the Big Five invested personal effort in pursuing reform, he became increasingly committed to the success of the overall effort. For the president, signaling that this was an issue of "intense interest" and "personal engagement" was critical.[69] It altered the calculus of congressional Republicans who had been reluctant reformers in the previous Congress. The president's engagement encouraged them to follow his lead even in areas of deep disagreement and made them more willing to accept compromise solutions. In short, President Bush provided the lion's share of *energy* and *direction* to this effort.

Each of the five remained committed to the basic compromise that had been worked out among the key political groupings whose interests had to be accommodated in order for reform to garner broad acceptance. The two bills crafted in the House and Senate committees included the same basic formula: "annual testing for Bush, more state and local flexibility for congressional Republicans and big increases in funding for Democrats."[70] As the legislation moved forward, maintaining *coherence* was the principal task of the committee leaders who had to resist pressures from their own partisans to reinstate terms that had been identified by the "partners" as unacceptable. Boehner and Gregg fended off challenges from conservative Republicans; Miller and Kennedy had the same problem with liberal Democrats. Resisting such efforts must have been difficult since the lead negotiators often shared the same concerns and commitments but had agreed to compromise those positions in order to secure a legislative success.

Putting aside old animosities was especially important on the House side. Representatives Boehner and Miller had a long history of strong disagreement in a combative setting, a committee known for its ideological battles. Both men occupied new committee roles that required them to behave differently if they hoped to make legislative achievements. In the Senate, Kennedy assumed a more familiar leadership role when Jeffords switched parties. Now in the majority, Kennedy worked with Gregg, an ideological opponent, in order to accomplish a common goal. Unlike its House counterpart, the Senate committee was not infamous for pitched ideological battles, but the leadership tandem faced a more difficult challenge on the Senate floor where far more difficult issues could arise to derail the compromise package. The lengthy Senate debate provided ample opportunity for the negotiated bargain to unravel. The efforts of Kennedy and Gregg kept it on track.

The "Big Five" could not have achieved success alone. All relied on key staff aides to monitor the day-to-day details of the legislative process and undertake the nuts and bolts of negotiations. Sandy Kress received the most media attention, but the reach of all the key players was extended by the able staff assistance they received. Kress, as the White House liaison in the process, was in an especially key role since he had to advise the president on both the substance and politics of developments. Resolving the enormously complex policy and political issues required determined assistance on all sides.

Sustaining momentum in the aftermath of 9/11 and in the face of the anthrax scare required commitment from all three institutions—the White House, the House, and the Senate. Party leaders in both the House and Senate were less committed to the effort than the committee leaders, and the latter had to keep pushing forward. Bush carved out enough time from his now more crowded schedule to provide the necessary *energy*, making it clear that he supported continued action even though policy discussions about the response to terrorism demanded the bulk of his time and attention. Although less personally engaged than before, Bush "bird dogged" the legislative process with the help of White House aides, intervening at key points when he was needed.[71] The president clearly signaled this continuing interest and commitment to his partisan allies.

Taking advantage of the strategic situation is part luck and part skill. While 9/11 indeed had the potential to be a disruptive force, it also encouraged many in government to maintain as much "normalcy" as possible. Boehner was especially effective in articulating ways that a continued pursuit of education reform demonstrated national unity in policy areas outside counterterrorism. It also demonstrated the bipartisan unity that reigned from September 2001 to February 2002. The president's comments at a Washington, D.C., rally celebrating the reform on the day after his signing of the law typified the new cross-party cooperation that NCLB symbolized:

> But I want to repeat some of the things I said yesterday. First of all, I know the folks in Crawford, Texas won't believe this, but Ted Kennedy is an able, good man. (Laughter and applause.) This bill would not have happened had he decided not to work to make it happen. He put his mind to it. (Applause.) I learned this: you want him on your side in a legislative battle.
>
> I also want to thank George Miller, from the state of California. (Applause.) George is a proud liberal, but also he's a proud author of this bill. He cares deeply about a system that quits kids—he wants to change it. (Applause.) I like him so much, I gave him a nickname: Big George. (Laughter.)
>
> But I've enjoyed working with these two Democrats. They are a credit to their party but, more importantly, a credit to our country. (Applause.)
>
> Yesterday, I signed the bill in Chairman Boehner's district. (Applause.) I knew Boehner had a big family—(laughter)—I didn't realize it was that big. (Laughter.) I did so because John was a steady influence in the process; he kept the process moving forward, even in the face of 9/11. He said, we've got to get a bill and he worked hard to bring people together to get it done. Mr. Chairman, you did a fabulous job and I thank you. (Applause.)[72]

Democrats were united in their desire to wrest substantial new investments in education from the Bush administration. Pursuing this goal was complicated by the falling federal revenues caused by tax cuts, a slowing economy, and the new demands placed on federal spending by the security crisis. Kennedy, Miller, and the New Democrats invested in the process had to determine when holding out for more money would be unsuccessful. Negotiators must make accurate evaluations of when the time is right to make a deal and stop pushing for an unachievable goal. Bargaining and negotiation skills are sometimes depicted in the media with a negative connotation—accepting less than total success appears to require compromising on principle. Yet, knowing the right point to stop pushing is a bargaining skill that is ultimately a form of leadership essential to navigating a long and complicated decision process.

Doing things differently from the past was also vital to the final success. Bipartisan working groups outside the formal legislative structure and the public eye enabled the Big Five to build trust, reach compromises, and construct *coherence*. These qualities made it possible for them to withstand opposition from the more extreme flanks of their parties. Resisting external pressures was also important. Both parties enjoyed the support of mobilized groups that had been especially effective in the 106th Congress in getting legislators to argue their agendas, an exercise in policy debate rather than reform. These groups were active in the 107th Congress, but the Big Five ensured that their influence would not prevent success.

Success required developing a new vocabulary of accountability that allowed the Democrats to support goals other than simply spending more money and Republicans to regard additional money as being used toward accomplishing new ends. Not everyone agreed on these new definitions; thus, the successful effort in 2001 contrasted with 2000 in that different actors employed different definitions and therefore different expectations. This worked well for the purpose of passing legislation but bodes ill for implementation.[73] As Andrew Rudalevige makes clear, " . . . the legislative process that created NCLB bequeathed statutory language that met the needs of an odd coalition wedded to diverging priorities but not always the needs of those doing the implementing."[74] In subsequent years, rule-making by the U.S. Department of Education proved to be enormously controversial; there were many demands for modifications to the original purposes of the law that arose from interest groups and even Republican-led legislatures. When Margaret Spellings became the secretary of education in the second Bush administration, she announced the need to adjust the original system of accountability to reality, an admission that rigorous adherence to the legislation was not working.

NCLB, as befits a precedent-shattering law, has been enormously controversial. Democrats argue that the administration reneged on its promise to increase education funding. Republicans argue that the law increased rather than decreased the power of federal bureaucrats who impose new strictures on state programs. And the issue was central to the president's reelection campaign in 2004, though it paled in comparison to the war on terrorism and the war in Iraq. Administration spokesmen were called upon to defend the "deal" that was made.

Question from Suzanne Miller, Associate Professor, University at Buffalo:
Around the country, schools and whole states have found that the amounts
of money promised by the Bush administration to fund NCLB have not mate-
rialized. If education is important, why doesn't the administration fund
NCLB fully?
Sandy Kress:
Suzanne, I've heard this concern around the country, and frankly it baffles
me. I was the president's chief negotiator on NCLB. I was there. The president never promised funding that failed to materialize. The Democrats
demanded during the negotiation that the administration agree at least to a
$4 billion increase in appropriations for K–12 education. As unusual as this
request was (usually appropriations are decided later in the legislative
process) and as controversial as it was for OMB and both Democrats and
Republicans on the Appropriations Committees, the president agreed to, and
helped deliver on this deal![75]

Who won, who lost? Will this change of direction in federal education policy help students, or will it prove to be another disappointment? Educators and
education policy specialists will continue to argue these questions into the
future. What we can be more certain of, however, is that the initiative would not
have succeeded without effective political leadership. This was provided by the
president, both at the outset and throughout the process. By advancing this proposal as his top priority, President Bush assured its place on the nation's agenda,
energizing legislators; the "blueprint" character of his proposal established a
direction for congressional deliberations and enabled him to construct a final
bargain among the multiple groups in Congress who were engaged by the
issue but who had been unable to design a grand solution in the previous Congress; and he effectively guided the process as it encountered significant tur-
bulence, making it possible to maintain forward progress. His continued
commitment made it clear to conservative Republicans, in particular, that it was
more important to craft a "solution" than to adopt dramatic positions that had
no hope of passage.[76]
    Nor would NCLB have been successful without the effective leadership of
the Big Four in Congress. Bush enlisted their help by providing them with the
opportunity to achieve some of their goals, and to receive a partial rather than
a full loaf, which enabled them to remain part of the common effort. Coordinating strategy across the parties was essential to successful passage of the legislation in both the House and the Senate, though the greatest challenges arose
at different stages of the legislative process. Meeting throughout the legislative
odyssey built trust that everyone was committed to achieving success, not to
using education as a way to gain partisan advantage.

NOTES

1. Washington Post/ABC News poll showed 55 percent approval on February 25, 2001, the lowest for a president at a comparable point in his presidency, with the previous low registered by Richard Nixon at 60 percent. Gary Langer, "Mixed Reviews," <http://abcnews.go.com/sections/politics/DailyNews/poll010226.html> (4 April 2005).

2. See chapter 3 for a discussion of the attacks.

3. Karen Foerstel, "More Anthrax, But Mail May Resume Soon," *CQ Weekly,* 24 November 2001, 2783. See chapter 5 for a discussion of the anthrax attacks.

4. Eric W. Robelen, "Amid Heartland Hoopla, Bush Signs the ESEA," *Education Week,* 16 January 2002. <http://www.edweek.org/ew/articles/2002/01/16/18bush.h21.html?querystring=No%20Child%20Left%20Behind> (19 April 2005); also see Dana Milbank, "With Fanfare, Bush Signs Education Bill," *Washington Post,* 9 January 2002, A3.

5. "An ESEA Primer," *Education Week,* 9 January 2002.

6. Eric W. Robelen, "States Sluggish On Execution of 1994 ESEA Act," *Education Week,* 28 November 2001; <http://www.edweek.org/ew/articles/2001/11/28/13comply.h21.html?querystring=No%20Child%20Left%20Behind> (19 April 2005).

7. Remarks of President Johnson following enactment of the Elementary and Secondary Education Bill, April 9, 1965, *Public Papers of the Presidents of the United States,* <http://www.presidency.ucsb.edu/ws/index.php?pid=26883&st=&st1=> (12 May 2005).

8. Remarks of President Clinton on signing the Improving America's Schools Act, Framingham, Massachusetts, 20 October 1994, *Public Papers of the Presidents of the United States,* <http://www.presidency.ucsb.edu/ws/index.php?pid=49332&st=Education&st1=> (9 March 2005).

9. Remarks of President Clinton.

10. William Jefferson Clinton's address to a Joint Session of Congress on the State of the Nation, 4 February 1997, <http://www.presidency.ucsb.edu/ws/index.php?pid=53358> (12 May 2005).

11. See our discussion of partisan conflict in chapter 1.

12. For a discussion of how the parties' positions on education evolved from 1960–2000, see Frederick M. Hess and Patrick J. McGuinn, "Seeking the Mantle of 'Opportunity:' Presidential Politics and the Educational Metaphor, 1964–2000," *Educational Policy* 16, no.1 (January and March 2002): 72–95.

13. The Pew Research Center for the People and the Press found that education led the list of voter priorities from 1997–2000. Survey Report January 17, 2002, <http://people-press.org/reports/display.php3?PageID=90> (28 May 2005). Also see Sue Kirchoff, "Schools Bursting with Issues," *CQ Weekly*, 22 January 2000, 112; Hess and McGuinn, "Seeking the Mantle of 'Opportunity,'" Table 1, 74.

14. Bush statement during the 1/15/2000 GOP debate in Johnston, IA, quoted in Sue Kirchoff, "Schools Bursting With Issues," *CQ Weekly*, 22 January 2000, 112.

15. David Nather, "Broad Support Is No Guarantee for Bush's Legislative Leadoff," *CQ Weekly*, 27 January 2001, 221.

16. Andrew Rudalevige, "Accountability and Avoidance in the Bush Education Plan: The 'No Child Left Behind Act of 2001,'" paper presented at Harvard University's Program

on Education Policy and Governance Conference on Taking Account of Accountability, Boston, MA, 10–11 June 2002, 23–24.

17. Amy Goldstein, "Bush's Schools Guru Expands Her Education," *Washington Post,* 28 March 2001, A21.

18. Sam Rosenfeld, "Soft Bigotry," *American Prospect,* online edition, 31 August 2004, <http://www.prospect.org/web/page.ww?section=root&name=ViewWeb&articleId =8440> (14 May 2005).

19. For a brief bio of Kress see <http://www.ets.org/aboutets/issues/kress.html> (6 June 2005).

20. Scott Parks, "The Big Man on Campus Reform," *Dallas Morning News,* 6 March 2005.

21. Emily Pyle, "Te$t Market," *Texas Observer,* 13 May 2005.

22. David Nather, "Boehner and Miller: Bipartisan Allies Determined to Pass ESEA Overhaul," *CQ Weekly,* 2 June 2001, 1314.

23. Nicholas Lemann, "Letter from Washington: Testing Limits," *New Yorker,* 2 July 2001.

24. David Broder, "Long Road to Reform: Negotiators Forge Education Legislation," *Washington Post,* 17 December 2001, A1.

25. Paul Manna, "Leaving No Child Behind," in *Political Education: National Policy Comes of Age,* ed. Christopher J. Cross (New York: Teachers College Press, 2004), 127.

26. David Broder, "Long Road to Reform: Negotiators Forge Education Legislation," *Washington Post,* 17 December 2001, A1.

27. Nather, "Boehner and Miller," 1314. Also see Michael Barone and Grant Ujifusa, *The Almanac of American Politics* (Washington, DC: National Journal, 2000), 1273.

28. *Congressional Quarterly Almanac* (Washington, DC: Congressional Quarterly, 2001), sec. 8, 5.

29. *Congressional Quarterly Almanac,* sec. 8, 5.

30. Diane Granat, "Special Report: The Class of 1974—Whatever Happened to the Watergate Babies?" *CQ Weekly,* 3 March 1984, 498.

31. "Committees: Rep. Miller Named Interior Chair," *CQ Weekly,* 10 May 1991, 1173.

32. George Miller's House website biography, <http://www.house.gov/georgemiller/bio.html> (3 March 2005).

33. Rudalevige, "Accountability and Avoidance," 27.

34. Nather, "Boehner and Miller," 1314; Manna, "Leaving No Child Behind," 132; David Nather, "Conferees Make Little Headway on Biggest Issues in Education Bill; Recess Talks Planned on Accountability," *CQ Weekly,* 4 August 2001, 1926.

35. Rudalevige, "Accountability and Avoidance," 23–24.

36. Also see Manna, "Leaving No Child Behind," 132.

37. Joetta L. Sack, "Democrats' 'Three R's' Bill Regains Currency," *Education Week,* 21 March 2001, <http://www.edweek.org/ew/articles/2001/03/21/27lieberman.h20.html> (14 May 2005).

38. David Nather, "The Leadership War," *CQ Weekly,* 19 January 2002, 181.

39. Michael Barone and Grant Ujifusa, *The Almanac of American Politics* (Washington, DC: National Journal, 2004), 774.

40. Rick Atkinson, "Why Ted Kennedy Can't Stand Still," *Washington Post,* 29 April 1990, W11.

41. Atkinson, "Why Ted Kennedy Can't Stand Still," W11.

42. Atkinson, "Why Ted Kennedy Can't Stand Still," W11.

43. Rudalevige, "Accountability and Avoidance," 26.

44. *Congressional Quarterly Almanac*, sec. 8, 5.

45. Manna, "Leaving No Child Behind," 130.

46. Broder, "Long Road to Reform," A1.

47. David Nather, "Education Bill Passes in House with Strong Bipartisan Support," *CQ Weekly,* 12 May 2001, 1079.

48. The administration's refusal to accept this mandatory provision was reportedly one of the reasons Senator Jeffords bolted from the Republican Party.

49. Kerry Kantin, "Rep. Boehner Soothes Conservatives' Nerves," *Hill,* 1 August 2001, 4.

50. Nicholas Lemann, "Letter from Washington: Testing Limits," *New Yorker*, 2 July 2001.

51. Rudalevige, "Accountability and Avoidance," 36.

52. David Nather, "Conferees Make Little Headway on Biggest Issues in Education Bill; Recess Talks Planned on Accountability," *CQ Weekly,* 4 August 2001, 1926.

53. Broder, "Long Road to Reform," A1.

54. Erik W. Robelen, "Amid Crisis, Outlook for ESEA Overhaul Unclear," *Education Week,* 26 September 2001. <http://www.edweek.org/ew/articles/2001/09/26/04esea.h21.html?querystring=No%20Child%20Left%20Behind> (5 April 2005).

55. Robelen, "Amid Crisis."

56. Rebecca Adams, Julie Hirschfeld Davis, Chuck McCutcheon, Ted Monoson, David Nather, and Keith Perine, "A Legislative Agenda in Limbo," *CQ Weekly,* 15 September 2001, 2134.

57. Erik W. Robelen, "Congress Refocuses on ESEA but Much Left to Resolve," *Education Week,* 3 October 2001. <http://www.edweek.org/ew/articles/2001/10/03/05esea.h21.html> (23 April 2005).

58. Transcript of interview with Representative George Miller, Morning Edition, NPR, Sept 11, 2001, <http://edworkforce.house.gov/democrats/npr.html> (3 June 2005).

59. Erik W. Robelen and Joetta Sack, "Policymakers Scramble to Deal with Closings," *Education Week,* 31 October 2001, <http://www.edweek.org/ew/articles/2001/10/31/09secure.h21.html> (23 April 2005); and Erik W. Robelen, "ESEA Conferees Reach Accord on Social Issues," *Education Week,* 7 November 2001, <http://www.edweek.org/ew/articles/2001/11/07/10esea.h21.html> (2 May 2005).

60. Robelen, "ESEA Conferees Reach Accord."

61. Erik W. Robelen, "Anthrax Incident Slows House-Senate Panel's Progress on ESEA Bill," *Education Week*, 24 October 2001, <http://www.edweek.org/ew/articles/2001/10/24/08esea.h21.html> (23 April 2005).

62. Joetta L. Sack, "ESEA Negotiators Near Accords, But Snags Remain," *Education Week,* 5 December 2001, <http://www.edweek.org/ew/articles/2001/12/05/14esea.h21.html> (5 May 2005).

63. Broder, "Long Road to Reform," A1.

64. Erik W. Robelen, "ESEA Passage Awaits a Deal on Spending," *Education Week,* 12 December 2001, <http://www.edweek.org/ew/articles/2001/12/12/15esea.h21.html> (3 April 2005).

Chapter 2

65. Erik W. Robelen, "House Overwhelmingly Passes Sweeping Education Reform Bill," *Education Week,* 13 December 2001, <http://www.edweek.org/ew/articles/2001/12/13/15esea_web2.h21.html> (14 April 2005).

66. Manna, "Leaving No Child Behind," 136.

67. Krista Kafer, "Education Reform's Final Odds," op-ed commentary, *Washington Times*, 19 June 2001, A18.

68. David Nather, "Compliments of the 107th Congress: Lessons for a New Congress," *CQ Weekly,* 14 December 2002, 3232.

69. Rudalevige, "Accountability and Avoidance," 41.

70. Nather, "Compliments of the 107th Congress," 3232.

71. Manna, "Leaving No Child Behind," 129.

72. Comments of President Bush, 9 January 2002, at Constitution Hall regarding education reform. White House press release "President Thanks Congress for Work on Education Reform," <http://www.whitehouse.gov/news/releases/2002/01/20020109-6.html> (24 April 2005).

73. "President Bush and members of Congress achieved an impressive legislative victory by holding firm to common language, avoiding extremes from both ends of the policy spectrum and subsuming the substantive divergences lurking beneath the surface of their 'terminology.' " Rudalevige, "Accountability and Avoidance," 42.

74. Rudalevige, "Accountability and Avoidance," 4–5.

75. Transcript of online chat, "The Bush Education Agenda," *EdWeek.org*, 24 July 2004, <http://www.edweek.org/chat/transcript_09-09-2004.html> (23 April 2005).

76. Manna, "Leaving No Child Behind," 129.

3

Intelligence Redesign and Reform

The terrorist attacks of 9/11 targeted on New York City and Washington, D.C.,[1] shocked all segments of American government from the president down to local emergency response agencies. Many questions needed answering: How could this have happened? Were the government's intelligence agencies asleep at the switch? Who was responsible for the failure to detect and defend against the terrorists? What errors were committed that allowed thousands of citizens to die and thousands of lives to be altered? And as the wife of one victim asked in public testimony, "Why hadn't our government fulfilled its foremost obligation—to protect our nation?"[2] Ultimately, answers to these questions would produce a set of changes in American intelligence gathering and analysis intended to prevent a recurrence. Time will tell whether these were the right changes and whether they were sufficient.

More than three years after the attacks, the search for answers produced the Intelligence Reform and Terrorism Prevention Act of 2004 (Public Law 108-408), signed into law by President George W. Bush on December 17, 2004. The path to reform was circuitous and rife with partisan conflict. Investigating 9/11 had the potential to influence both the 2002 and 2004 elections, and party strategists realized the stakes were great in the highly partisan atmosphere that reemerged after the brief, temporary truce in partisan warfare that followed the attacks of 9/11. Political leaders in both the White House and Congress steered these efforts because they were concerned about the political consequences likely to flow from blame for government failures. In fact, the final product was delayed until after the presidential and congressional elections of November 2, 2004, and much of the delay was occasioned by the respective parties' concern about their political adversary, not the terrorist adversary, gaining advantage. It is doubtful whether even this product would have been achieved without the steady pressure applied by persistent citizens' groups; some have suggested that government agencies' and elected officials' resistance to reform, avoidance of responsibility, and tendency to accept partisan stalemate was only overcome because of the pressure mounted by groups representing the families of victims of 9/11.

This case allows us to examine the roles played by those who significantly shaped the reform effort. In particular, we will look at several examples of "tandem leadership," pairs of leaders, most often from different parties, who played particularly constructive roles in shaping compromise solutions. Senators Susan Collins (R-ME) and Joseph Lieberman (D-CT), 9/11 Commission chair Thomas Kean and vice-chair Lee Hamilton, and Representatives Christopher Shays (R-CT) and Carolyn B. Maloney (D-NY) sought to exercise such joint leadership. We will also examine how "group leadership," a collection of individuals, can exercise influence by acting in concert. Both the members of the 9/11 Commission and the 9/11 Family Steering Committee, the principal group representing the interests of family members of 9/11 victims, provide good examples of such leadership.

In this chapter we first discuss the intelligence community and the September 11 attacks followed by an analysis of early congressional efforts to investigate intelligence failures. Next we focus on congressional and public efforts to pressure President Bush into establishing the 9/11 Commission and the president's eventual agreement. We then discuss the Commission's final report before analyzing policymakers' efforts to implement the Commission's findings. Finally, we will analyze how "tandem leadership" and "group leadership" were critical in producing intelligence reform.

BACKGROUND: THE SEPTEMBER 11 TERRORIST ATTACKS

On Tuesday morning at 8:46 a.m., American Airlines Flight 11 from Boston slammed into the North Tower (Building 1) of the World Trade Center in New York City. The plane is estimated to have contained ten thousand gallons of jet fuel for its trip to Los Angeles and to have been traveling at 470 mph upon impact. Eighty-one passengers and eleven crew members died instantly. But the death toll was far higher in the building. No one above the crash line of the 93rd to 98th floors survived the collision, and approximately 1366 people died. Below the crash line, more than four thousand survived and seventy-two died. Three of the five hijackers were stopped that morning when they tried to board the plane at Boston's Logan Airport, but the only consequence was that their checked luggage was held off the plane until it was confirmed that they had boarded the plane. CNN began live coverage of the crash scene at 8:48 with other networks soon joining in. As a result, millions of Americans watched the catastrophe unfold live on television.

United Airlines Flight 175 also took off from Boston that morning for Los Angeles. The pilot of Flight 175 heard a suspicious transmission from Flight 11 that suggested something was amiss, but the transmission did not elicit enough concern to raise alarm. In a matter of minutes, terrorists attacked the flight attendants on Flight 175, breached the cockpit, and took control of the plane. Flight 175, carrying fifty-six passengers and nine crew members, crashed into the South Tower (Building 2) at 9:03 a.m., hitting the building between the 78th through 84th floors. Six hundred people eventually died in the building, all but four of whom worked above the crash point; a handful of workers from the upper floors escaped. The lower death toll resulted from the evacuation of many workers during the seventeen minutes that followed the earlier crash, even though they were given conflicting directives. The combined death toll of these crashes (excluding hijackers) has been estimated at 2,998, including emergency personnel responding to the crisis.

American Airlines Flight 77 took off from Dulles Airport outside Washington, D.C., for Los Angeles. At least three of the five hijackers were stopped and screened before boarding. Although its takeoff was late, a general alert of the other hijackings had not yet been posted. After the plane was hijacked, it reversed course and flew toward Washington, D.C., crashing into the Pentagon at 9:37 a.m. More than 25,000 people normally work in the building, but the wing that was struck had recently been renovated so the workforce was unusually small (about 800). The new structural renovations to the wing also limited the damage. The death toll on the ground was approximately 125, and all fifty-eight passengers and six crew members died in the collision.

United Flight 93 was to have taken off for San Francisco at 8:01 a.m. but was delayed for more than forty minutes on the ground at Newark International Airport. Sometime between 10:03 and 10:10 a.m. the plane crashed in an empty field near Shanksville, Pennsylvania, after the thirty-seven passengers attempted to seize the plane back from its four hijackers. The plane was about 15 minutes from Washington, D.C., its presumed destination. All thirty-seven passengers and seven crew members died in the crash.

The death toll from the four incidents was 2,998 on the ground in New York City, 125 at the Pentagon, and a combined 265 airline passengers and crew members. More than one thousand of the dead in New York City could not be identified in subsequent weeks due to the devastating effects of fire and the structural collapse of the two towers. The nineteen terrorists, almost certainly associated with Al-Qaeda, the organization headed by Osama bin Laden, coordinated their actions and produced the largest man-made disaster in American history. The economic impact was severe as the three New York–based stock exchanges did not open on September 11 and remained closed until September 17 when they suffered historic declines. Domestic airlines halted operations for several days and then suffered from severe declines in business as travelers avoided air travel, a shock from which the airlines had not recovered four years later. In addition, future health problems are anticipated among Manhattan residents, especially for rescue and recovery workers, who were exposed to tons of dust including glass fibers and asbestos that spread over the city in a thick cloud after multiple World Trade Center buildings collapsed.

The Intelligence Community

On the morning of the hijackings, few agencies of the United States government distinguished themselves. The Federal Aviation Administration, overseer of the air traffic control system, was slow to identify the problems and notify others. The North American Air Defense Command (NORAD) responded slowly to the information and dispatched jet fighters to the wrong locations. Decision-makers in Washington scrambled for cover; both Capitol Hill and the White House were evacuated. Vice President Richard Cheney and National Security Advisor Condoleezza Rice set up operations in the secure White House Situation Room. Both President Bush and Secretary of Defense Rumsfeld, when notified of the attacks, continued to complete their current activities, a photo opportunity in a Florida elementary school in Bush's case and a routine briefing in Rumsfeld's. Although firefighters and police responded quickly on-site, coordination of larger emergency efforts was halting in New York City. Although all of these agencies and actors received scrutiny during the subsequent investigation of events, most attention focused on why the CIA, FBI, and other units in the intelligence community had failed to apprehend the terrorists and prevent the attacks.

In September 2001, the U.S. intelligence community consisted of fifteen units. The CIA is an independent agency operating under the direction of the president. The Department of Defense houses four separate service intelligence agencies (Air Force, Army, Marine Corps, and Navy), the more general Defense Intelligence Agency (DIA), and three specialized units: the National Geospatial-Intelligence Agency, the National Reconnaissance Office, and the National Security Agency. The FBI is located in the Department of Justice, which also contains the Drug Enforcement Administration's Office of National Security Intelligence. The Departments of Energy and State have units of their own intelligence units, the Office of Intelligence in the former and the Bureau of Intelligence and Research in the latter. Finally, the Department of Transportation has the Office of Intelligence Support. Coast Guard Intelligence was the fifteenth unit, which since 2003 has been housed in the Department of Homeland Security, created in November 2002, which then added the Information Analysis and Infrastructure Protection Directorate, a sixteenth unit. Collectively, these agencies and offices represent the United States intelligence community, but that community is frequently characterized by competition for dollars and conflict over interpretations of threats and recommendations for action. The performance of these federal agencies came under close scrutiny in the wake of 9/11.[3]

Just as there are multiple centers of intelligence gathering and evaluation in the executive branch, there are multiple centers of congressional oversight. Both the House and Senate have separate intelligence committees and appropriations committees that exercise considerable influence. Each chamber has an armed services committee, as well, that is especially attentive to the extensive intelligence activities of the Department of Defense and the branches of the armed services. Both chambers also have government affairs committees that are especially interested in issues of government structure and ways to enhance efficiency. After 9/11, both of the chambers' judiciary committees also exercised greater attention to how civil liberties were affected by expanded counterterrorism powers of detention and surveillance granted by the Uniting and Strengthening America by Providing Appropriate Tools Required to Intercept and Obstruct Terrorism Act of 2001 (USA Patriot Act) passed on October 26, 2001. Three special topics deserve additional mention. During the post-9/11 period, the House created a special ad hoc committee to coordinate the chamber's response; the House and Senate Select Intelligence Committees undertook a bicameral, bipartisan joint inquiry; and interlocking memberships, especially in the Senate, played an important role as members on the intelligence committees also serving on the Armed Services Committee defended the DOD units from change.

In addition to investigations, Congress had several other ways to influence intelligence issues. Annual authorizations are an especially powerful way to shape bureaucratic actions, and these decision points were used repeatedly as a means to redirect intelligence efforts or blunt broader calls for reform and investigation. Finally, individual members found ample opportunity to make their views known in the media and seek to shape action.

EARLY EFFORTS TO LAUNCH A 9/11 INQUIRY

Soon after 9/11, some members of Congress called for an investigation into intelligence failures. Such calls often included proposals to create an independent commission to investigate the intelligence failures before the attacks and propose a major overhaul of the intelligence community. For example, Senator Robert Torricelli (D-NJ) proposed the formation of a commission of inquiry on December 18, 2001, and Senators John McCain (R-AZ) and Joseph Lieberman (D-CT) proposed creation of an independent 9/11 Commission on December 20 (S 1867). Lieberman, as chair of the Senate Governmental Affairs Committee, was able to keep the proposal alive throughout the year by using his committee to work on the idea. The administration and the House, however, opposed creation of such an independent group. Furthermore, the chairs of the House and Senate Intelligence Committees rejected such a proposal, citing Congress's traditional investigatory role, and pledged instead to conduct congressional inquiries.[4]

The Joint Congressional Inquiry

On December 20, 2001, House and Senate leaders arranged a bicameral, bipartisan congressional inquiry with participation from both the House Permanent Select Committee on Intelligence and the Senate Select Committee on Intelligence. Such a bicameral initiative was virtually unprecedented and reflected the intent of Republican Party leaders to meet the Congress's desire to conduct an investigation.[5] The administration, like many others before it, argued that investigations consume time and deflect the administration's attention from the major work at hand—in this case, fighting terrorism. Such inquiries also have enormous potential to provide administration critics with ammunition, a danger made greater by Democrats' control of the Senate. By having the standing intelligence committees conduct the investigation, the intelligence community and the administration hoped for a more sympathetic and less intrusive review because of the close working relationships between the committees and the agencies. The committee chairmen, both from Florida, were longtime political friends and one, Representative Porter Goss, had served in the CIA. The initial staff director for the joint inquiry, L. Britt Snider, chosen by the committee chairs, had served as the CIA's inspector general and was a close associate of CIA Director George J. Tenet.

Over the course of the joint inquiry, committee staff reviewed five hundred thousand pages of government documents. They also conducted about three hundred interviews and held discussions with another six hundred members of the intelligence community and other officials. Although this effort represents a significant amount of work, it did not go smoothly. Several sources of conflict, including partisanship, electoral competition, personal ambition, and staff turnover prevented the inquiry from making greater strides.

The first source of partisan conflict was that the Democrats controlled the Senate, and the Republicans controlled the House. Divided party control added further fuel to the interbranch rivalry that would have existed even if one party had controlled both chambers. Second, the Democrats' criticism of the administration's performance both before 9/11 and in the war against terrorism played a prominent part in the 2002 midterm elections.[6] Since the Republicans used the 9/11 attacks and security issues to maximum effect in the election, both sides had a reason to distrust the other—the investigation became a political football that both sides wished to exploit. Third, personal ambition played a role in limiting the investigation's effectiveness. The Senate committee was chaired by Senator Bob Graham (D-FL), who later sought his party's presidential nomination, and the House committee was chaired by Porter Goss (R-FL), who later became director of the CIA. The committees' ranking members were Senator Richard Shelby (R-AL), a former chair of the committee but a strong critic of the intelligence community, and Nancy Pelosi (D-CA), an outspoken administration critic who became the House minority leader after the 2002 election. Finally, the joint inquiry's progress was disrupted when the original executive director, L. Britt Snider, resigned on May 1, 2002, after numerous conflicts with his own staff and committee members.[7] This staff turnover delayed initial hearings that had been expected in May 2002 but did not begin until September 18, 2002, when a new staff director, Eleanor Hill, was in place.[8]

A Recalcitrant White House

The last mitigating factor preventing greater success by the joint inquiry was the increasingly strained relationship between the Congress and the White House over intelligence. Although the committees had been promised full cooperation and ready access to documents by the White House, the CIA director, and other leaders in the intelligence community, the administration denied, limited, or severely delayed numerous requests for information and testimony.[9] For example, the inquiry was denied access to the President's Daily Brief (PDB), a summary of worldwide developments produced by the CIA and delivered daily by its director to the president. Not only were the contents declared off-limits, but the CIA also refused to describe the process by which the brief was developed. Thus, the committee could learn neither *what* Presidents Clinton and Bush were told about Al-Qaeda threats nor *when* they were told.[10]

There were many other examples of the administration's unwillingness to provide materials to the inquiry. The administration rejected requests for information about CIA cooperation with foreign governments, information about annual budget requests submitted by the intelligence agencies, and how the White House had acted on those requests. The administration also denied requests for information used by the National Security Council to guide intelligence community activities.

There were also many examples of the administration granting requests for information but delaying its submission and the process for usage. Both the CIA and the National Security Agency insisted that documents be reviewed in their offices with restricted rights to copy those materials, although notes could be taken and removed from the premises. The agencies insisted that representatives (monitors) had to be present at all interviews with personnel; the joint committee insisted on independent access and succeeded in achieving it on several occasions. Those documents that were supplied came only in paper, not in electronic form, as the inquiry staff had requested, and even those materials made available had substantial portions blacked out, or "redacted."

Finally, the administration was particularly protective of senior staff. The national security advisor, Condoleezza Rice, refused to testify, and when the deputy national security advisor, Stephen J. Hadley, agreed to respond to written questions, there was a five-month delay between the submission of the questions and the response. (Hadley later replaced Rice as the national security advisor when she became secretary of state.) Ultimately the congressional inquiry did not hear from the most senior national security officials in the Bush administration; it was unable to interview the secretaries of state and defense, the attorney general, or the National Security Advisor.

In short, from the joint inquiry's perspective, the congressional investigation was severely hampered by the administration's noncooperation and delay. Even Republican Senator Richard Shelby (R-AL) ran the risk of being openly critical shortly before the 2002 midterm elections, saying that, "You know, we were told that there would be cooperation in this investigation, and I question that. I think that most of the information that our staff has been able to get that is real meaningful has had to be extracted piece by piece."[11]

Despite the favorable circumstances of the joint inquiry, with intelligence committees leading the investigation, the administration dragged its feet rather than cooperate during the joint inquiry. Even after it was completed, the administration delayed release of the final report because it drew upon confidential material, and the report was withheld from the public, ostensibly to prevent damage to ongoing intelligence efforts. The declassification review process took many months to complete, and the full text of the report was not released until July 24, 2003, a full six months after the inquiry released a list of nineteen recommendations on December 11, 2002.

ESTABLISHING THE 9/11 COMMISSION

Because the congressional inquiry floundered through most of its investigation, there were renewed calls for the creation of an "independent" inquiry that was less likely to be mired in politics. President Bush initially opposed launching such an independent investigation but ultimately reversed course on September 20, 2002. This reversal was the result of mounting pressure brought to bear on the administration by Congress and 9/11 family groups, pressure that was amplified by unfavorable media coverage for the administration just as the midterm elections were approaching.

Pressure Mounts on the White House for an Independent Commission

In the immediate aftermath of the 9/11 attacks, the White House made efforts to head off a potential independent commission investigating intelligence failures, including personal lobbying by Bush and Cheney. *Newsweek* reported in its February 4, 2002, issue that Vice President Cheney called Senate Majority Leader Tom Daschle on January 24, 2002, to oppose creation of an independent 9/11 inquiry; President Bush reportedly followed with a similar call to Daschle on January 28. The president and vice president reportedly argued that the administration was too busy running the war on terrorism to contend with an independent inquiry, and they were concerned that delving into sensitive information could reveal critical intelligence sources that would compromise their efforts. Bush and Cheney's efforts to prevent an independent inquiry came during a period of extraordinary bipartisanship following 9/11. In this bipartisan spirit, Daschle chose not to push for creating the independent inquiry early in 2002, but Senator Lieberman kept the option alive in his committee.

Public pressure to launch an independent inquiry surged in May 2002 when it was revealed that Bush had been briefed on August 6, 2001, a month before the terrorist attacks, about the possibility Osama bin Laden might hijack commercial aircraft. Amidst a flurry of explanations from Condoleezza Rice about how the briefing materials had not been very precise, Vice President Cheney warned about the potential damage investigations could cause, particularly when "the United States faces the threat of a new attack even worse than the Sept. 11 assaults." He went on to condemn "Democratic Party criticism of the White House's handling of the terror warnings as 'thoroughly irresponsible . . . in a time of war.'"[12] Any suggestion that the White House may have had advance knowledge of the terrorist attacks was political dynamite, as demonstrated again in 2004 when such charges became part of the presidential campaign. When asked about the issue during a trip to Europe on May 23, 2002, the president echoed Cheney's warnings about damage that might be done to the war effort and opposed creation of an independent investigation, saying that sources could be compromised if people outside the administration had access to sensitive information.

The administration's warnings notwithstanding, pressure continued to build in Congress to launch a separate investigation. Members of Congress with previous interest in an independent commission, like Senators McCain, Lieberman, and Shelby, and Representatives Tim Roemer (D-IN), Chris Shays (R-CT), and Chris Smith (R-NJ), once again sought to create an independent inquiry.[13] As the FY 2003 Intelligence Appropriations bill (H.R. 4628) moved through the House, Tim Roemer secured approval of an amendment that "required the establishment of a bipartisan 'blue ribbon' commission to investigate intelligence failures that led to the September 11th terrorist attacks and recommend actions to help prevent future attacks."[14]

This amendment, approved on July 25, 2002, by a floor vote of 219 to 188, was opposed by the administration and the Republican Party leadership. The Republican leadership feared that the proposed commission would seek to lay blame at the president's door: as Ray LaHood (R-IL) complained, "This is the blame-game commission. It's [the Democrats'] attempt to try and blame Bush somewhere along the way."[15] The amendment received support from 193 Democrats, 1 Independent, and 25 Republicans. The Republican support largely drew from Northeast districts that suffered sizable losses in the terror attack, as well as a few conservative Republicans highly critical of the government's performance in collecting intelligence. One hundred eighty-three Republicans, 4 Democrats, and 1 Independent voted to oppose the amendment. This break in Republican ranks signaled growing frustration at the lack of progress in the joint inquiry and a response to the administration's proposal for a 25 percent increase in the intelligence budget for the upcoming fiscal year.

Representative Christopher Smith (R-NJ) offered another amendment, approved by voice vote, requiring two victim family members to be included on the commission. Significantly, Roemer served as a member of the congressional joint inquiry and was sufficiently critical of the administration's noncooperation to include a separate statement in the final report that detailed the administration's delay tactics. The consensus opinion at the time was that the call for an independent commission would be removed in conference committee, but that ultimately did not happen.

9/11 Family Steering Committee

Twelve family members—mothers, wives, daughters, one husband, and one sister—of 9/11 victims came together after the 9/11 Commission was organized in order to monitor its activities after working together during the preceding year trying to get an independent inquiry launched. Members of the 9/11 Family Steering Committee (FSC) also belonged to other survivor/victims' organizations and frequently were chairs, cochairs, or founders of those organizations. In some respects, then, the FSC served as a coordinating council representing many other organizations although they did not have such a formal standing. Their task was to shame the government into action. As Dana Milbank of the *Washington Post* argued the day after the reform was adopted,

> It is no exaggeration to say that yesterday's reorganization of the nation's intelligence structure would not have happened without [Mary] Fetchet, [Carol] Ashley and the 10 other self-appointed representatives of September 11 victims' relatives who formed the Family Steering Committee. Though they started out with little understanding of politics or national security, and they did not truly represent the thousands of victims' relatives (in fact, many other relatives opposed

the legislation), they used the moral authority they earned from their losses—invoked freely in vigils, at news conferences and in the lobbies of Congress—to shame the government into action.[16]

Individuals began to visit Washington in the fall of 2001, meeting with sympathetic members of Congress while others contacted legislators by fax and phone. Other family members offered testimony to the congressional joint inquiry, other congressional committees, and the 9/11 Commission or appeared on television to promote the idea of creating an independent inquiry. These public statements humanized the inquiry, linking the details of intelligence reporting systems and organizational procedures to real costs in very human terms.

The group closely monitored the progress of the 9/11 Commission, issuing "Report Cards" and commentary along the way. At the same time that they criticized the administration for "stonewalling" Commission requests for information, they also criticized the Commission's performance: "This investigation was supposed to be hard hitting and transparent. So far it has been neither. Instead it appears that the Commission has acquiesced to every condition imposed by recalcitrant government officials."[17] After the Commission issued its report, the FSC became aggressive advocates for adoption of the recommendations.

Media pressure also became a significant factor. During a television interview with Phil Donahue on August 13, 2002, Kristen Breitweiser, the wife of a 9/11 victim, presented a highly sympathetic case for why the joint congressional inquiry was not sufficient:

We don't feel comfortable with Congress investigating itself, basically. You have congressional committees that had oversight duties with the FBI and the CIA. We want politics removed. We want pure accountability, and we feel that an independent investigation is needed to have that. We've had independent investigations with regard to Pearl Harbor, with regard to the [NASA] shuttle accident. If there's a car accident, you have an investigation. We have waited 11 months.

And at the height of media revelations about widespread corporate scandals she explained,

You have President Bush out there saying that he wants transparency and accountability on behalf of Fortune 500 CEOs. I would like some transparency and accountability on behalf of, you know, President Bush and his workers, who were the individuals that failed my husband and the 3,000 other people that day.[18]

In September, the first anniversary of the 9/11 attacks was marked with numerous newspaper editorials decrying the lack of clear answers about what had transpired a year earlier, but the most important surge in public pressure came during the initial public hearings of the joint congressional inquiry, on September 18, 2002. The dramatic testimony from two surviving spouses of 9/11 victims, who highlighted their frustration and repeated their call for an independent inquiry, led to widespread coverage in the media. One of the spouses was Kristen Breitweiser, serving as a spokesperson for the victims' families. She poignantly explained that, "My 3-year old daughter's most enduring memory of her father will be placing flowers on his empty grave." She also recounted the last conversation with her husband that concluded just minutes before the second plane slammed into the towers.[19] Breitweiser calmly explained that,

> September 11th was the devastating result of a catalogue of failures on behalf of our government and its agencies. My husband and the approximately 3,000 others like him went to work and never came home. But, were any of our governmental agencies doing their job on that fateful morning? Perhaps, the carnage and devastation of September 11th speaks for itself in answering this question. . . .
>
> Soon after the attacks, President Bush stated that there would come a time to look back and examine our nation's failures, but that such an undertaking was inappropriate while the nation was still in shock. I would respectfully suggest to President Bush and to our Congress that now, a full year later, it is time to look back and investigate our failures as a nation. A hallmark of democratic government is a willingness to admit to, analyze, and learn from mistakes. And it is now time for our nation to triumph as the great democracy that it is. . . .
>
> The families of the victims of September 11th have waited long enough. We need to have answers. We need to have accountability. We need to feel safe living and working in this great nation.[20]

Bush Reverses Course: Building the 9/11 Commission

Two days after these hearings and the ensuing public pressure for an independent investigation, President Bush reversed his earlier position and endorsed a "focused inquiry" in a letter to congressional leaders. Support for an independent inquiry had also grown among members of Congress, including the members of the intelligence committees who had earlier resisted the suggestion, as the research portion of the congressional joint inquiry came to a conclusion. Two considerations figured prominently in the change of heart: many intelligence committee members were scheduled to rotate off the panels in the next Congress so there would be little continuity; and some of the initial findings made them believe that the February 2003 deadline for the joint inquiry did not provide enough time for a full evaluation of the nation's intelligence needs. In July, the House had gone on record supporting the independent inquiry by supporting Roemer's amendment; on September 19, the Senate overwhelmingly approved an amendment sponsored by Senators Lieberman and McCain to establish an independent inquiry by a vote of 90–8. This strong endorsement of the Lieberman-McCain amendment could be viewed as a rebuke to the administration which had initially opposed the senators' effort.[21]

The House and Senate, however, had different conceptions of how to design an independent investigation. The Senate called for a broader inquiry than the House or the administration wanted, so supporters in the Congress sought to build consensus through negotiations among Representative Porter Goss, chairman of the House Select Committee on Intelligence, Nancy Pelosi (D-CA), ranking Democrat on the House Intelligence Committee, Senate Intelligence Committee Chairman Bob Graham (D-FL), and Senator Richard C. Shelby (R-AL), the panel's ranking Republican.[22] In addition to the interchamber negotiation, the White House insisted on several procedural points that would protect the president from a congressional witch hunt: the president would name a single chair, instead of the Democrats' preference for cochairs, and Congress would select the other nine members; and subpoenas for information would require six votes on a committee that would include five Republicans and five Democrats, a way, it was argued, to reduce partisanship.[23]

Talks dragged on, but the party and chamber differences seemed to be resolved on October 10 when congressional negotiators announced a tentative agreement on two procedural provisions very different from those the White House had advanced: the committee would have cochairs, meeting the Democrats' demand, one named by the president and one by Congress; and subpoenas would be issued with the support of five votes, meaning that either bloc of party nominees could insist on a direction of inquiry. Negotiators publicly declared success before the cameras with members of the victims' groups in attendance.

During the press conference, however, Representative Goss took a phone call in his office from Vice President Cheney objecting to the terms of the deal, and after discussion with his colleagues, Goss announced that they had not been able to agree on the deal that would satisfy the White House. Victims' family members, and other supporters of an independent investigation, were disappointed at the last-minute collapse as they interpreted the White House backing away from the president's earlier announcement of support as potentially undermining the entire effort. White House spokesmen, however, reaffirmed the administration's continued commitment and explained that the way an inquiry would be conducted was critical to its eventual success and therefore worthy of continued discussion. Victims' families held a candlelight vigil at the White House to call attention to the delay and insist that the White House drop its objections.

With negotiation over an independent investigation at a standstill and Election Day rapidly approaching, Senator Lieberman convened a meeting in his office on October 16 that included White House representatives and ten members of family groups to try to resolve the 9/11 Commission impasse before the Congress adjourned. When the family members became agitated at what they regarded as unreasonable intransigence on the part of the administration, the White House aides retreated from the room. As a result, no agreement was reached before Congress adjourned prior to the November 5 elections.[24]

Differences over the structure and rules of the independent inquiry were not resolved until November 15 when both chambers approved the FY 2003 Intelligence Authorization conference reports, which the president signed into law with a provision creating the National Commission on Terrorist Attacks Upon the United States, or more commonly, the 9/11 Commission. In the end, the administration compromised on several issues it had staked out prior to the election. As finally constituted, the Commission was to have

- ten members, divided evenly between Republicans and Democrats including one Republican approved by Senators McCain and Shelby, strong proponents of the inquiry;[25]
- a finite life span of eighteen months that would ensure its expiration well before the 2004 elections;
- a tight budget of $3 million;
- subpoena power exercised through six votes or through agreement of the chair and vice-chair;
- a focus on nine specified areas of inquiry in hopes of keeping the Commission's activities on track;
- a chair named by the president, and a vice-chair named by the Democrats.

President Bush initially named Henry Kissinger as the chair, and the Democrats named George Mitchell to serve as vice-chair. Within a month, both of these choices resigned due to potential conflicts of interest and reluctance to reveal client lists for their consulting and law firms that included Middle Eastern interests. The resignations did not constitute an auspicious beginning, as a *New York Times* editorial pointed out: "The Commission to investigate U.S. failures leading up to the September 11, 2001, attacks is in disarray, which is no small trick given that it has yet to meet."[26]

Both the president and the Democrats moved quickly to select new leaders. The president named Thomas Kean, former governor of New Jersey and current president of Drew University, to the Commission on December 16 to replace Kissinger; the Democrats named Lee Hamilton, a former congressman from Indiana and a fellow at the Wilson Center in Washington, D.C., as the vice-chair soon afterward. Upon his appointment, Kean made a controversial decision to remain full-time as president of Drew and commit one day a week to the Commission's work—a level of involvement that some considered too low. The other Republicans named to the Commission were Fred F. Fielding, an attorney; Slade Gorton, former senator from Washington state; John F. Lehman, a former secretary of the navy; and James R. Thompson, a former governor of Illinois. Democratic members were Richard Ben-Veniste, a Washington attorney and former chief of the Watergate Task Force; Jamie Gorelick, a former deputy attorney general from the Clinton administration with experience in the Department of Defense and earlier service on the Scowcroft Commission on Intelligence; Max Cleland, former senator from Georgia who had just been defeated in the November elections; and Timothy J. Roemer, the former congressman from Indiana who had served on the congressional joint inquiry and retired from Congress at the end of the term. Cleland later resigned from the Commission in December 2003 and was replaced by Bob Kerrey, the former senator from Nebraska.

9/11 Commissioners Thomas W. Kean and Lee Hamilton

The chair and vice-chair of the 9/11 Commission had long histories of bipartisan cooperation. At the time of his selection, Thomas W. Kean, president of Drew University, was described by the *New York Times* as "a moderate Republican known for his integrity and independence."[27] This record had been compiled as governor of New Jersey for two terms from 1981–1989. His family's political roots date back to the seventeenth- and eighteenth-century American leaders Peter Stuyvesant and William Livingston and extended into the recent past: "his father represented New Jersey for twenty years in the U.S. House of Representatives; his grandfather and his great uncle were U.S. senators from New Jersey."[28] Kean spent a decade in the New Jersey state assembly, becoming the party leader and speaker while losing primary bids for House and gubernatorial nominations. His narrow victory for governor in 1981 came at age forty-six after he defeated seven other Republicans for the nomination—he won the closest gubernatorial race in New Jersey's history. He was reelected in 1985 by the largest margin in New Jersey history with extensive support from traditionally Democratic groups, such as labor and environmental activists.

Kean followed a bipartisan strategy by necessity. New Jersey was a traditionally Democratic state, making it essential that a Republican governor cooperate with the Democrat-controlled legislature, a style he had mastered as a minority member in the state assembly.[29] His success in broadening the Republicans' electoral base brought him national attention, and he served as the keynote speaker for the Republican national convention in August 1988. But his selection and message was controversial among Republican conservatives,[30] and he decided in the 1990s not to seek a Senate seat when Frank Lautenberg seemed vulnerable in 1994 or when Bill Bradley retired in 1996. At the time, his public criticism of the new tone that Republican radicals had injected into Congress was quite pointed.

At the time of his selection, Lee Hamilton was director of the Woodrow Wilson International Center for Scholars in Washington, D.C. He had moved to this position after serving as the congressman from the 9th district of Indiana from 1964 until his retirement in 1998. During this long career, Hamilton served as chair of the Intelligence (1985–1987), Joint Economic (1989–1990), and International Relations (1993–1995, now Foreign Affairs) Committees. Hamilton defeated a Republican in the Democratic electoral landslide of 1964 and came to national attention in 1987–1988 as chair of the House select committee that investigated the Iran-Contra affair. Hamilton was known as a member of Congress who shunned publicity, so it was assumed that he would not take advantage of the sensitive investigation to seek partisan advantage. Nor was he a risk for leaks to the media. "In all of his leadership positions—and especially as Intelligence chairman—he has made a point of refusing to divulge classified information, even when other members appeared willing to do so."[31] Richard Cheney, then the representative from Wyoming, was ranking minority member on the committee, a connection that probably made Hamilton acceptable to the Bush administration as vice-chair of the 9/11 Commission.

Hamilton gained national prominence and respect. "Among his colleagues in Congress, he is respected primarily for his thoughtful, nononsense approach to issues. Hamilton rarely raises his voice, but other members listen when he does."[32] Both Michael Dukakis and Bill Clinton considered Hamilton for the vice presidential nomination. And he was repeatedly appointed to difficult leadership positions; the Iran-Contra investigation gained national coverage, but he also chaired a House task force created in late 1992 designed to investigate charges that the Reagan presidential campaign in 1980 had sought to avoid an "October surprise," actively working to delay the release of American hostages held in Iran until after the November election. This was political dynamite at the outset of a presidential election year. Under Hamilton's guidance, the committee exploded the charges as a myth and resisted the temptation to engage in highly partisan rhetoric.[33] This experience was a virtual dress rehearsal for the 9/11 Commission.

Controversies Surrounding the Commission

When Tim Roemer proposed creation of the independent commission, he argued, "It is imperative that we establish a commission that is free of partisanship and independent of the intelligence community that can make a full and complete accounting of the circumstances surrounding the awful tragedy of September 11."[34] His optimistic hopes were not fully realized as the Commission encountered partisanship and administrative resistance—similar to the problems that had plagued the congressional joint inquiry. And partisanship, far from being absent, emerged at several points, although the chair and vice-chair made a special effort to prevent it from damaging the overall effort. For the sake of organizing discussion, we will explore three areas of controversy that plagued the Commission: potential conflicts of interest, partisan purpose, and administration noncooperation, with the last receiving the most attention.

Potential Conflicts of Interest

Virtually all the Commission members had some association that critics assailed as a conflict of interest likely to impair a full and fair investigation, including corporate ties with Saudi Arabia, the country of origin for fifteen of the nineteen hijackers and a probable source of financing for the attacks, connections with Democratic and Republican election campaigns and organizations, ties to the airlines and airline manufacturers, or membership on government advisory boards. What these surely demonstrated was that important people—the kind to be named to a blue ribbon commission—had important connections. It was unlikely that anyone worthy of serving on the Commission would be wholly lacking in powerful connections and the potential conflict of interest they bring.

Probably of greatest concern, particularly for members of the 9/11 Family Steering Committee, the family group most active in monitoring the Commission's work, were the ties between the staff director, Philip Zelikow, and the Bush administration. Because Zelikow would guide the investigation, a significant conflict of interest could lead him to direct attention away from administration errors or oversights and make him uninterested in establishing individual culpability. After investigating his past, the family group called publicly for his resignation. Zelikow was an appointee of George W. Bush to the President's Foreign Intelligence Advisory Board; he had served three years on the first President Bush's National Security Council staff; moreover, he had worked closely, and coauthored a book, with National Security Advisor Condoleezza Rice.

Partisan Purposes

President Bush's initial reluctance to have an independent commission no doubt reflected his concern that Democrats would use the forum as a means to attack him during his reelection campaign, a fear that was fully justified when his opponent, John Kerry, made the Bush administration's intelligence failures an important part of the campaign.[35] As detailed above, during the negotiations to establish the Commission, the administration had sought to focus the inquiry, limit its budget and duration, minimize politically dangerous use of the subpoena power, and establish bipartisan operating rules. Nonetheless, partisanship could be clearly discerned in its operations. Democratic commissioners pushed Bush administration witnesses harder than their Republican colleagues who seemed anxious to help witnesses get through their questioning unscathed. Conversely, Republican commissioners grilled Clinton administration witnesses more fully than the Democrats. The Commission's chair and vice-chair faced the difficult task of summoning knowledgeable witnesses and encouraging their colleagues to ask tough questions while also maintaining a constructive relationship with the administration whose cooperation was critical to success of the effort, but which was understandably concerned about political fallout.

The most dramatic example of partisanship came in testimony from Richard Clarke, a terrorism expert in the Clinton White House who had remained a member of the Bush National Security Council (NSC). Clarke's televised testimony came on March 24, 2004, three days after he appeared on CBS's *60 Minutes*, where he assailed the Bush administration's handling of terrorism. Furthermore, Clarke's book *Against All Enemies* was available in bookstores on March 25. In short, there was a media blitz surrounding Clarke that highlighted critical statements about Bush's inattention to terrorism issues before 9/11 and the ineffectiveness of the administration's efforts afterward.

The administration and its allies, including those on the Commission, launched a multipronged counteroffensive against Clarke and his claims of a Bush failure. Reportedly, White House Counsel Alberto Gonzales called Republican Commission members Fred Fielding and James Thompson on the day before Clarke's testimony to suggest lines of questioning.[36] Questions were raised about Clarke's motives, whether he was angry over his demotion in the

Bush NSC and whether he was actively seeking a position in a Kerry administration by being so critical.

Condoleezza Rice, the president's National Security Advisor and Clarke's former boss, took the offensive in publicly defending the administration's record and ultimately appeared in person before the Commission to rebut Clarke's testimony. As in the case of the joint congressional inquiry, until this point, Bush had resolutely refused to allow her to testify, invoking "executive privilege," a claim made by presidents since Dwight D. Eisenhower that in order to preserve the quality of advice they receive, presidents must declare some materials and advisors off-limits. But under enormous public pressure, the White House and the Commission made an agreement whereby Rice would be the only White House figure to testify before the Commission.

A Noncooperative Administration

Allowing Rice to testify, allowing the Commission to have access to heretofore secret Presidential Daily Briefs, even allowing the president and vice president to meet with commissioners in a nonpublic setting were steps that followed painful, private negotiations between the Commission's leadership and the White House. If it appeared to be uncooperative, the administration ran the risk of potentially greater political damage than if it allowed controlled access to documents and people. The Commission and the White House engaged in the same dance as the congressional joint inquiry but in a different setting, one that produced far greater pressure on the administration to cooperate.

Problems arose from the outset when some Commission members had difficulty receiving security clearances, even though one might assume their prominence in public life would ensure clearance (for example, former Senator Slade Gorton was not immediately granted clearance). Similarly, there were problems in getting access to materials; Tim Roemer, a member of the joint congressional inquiry, was denied access to the final report that he had previously read as a member of the congressional joint inquiry. When the Commission chairs sought supplemental funding beyond the original $3 million appropriation that would be consumed by August 2003, the administration was very slow in agreeing to the additional appropriation (eventually totaling $12 million). A *New York Times* editorial speculated, "Reasonable people might wonder if the White House, having failed in its initial attempt to have Henry Kissinger steer the investigation, may be resorting to budgetary starvation as a tactic to hobble any politically fearless inquiry."[37] Similarly, when it was clear that the May 2004 deadline for completion of the Commission's work could not be met, the administration only reluctantly agreed to extend the deadline to July 2004.

The greatest problems involved access to administration documents and unfettered access to personnel. Conflict escalated during the summer of 2003.

The Justice Department insisted that a department official be present during any interview with a federal official, a practice that Commission Chairman Kean (the Republican) referred to as "intimidation." Several departments, particularly the FBI, CIA, and DOD were especially slow in responding to requests for information. Commissioners began complaining publicly: "We need a steady stream of information coming to us . . . Instead, we're getting a trickle."[38] Finally, the Commission members authorized in October and November 2003 that subpoenas be issued to the Federal Aviation Administration and the Pentagon to secure necessary documents. There were extended negotiations between the Commission's leadership and the White House, handled by Gonzales, about the release of documents shielded by the president as too sensitive, including the President's Daily Brief.

Pressure mounted on the administration, and an agreement was finally announced on November 12, 2003. Not all commissioners were to have access to classified intelligence documents, though all documents could be viewed by *some* commissioners; notes taken about documents that could not be removed or copied were also subject to administration review. This arrangement was changed in February 2004 when it was announced that all commissioners would be able to see summaries of the PDBs, but only three would be allowed to view the originals.

But the agreement on expanded access did not ensure smooth sailing. As late as April 2004 there was a flap about access to papers requested from the Clinton years in order to determine the relative efforts of the Clinton and Bush administrations in combating the terrorist threat. Coming in the wake of Richard Clarke's testimony, the White House withheld a large percentage of Clinton documents requested by the Commission's staff, turning over "1,966 pages of 10,790 total, or about 18 percent. Another 90 pages of Clinton documents are also in dispute," but that meant that nearly 75 percent of the requested documents were not produced. Commission member Jamie Gorelick delivered the Democrats' argument: "We can't afford to have documents that are relevant to our inquiry being withheld on a technicality. This is not litigation. This is finding facts to help the nation, and we should not treat this as if we're adversarial parties here."[39]

Finally, on April 29, 2004, President Bush and Vice President Cheney met with the 9/11 commissioners in the White House for an interview that lasted just over three hours. (Former President Clinton had previously met with the Commission as had former Vice President Gore in separate sessions.) Bush had resisted such an appearance and initially said he would meet only with Kean and Hamilton. He altered his position on March 30 in the wake of Richard Clarke's damaging testimony. But there were extensive conditions that limited the interaction: Cheney would also be included in the meeting; no stenographer would be present, so no transcript of the meeting would be available; neither would be sworn in; commissioners' notes would be reviewed for classified information and then returned to them.[40] Critics portrayed the joint testimony as evidence of the "Wizard of Oz" presidency, a direct contrast with the Bush campaign's portrait of the president as being on top of events.

> At the center is an incurious president who is so inarticulate that he can't be left on his own to make a sustained argument on behalf of his policies without falling back on rehearsed talking points and sound bites . . . the arrangement confirms Bush's inability to articulate anything without a script—or a tutor by his side.[41]

THE COMMISSION'S FINAL REPORT

On July 22, 2004, the 9/11 Commission released its 567-page report a few days earlier than its extended deadline. The final report was adopted unanimously, an effort to maintain unity that disappointed some. As Richard Clarke argued in a *New York Times* op-ed piece, "Americans owe the 9/11 commission a deep debt for its extensive exposition of the facts surrounding the World Trade Center and Pentagon attacks. Yet, because the Commission had a goal of creating a unanimous report from a bipartisan group, it softened the edges and left it to the public to draw many conclusions."[42] There were "failures" identified in the report, but the blame was spread broadly, not particularly focused on the Bush or Clinton administration. As one *Washington Post* article summarized, "Though openly dreaded for months by many Republicans and quietly feared by the White House, the report was much gentler on the Bush administration than they feared. Rather than focus criticism on the Bush administration, the Commission spread the blame broadly and evenly across two administrations, the FBI, and Congress."[43]

President Bush praised the Commission's work in a Rose Garden meeting when the chair and vice-chair delivered the report. The president promised to consider the Commission's recommendations but did not make any commitment to implement them. Speaker of the House Dennis Hastert made it clear the House would be very deliberate in taking action, suggesting that nothing would be completed before the November elections. Democrats, led by John Kerry, rushed to embrace the forty-one recommendations and promise rapid adoption. For their part, Kean spoke for the commissioners in announcing that "All 10 of us have decided to . . . do everything we can, whether it's testimony or lobbying or speaking or whatever's necessary, to let the American people know about these recommendations, know how important they are, our belief that they can save lives."[44]

This collective commitment to changing policy helped the commissioners overcome the conflict that would have arisen if the goal had been to assign

blame. For example, several members of the Commission found major dis-
crepancies in the account given by the president and vice president of who
authorized Air Force interceptors to shoot down commercial jets that might have
been hijacked and headed for Washington, D.C. The vice president said that the
president had relayed such approval to him during a phone call whose existence
could not be confirmed. One journalistic account summarizes the views of skeptical commissioners:

> One member of the commission, who would speak only if promised
> anonymity, was blunt: "We purposely did not reach a conclusion. We just
> laid it out. Some people may read what we wrote and conclude the autho-
> rization call had not preceded the [shoot down] order. People can come to
> their own conclusion. We didn't want to be in the position of saying the pres-
> ident and the vice president were lying to us."
>
> Bob Kerrey, the former Democratic senator from Nebraska and an out-
> spoken member of the 9/11 commission, put it this way: "We don't see that
> it happened the way he [Cheney] 'recalled it."
>
> One commissioner said frankly that the panel's members simply did not
> buy Cheney's account. "We tried to work out language that allows the reader
> to get that," he said, "without saying the vice president did not tell the truth."[45]

Rather than drive the point home, however, the Commission's language in the
final report merely suggested reason for doubt.

Looking the other way was especially distasteful to administration critics
during the heat of an election year. One of the harshest evaluations of the report
came from Benjamin DeMott in a *Harper's* article entitled "Whitewash as Public Service."

> In the course of blaming everybody a little, the Commission blames
> nobody—blurs the reasons for the actions and hesitations of successive
> administrations, masks choices that, fearlessly defined, might actually have
> vitalized our public political discourse.
>
> The most momentous subject before the 9/11 Commission was: What did
> President Bush know about the Al Qaeda threat to the United States, when
> did he know it, and if he knew little, why so?
>
> Given the evidence, the commissioners who meant to serve fact—meant
> truly to foster the future security of this country—would have had to con-
> front, through words and acts, the gap between the President's absurd,
> nobody-told-me assertions and the plain record before them of repeated
> attempts to draw his attention away from Iraq to the threat that closed the
> very street on which he and his family lived. They would have been forced

to raise the question, to themselves and to their audience, of whether this level of ignorance and obliviousness, this much incontrovertible proof of neglect and indifference, could be passed over in silence by men and women of patriotic good conscience. They would have been forced to admit to themselves that they knew what they knew.[46]

For the commissioners, the ultimate value of adopting such a strategy would lie in whether meaningful changes could be put into legislation and then implemented. Like everything else about the Commission, that path was not easy.

PREELECTION EFFORTS TO ACT ON THE COMMISSION'S REPORT

Congress seldom moves quickly, but a crisis situation or perceived urgency can sometimes move it into action. Both the Senate and the House devoted much of the August recess time to crafting legislative responses to the Commission's recommendations; these emerged in September. While bipartisanship dominated the Commission's recommendations, intense partisanship emerged when the Congress sought to act on the Commission's recommendations. The congressional debate, however, went beyond partisanship to include organizational turf—Congress began to answer the question of who would control the nation's intelligence apparatus. The central question quickly became. How much power would the Pentagon continue to exercise over intelligence?

The Director of National Intelligence

The focal point of the debate was the authority of a new director of national intelligence (DNI), a position recommended, under the different name of national intelligence director, by three groups: in early 2002 by a task force headed by former National Security Advisor Brent Scowcroft; in late 2002 by the joint congressional inquiry; and again in July 2004 by the 9/11 Commission. As one analyst summarized, "Just how powerful the intelligence director becomes under a new law will determine whether the true center of power in the war against terrorism rests with a new spy chief or remains centered in the Pentagon."[47]

To summarize this struggle, defenders of the Pentagon's power lost in the Senate but succeeded in the House, ultimately winning most of their points in the Intelligence Reform and Terrorism Prevention Act of 2004 that was signed into law on December 17, 2004. Getting there, however, was a long, circuitous process.

Senate Consideration: Bipartisan Agreement

The 9/11 Commission members, their allies in the Senate, and the most promi-nent 9/11 family groups hoped that the approaching November 2004 election would make it possible to secure major changes in the intelligence system. And their hopes seemed well on the way to being realized on Wednesday, October 6 when the Senate adopted a bipartisan reform bill (S. 2845) by a vote of 96–2. All fifty-one Republicans supported the proposal which the White House sup-ported and the 9/11 commissioners endorsed.[48] Senators Susan Collins (R-ME) and Joseph Lieberman (D-CT), the chair and ranking member of the Senate Governmental Affairs Committee, had been given the task of putting together the Senate response to the 9/11 Commission Report. Their bill remained true to the Commission's report and hewed a middle-of-the road path—not as much power given to the DNI as three former chairs of the Intelligence Committee (Republicans Arlen Specter [PA], Richard Shelby [AL], and Pat Roberts [KS]) sought, but greater control over budgetary and personnel decisions than another group of senators from the Armed Services and Appropriations committees (Republicans John Warner [VA] and Ted Stevens [AK] and Democrats Sander Levin [MI] and Daniel Inouye [HI]) would have preferred.[49] Pentagon defend-ers were not only helping the military avoid losing control over intelligence agencies but were also defending their own turf within Congress, their com-mittee's jurisdictional power that would be reduced if control shifted to the new position. The Pentagon's defenders lost most of the battles in the Senate, and a DNI emerged with strong authority over intelligence budgets, personnel, and collection and analysis priorities.[50]

Susan Collins (R-ME) and Joseph Lieberman (D-CT)

Susan Collins's first successful campaign for public office came in 1996 when she won a seat in the U.S. Senate. Until then, she had extensive exposure to politics through her family (her father was a state senator, her mother a mayor) and through her career as a Senate staff aide (twelve years), an appointed official in Maine government, and a New England Small Business Administration official (one year). Two years after badly losing a campaign for governor of Maine, she succeeded her earlier men-tor and boss, Senator William Cohen. Her initial margin of victory (49 to 44 percent) grew considerably six years later (58 to 42 percent). As a moderate Republican, Collins has frequently found herself in a critical position on hotly contested issues, such as tax cuts, annual budget votes, and social issues (for example, partial-birth abortion).

Joe Lieberman was narrowly elected to the Senate in 1988 after ten years in the Connecticut state Senate and six years as the state's attorney general. He also practiced law for three years after earning both B.A. and law degrees at Yale and again after losing a bid for the U.S. House in 1980. A devout Orthodox Jew, Lieberman refuses to engage in political activities on Saturdays, even when they are critical to his campaigns. He has consistently advocated closer ties between government and religion and is described as well "to the right of most Democrats on cultural issues and foreign policy."[51] Lieberman was the running mate of Al Gore in 2000 as Democratic nominee for vice president, and he ran for the presidential nomination in 2004, ultimately withdrawing in February 2004 after losing badly to John Kerry in the New Hampshire primary. He has been an outspoken figure on foreign policy, public morals, Bill Clinton's personal transgressions as president, and the needs of homeland security. Lieberman proposed creation of a Department of Homeland Security well before President Bush, but his version lost in the Senate after the November 2002 elections. He has been a consistent supporter of Bush's policies in Afghanistan and Iraq but a critic of the administration's performance on intelligence collection and analysis. His reelections in 1994 and 2000 were by comfortable margins of 67–31 percent and 63–34 percent. In 2006, Lieberman was forced to run as an Independent after losing the Democratic primary, but he won reelection with 49.7 percent of the vote and caucuses with the Democrats.

Collins was a relatively new committee chair (2003) when intelligence reform came within her jurisdiction. Lieberman has often partnered with Republicans including John McCain (R-AZ), Rick Santorum (R-PA), and John Kyl (R-AZ) in the Senate as well as former cabinet secretary William Bennett. Thus, in his role as ranking minority member on the Senate Governmental Affairs Committee (now renamed Homeland Security and Governmental Affairs), his cooperation with Chairperson Susan Collins was not unusual. The more experienced Lieberman helped defend their joint legislation against the onslaughts of more senior senators (Byrd [D-WV], Stevens [R-AK], Warner [R-VA], and Levin [D-MI]) in the committee and on the Senate floor. Collins, however, ultimately conducted the negotiations with the White House as deal-making in the House dragged on. The final outcome—deleting immigration provisions and delaying full language on preserving the chain of command until after the law had passed—was viewed as a success for Collins.[52]

House Consideration: Partisan Rancor

Action in the House was quite different. Speaker Hastert created a task force that consisted exclusively of senior Republican Party and committee leaders to draw up the chamber's response, H.R. 10, which was introduced on September 24. This allowed Hastert to exercise much greater control over the legislation than if it had been referred to a committee. The resulting bill was more protective of the Pentagon's powers than the Senate version and addressed antiterrorism issues beyond intelligence such as immigration reforms. By wholly excluding Democrats from the drafting process and developing a Republican response to terrorism, partisanship was certain to play a major role.

The five committees that ordinarily exercised jurisdiction over issues addressed in the proposal (Armed Services, Judiciary, Select Intelligence, Government Reform, and Financial Services) conducted "mark-up" hearings on the same day. Most debate followed the same pattern: Democrats and a few moderate Republicans sought to substitute language from the Senate's reform bill for that in the House version but were defeated. On October 7, the House rejected a bipartisan bill (H. B. 5150) developed by Christopher Shays (R-CT) and Carolyn B. Maloney (D-NY) very similar to S. 2845, the Senate version; the next day, the House approved a strikingly different reform proposal by 282–134. This outcome ensured that the conference negotiations between the two chambers would be difficult.[53] Senate Republican leaders might well have expected this action in the House and allowed their own bill to proceed without fragmenting their membership.

Democrats and supporters of a bipartisan strategy were predictably outraged. Representative Maloney argued, "It's not hard to see what's going on here . . . Some say that the goal of the Republican leadership is to pass a bill that cannot be reconciled with the Senate bill before the election. The Republican leadership knows that after the elections, when the political pressure is off, the prospects for reform will vanish."[54] Representative Nancy Pelosi (D-CA), the House minority leader, raged that "House Republicans stand alone as the only obstacle in the way of passing a 9/11 bill that will make America safer." Senator Tom Daschle (D-SD), the Senate Democratic leader, said that while "everybody's been on their best behavior" in the Senate, provisions in the House bill could turn the intelligence debate "into a political football again" and then "all bets are off."[55] The partisan divide escalated when Republican Majority Leader Tom DeLay (R-TX) called a news conference at which he held up a summary of the House bill and ripped it in two "suggesting that Democrats were trying to shred the recommendations of the 9/11 Commission. 'The Democrats want to rip up the 9/11 Commission recommendations that they don't like and throw them out.'"[56] All this occurred, of course, with the backdrop of the election one month away.

More generally, House Republicans defended their action by arguing that they had taken the 9/11 Commission recommendations and improved them; new law enforcement provisions made it more difficult for immigrants to establish asylum and easier to deport illegal immigrants who had been in the country for less than five years. A different victims' group, 9/11 Families for a Secure America, endorsed these changes as critical. But more significantly in the view of reformers and the 9/11 commissioners, the House bill substantially reduced the power of a new director of national intelligence (DNI) to coordinate the work of the Defense Department's intelligence units whose expenditures constituted an estimated 80 percent of the total intelligence budget. Personnel and budget powers granted to the DNI in the Senate bill were absent from the House version. Skeptics argued that it was the old Washington turf game at work—the Pentagon and its congressional allies were trying to block reform. Neither the civilian nor the military officials in the Pentagon nor the members of defense oversight committees in Congress wanted to see their influence reduced by shifting budget authority to a new intelligence czar. While members of the Senate Armed Services Committee had lost their battle to preserve influence, those in the House had been more successful.

The Conference Committee: Failed Negotiation

The Republicans' congressional leaders, Hastert and Frist, promised that a conference committee would work through the upcoming August congressional recess and produce a compromise bill that would be passed before the November elections. But that did not happen. As usual, initial discussions occurred largely behind the scenes but soon moved very much into the open. Serious negotiations did not commence until October 20 and by Sunday the 24th, Senators Collins and Lieberman, the leaders of the Senate conferees, announced publicly that their group had unanimously (that is, Republicans as well as Democrats) rejected a House compromise proposal that would have weakened the DNI too greatly. A number of "big guns" then weighed in on the public debate. Tom Kean, chair of the 9/11 Commission, announced that he agreed with the Senate position. But the House had its supporters, too. General Richard B. Myers, chairman of the Joint Chiefs of Staff, sent a letter to House members supporting their position. Myers had testified earlier on Capitol Hill on his concerns that Senate-backed changes endangered the kind of "real time" intelligence needed to be successful. The new DNI would add another link to the chain of command. As one analyst summarized,

> The Pentagon's primary case for keeping operational and significant budgetary control over its agencies rests on a simple principle: The ability to act quickly is essential to accomplishing battlefield goals. The military argues

that critical intelligence for troops in battle zones should not have to be sifted through another layer of bureaucracy such as the NID [DNI] before it can be acted on in the field.[57]

Duncan Hunter (R-CA)

Duncan Hunter entered the House in 1980 and represents the 52nd district in California, an area in San Diego County that has supported his reelection with margins of 65 percent and greater in all but one of his subsequent campaigns. He became chair of the House Armed Services Committee in 2002 after chairing subcommittees on Military Procurement and Military Research and Development during the previous eight years, where he was able to advance a number of high-tech weapons systems. After service in Vietnam as an Army Ranger when he earned a Bronze Star, Hunter completed his education, earned a law degree, and practiced briefly before starting his political career. Throughout his career, Hunter has been an ardent, unapologetic advocate of increased defense spending for both weaponry and troops, sometimes opposing the lower budget recommendations of presidents from his own party and more often the preferences of Republican senators.[58] *Congressional Quarterly* has described him as "the embodiment of a congressional defense hawk."[59] His aggressive defense of the military during the furor that followed revelations about prisoner abuses in the Abu Ghraib prison in Iraq brought him into conflict with his Senate counterpart, John Warner (R-VA), who launched an investigation by his own committee.

In November 2004, Hunter "was able to stall intelligence overhaul legislation by convincing enough Republican colleagues that an intelligence czar would interrupt the flow of critical information to U.S. troops in battle." He argued that the proposed reform "would cause confusion in the chain of command, which could lead to casualties in the battlefield,"[60] an accusation that no member of Congress wanted to face. "In an emotional November 20 caucus of House Republicans in the basement of the Capitol, [Hunter] was able to persuade a majority of his colleagues that the conference agreement would endanger U.S. troops on the battlefield — including his own son, a Marine who had fought in the first assault on Fallujah in April."[61] By arguing for the Pentagon to retain control over its intelligence sources (including satellite reconnaissance), Hunter preserved the budget power of the secretary of defense and that of his own committee. Hunter sought the 2008 Republican presidential nomination.

When Senate conferees refused to budge on this issue, Duncan Hunter, chair of the House Armed Services Committee and a member of the conference committee, called General Myers late on the night of October 20. Myers confirmed his concerns and agreed to put them in writing. Hunter then released the letter and thereby publicly contradicted the president's earlier endorsement of the Senate bill, a less serious breach of loyalty for Hunter than for Myers who was openly disagreeing with his commander in chief.[62]

Myers's open split with the president further fueled media speculation about Defense Secretary Donald Rumsfeld's role in behind-the-scenes lobbying against the Commission's recommendations, something he had been charged with as the recommendations were considered in both chambers. Given this very public division in the administration, a clear question arose: Did President Bush really support the 9/11 Commission's reform proposals? Since doubts about his support for the reforms had the potential to damage his own reelection campaign, the White House press office made sure that the media learned of the president's phone calls to both Senator Frist and Speaker Hastert asking them to get the reform legislation to him as quickly as possible and before the elections.[63] This may have mollified some critics, but advocates of the Senate's reform proposals believed that presidential phone calls signaled negligible White House support.

With the election just a week away, the last push for reform prior to November 2nd had failed. Supporters of the Senate's version became increasingly distraught, fearing that the pressure for genuine reform would disappear after the election, and the opponents of change would emerge victorious. After the election had come and gone, their only remaining hope was for a "lame duck" session of Congress, convening after the elections but before the new Congress was in place, to take action, much as had happened in 2002 when disagreements over the Department of Homeland Security were resolved after the midterm elections. In that case, however, there had been distinct party alternatives on the table—a Democratic and a Republican version of the department.[64] In this case, there were two Republican versions on the table, one bipartisan and one partisan, so the election would render a judgment less clearly drawn on partisan lines. Rather than start down the path of another round of committee hearings and contending bills, reformers believed that pushing the process to a conclusion in 2004 was critical. Of course, opponents, largely supporting the status quo, took the opposite view, hoping that action would be delayed. It was less clear which position was preferred by the "super reformers," those in the Senate who had argued that the only cure for the many ills of intelligence was even greater restructuring than the Senate-approved version prescribed.

POSTELECTION EFFORTS TO ACT
ON THE COMMISSION'S REPORT

Rather than disappearing from the national agenda as some expected, intelligence reform received a further lease on life following the November 2004 elections. President Bush came under intense pressure to do more to coerce his congressional allies, especially after his postelection statements. Basking in an aura of victory that had eluded him in 2000 with the protracted conclusion to that hotly contested election, Bush on November 4, 2004, explained during a press conference how he would move on the agenda he had laid before the American people during the campaign and which they had endorsed.

> I earned capital in the campaign, political capital, and now I intend to spend it. It is my style. That's what happened in the—after the 2000 election, I earned some capital. I've earned capital in this election—and I'm going to spend it for what I told the people I'd spend it on, which is—you've heard the agenda: Social Security and tax reform, moving this economy forward, education, fighting and winning the war on terror.[65]

Already criticized before the election because of what some believed was tepid support for intelligence reform, President Bush now offered a strong statement of purpose that contrasted sharply with the modest call for action also included in the press conference's opening statement:

> Our government also needs the very best intelligence, especially in a time of war. So I urge the Congress to pass an effective intelligence reform bill that I can sign into law.[66]

There were calls from reformers for a redoubled effort, and Senator Collins, leader of the Senate conferees, spoke with Condoleezza Rice about the need for the president to intervene.[67]

Another Failed Attempt

But the path to reform still proved difficult. A lame duck Congress reassembled in Washington on November 16 for what was expected to be a brief session to resolve an appropriations problem and to hammer out an agreement on intelligence reform. Senate negotiators made an important concession—they dropped their call for the overall total of the intelligence budget to be made public, allowing budget decisions to continue to be channeled through secret accounts in the Pentagon's budget. They remained, however, committed to giving the DNI control over how that budget would be spent.[68] Representative Hunter used his

retreat to plan strategy for the upcoming Congress. When the president's aides pressured the House party leaders to bring their troops into line the way they had on a major Medicare vote in 2003 when conservative Republicans had also resisted the White House, they were bluntly told this would not happen again; the president and his aides would have to find a way to mollify the recalcitrant chairs.[81] Reportedly, President Bush and Vice President Cheney peppered Representative Hunter with calls seeking to develop compromise language. Air Force Gen. Richard B. Myers, the chairman of the Joint Chiefs of Staff, retreated publicly from his earlier support of Hunter's position, presumably under White House pressure. Bush called for approval of the reform during his December 4 radio address and sent a letter to conferees and Republican Party leaders two days later announcing an agreement with Hunter.

Blankley was right; Chairman Hunter and his Senate Armed Services Committee counterpart, Senator Warner, discussed the issue with both President Bush and Vice President Cheney who oversaw the final negotiations. In a major breakthrough, Hunter accepted new language that specified the new DNI's authority would not "abrogate the statutory responsibilities" of the secretary of defense, language designed to protect the military chain of command.[82] By recognizing that the secretary of defense would retain the power to manage his own intelligence agencies, Collins and Lieberman (who learned of the new language through a cellular phone call from Collins while attending a concert the night of December 5) reduced the clout of the new DNI. With this victory in hand, even if it was more face-saving than real, Hunter agreed to support the amended conference report, thus leaving Sensenbrenner to fight his own battles for immigration reforms. (Sensenbrenner ultimately voted against the final bill.) Lopsided votes of approval followed: 336–75 in the House on December 7 and 89–2 in the Senate on December 8. The bill became law on December 17 when President Bush signed PL 108-458.

The final product was indeed a compromise. "What the conferees eventually settled on was a less powerful post than the 9/11 Commission and the Senate had recommended, but still more powerful than the Pentagon wanted."[83] The DNI would be able to set the direction for the intelligence community by developing overall budget levels but would not be able to manage daily operations of units in the Department of Defense. He would play a role in choosing the heads of intelligence agencies but would not have the final word. The president was given authority to develop specific guidelines for how the new director would relate to the secretary of defense so the chain of command would remain solid. Further, the agreement established that:

- annual intelligence spending would remain classified rather than revealed publicly as the Senate had wanted (most authorities suggest that it totals $40 billion annually);

- the Director of National Intelligence (DNI) would be able to transfer up to 5 percent of an intelligence agency's funding, far short of the unlimited authority recommended by the 9/11 Commission;
- a new Civil Liberties Oversight Board would be created, but its power was curtailed by denying it subpoena powers to investigate government wrongdoing;
- the National Counterterrorism Center previously created by executive order would be overseen by the DNI;
- the DNI would appoint a National Intelligence Council responsible for creating administration-wide intelligence estimates;
- the DNI would create structures that encourage information-sharing within the intelligence community;
- some of Sensenbrenner's immigration provisions were accepted (for example, a process to develop uniform national standards for issuing drivers' licenses), but most were dropped;
- changes in congressional oversight of intelligence, another recommendation of the 9/11 Commission, would not be included in the reforms.

The compromise, while winning overwhelming support in the House and Senate, drew fire from both the conservative and liberal ends of the political spectrum. Representative Dana Rohrabacher (R-CA), one of the diehard conservatives who voted against the final bill, called it "a piece of illusion legislation" that was more of an impediment than a benefit. On the other side, Representative Nancy Pelosi (D-CA) thought the DNI had been so weakened that he might be a figurehead.[84] Liberal commentators saw the DNI's limited powers as evidence of a Bush strategy to endorse reform publicly while working to minimize its reach.[85] Critics of the Pentagon's power saw the "abrogation" clause as preserving control of the three large, and expensive, agencies under the Defense Department's control—the National Reconnaissance office, the National Imagery and Mapping Agency, and the National Security Agency—that together comprise more than half of the total intelligence budget.[86]

THEMES OF INDIVIDUAL LEADERSHIP ON INTELLIGENCE REFORM

In this case study we found that President Bush, from whom leadership would normally be expected on a time-sensitive issue, preferred to delay action as long as possible and only the persistent actions of rank-and-file members of Congress and public pressure kept the issue alive. Time and again, the administration sought to derail a thorough inquiry, first by sympathetic congressional allies in the joint inquiry and later by the 9/11 Commission. Moreover, the administration was largely successful in securing reforms that preserved the president's maximum flexibility to structure the intelligence community as he wished. In the end, a strategy of delay worked for the president.

Outside the presidency, we found that leadership was seldom exercised alone in this case but was exercised by pairs, which we call "tandem leadership," or by a larger group, which we will term "group leadership." Examples of "tandem leadership" include Senators Collins and Lieberman, Representatives Maloney and Shays, and Tom Kean and Lee Hamilton, chair and vice-chair of the 9/11 Commission. Two examples of group leadership include the full membership of the 9/11 Commission, both during its work and afterward, and the 9/11 Family Steering Committee. More than the president and party leaders, these tandems and groups provided the *direction, coherence,* and *energy* that ultimately produced reforms, whether one sees those reforms as modest or substantial.

Each of the three tandem leadership teams bridged the partisan divide that has become so prevalent in Washington, D.C., over the past two decades. In Congress, of course, there is a long tradition of committee chairs and ranking members working together across party lines to address common areas of concern. Not all committees develop such norms of cross-party cooperation, but many do. As a committee's formal leader and leader-in-waiting, the two senior members of their party often find it in their best interest to cooperate, at least procedurally, in addressing the group's common jurisdictional issues. One can argue that such institutional practices are especially valuable during periods of heightened partisan conflict to ensure that the institution's work gets done.

In this case, *energy, direction,* and *coherence* were much like batons handed off to different runners for their leg of a relay race. Senator Lieberman was one of several members of Congress who injected early *energy* into the reform effort when he joined Senator McCain in a call for an independent investigation in December 2001. This initial effort was sidetracked by Republican Party leaders who responded to the president's preferences, but by working closely with increasingly disaffected members of the Senate Intelligence Committee and family groups, Lieberman kept the option of an independent inquiry alive and revived the proposal for launching such an inquiry prior to the 2002 election. After the 2002 elections, the jurisdiction of the Government Affairs Committee was broadened to include Homeland Security, and Senator Collins became the new chair but continued to work closely with the ranking member, Lieberman.

In the Senate, Collins and Lieberman shaped a compromise proposal that provided *coherence* to the reform efforts; the proposal was true to the 9/11 Commission's recommendations, less radical than the maximum reformers (mostly Senate Republicans) wanted but more aggressive than defenders of the Pentagon hoped to preserve. This reasonable position attracted broad bipartisan support that was reflected in the unified position maintained by the Senate team throughout negotiations with House conferees. Collins occupied a difficult position as leader of the Senate's conferees; as a moderate Republican, she confronted a far more conservative group of partisans in the House with a very different reform agenda.

Kean and Hamilton provided most of the *energy, direction,* and *coherence* during the middle stages of this process. Although Kean had never served in Congress, Hamilton had many years of exposure to shared responsibility for conducting committee business, and Kean's background as governor of New Jersey, and as a state legislator, also ensured that he had been exposed to similar practices. Thrust into the role of serving as leaders of a group with an equal number of Republicans and Democrats, the heads of their respective camps found themselves in a situation remarkably similar to a closely balanced congressional committee with similar patterns of cooperation. Together, Kean and Hamilton walked a difficult path. They worked hard to *energize* the inquiry's forward progress by being respectful of the president and the administration even when the latter were trying to delay and dissemble; ultimately, the Commission could only do its job by winning presidential cooperation. They identified a focus that unified the Commission's members and gave the inquiry *direction.* They also provided *coherence* by fashioning a set of consensus recommendations that attracted unanimous Commission support. They encouraged their more partisan Commission colleagues to be aggressive in their questioning but kept the conflict from getting out of hand. At the end, they designed a media strategy that emphasized speaking with a single rather than multiple voices as a way to maximize their effectiveness. Thus, their task was to find areas of agreement that could maximize the Commission's collective impact.

Tandem leadership promotes cross-party cooperation, resists the calls for more conflictual action from those with more extreme views either inside the group or outside its operations, and helps develop positive solutions. It is illustrative that no such tandem leadership team was allowed to exercise influence in the House of Representatives where Speaker Hastert quickly moved to make intelligence reform a party issue by developing a Republican response through a structure that excluded Democratic participation. As a result, the bipartisan proposals put forth by Representatives Maloney and Shays—roughly the same as those developed in the Senate—were systematically rejected by party loyalists in the five committees that shared jurisdiction over the House plan. The bipartisan plan probably had sufficient support to be adopted in the House, but Hastert's refusal to bring it up made the question moot. It remains unclear whether this Republican resistance was encouraged, tolerated, or opposed by President Bush and his aides in the White House and the cabinet.

Group leadership is probably less common in American politics than the tandem pattern which is encouraged by congressional structures. Particularly noteworthy in this case is the impact that the 9/11 Family Steering Committee had on intelligence reform. Formed by a small group of wives and mothers of victims killed in the terrorist attacks on the World Trade Center, the group was self-appointed—they were not the elected spokespersons for a large membership group. A few highly motivated and committed individuals brought enormous pressure on elected officials by pooling their efforts, working with congressional allies, and winning favorable coverage by the media, who loved the *Mrs. Smith vs. Washington* qualities of the effort. At critical points in the process, the Family Steering Committee issued public statements, lobbied White House and congressional leaders, held press conferences to denounce inactivity, testified before congressional hearings, and appeared on national television to insist on old-fashioned government virtues of accountability and responsiveness. Not all of their efforts produced success, but they became a consistent force that was vital to maintaining momentum—giving the reform effort *energy*. Their emotional statements of personal loss evoked sympathetic media treatment and, as opponents to reform realized, likely public support.

After submitting their final report, the ten members of the 9/11 Commission transformed themselves into the 9/11 Public Discourse Project, an effort designed to ensure that the president and Congress would effectively implement the changes they agreed to. Such diligence reflected a realism about Washington gained through painful experience—too often, reforms are embraced on paper as short-term responses to public demands for solutions, but no changes occur in bureaucratic behavior. Not only did the commissioners collectively commit themselves to the original goal of identifying the intelligence failures preceding the 9/11 terrorist attacks, but they also put aside partisan differences to identify a common, *coherent* set of recommended changes. Some of that success can be attributed to the efforts of their leaders, Kean and Hamilton, but the members deserve much of the credit, as well. Sticking together was not easy since it often put them at odds with the administration and agencies that had stonewalled the earlier joint congressional inquiry. The testimony of some witnesses (for example, Richard Clarke) severely tested their bipartisan cooperation, but they persevered and were able to sublimate the urges for partisan bickering that so fill the national environment.

At some points, the 9/11 Commission members rallied around their own in the face of external attacks. The best example of this occurred when Attorney General John Ashcroft suggested that commissioner Jamie Gorelick had been an architect of the "wall" between intelligence agencies and the FBI when she served as the assistant attorney general in the Clinton administration. Ashcroft released a memo drafted by Gorelick in 1995 and additional materials were later released. A republican congresswoman publicly questioned the Commission's objectivity:

"If she stays on the commission, its findings will be suspect," agreed Republican Representative Ginny Brown-Waite of Florida, who sent a letter to the commission, signed by 75 House Republicans, on April 23. "If you have one rotten apple, the whole basket starts to smell. And Jamie Gorelick is that rotten apple."[87]

Kean and Hamilton came to Gorelick's defense, and no Republican commissioner publicly criticized her.

Once the final report was issued, the commissioners provided *energy* by campaigning for adoption of the recommendations by Congress, pushing at key points in the process to keep the prospects for reform alive even when they seemed to have vanished. And, finally, multiple commissioners have been engaged in the effort to ensure that change is actually accomplished; the 9/11 Public Discourse Project held public hearings in summer 2005, unsuccessfully sought information from the administration, and issued a report that expressed concern about the legislated reforms.[88]

One figure merits special discussion for his individual leadership in this case. Representative Hunter, chair of the House Armed Services Committee, became the most effective congressional critic of proposed intelligence reforms and exacted major concessions before agreeing to a final package. For a time, Hunter was also part of a tandem leadership team when he and Representative James Sensenbrenner mobilized opposition in the House Republican caucus. But consideration of Sensenbrenner's priorities was delayed for the future, and Hunter and his allies in the Pentagon emerged as the big winners. Hunter's success was a remarkable performance, enhanced at times by his emotional description of the need to protect soldiers' lives in Iraq, a personal concern since his son was on the battlefield at the time of the discussions. Hunter's efforts were fully consistent with a pattern that students of Congress have identified for decades: powerful committee chairs are in a position to block changes inimical to the interests of themselves and their bureaucratic allies. Even presidents frequently have difficulty forcing change in the executive branch, and that may have been the case in this instance with Bush's best efforts being thwarted, though the precise role played by the Bush White House remains cloudy. John Lehman, a Republican member of the 9/11 Commission and former secretary of the navy, criticized Hunter's argument as being all about self-aggrandizement. "It's a red herring that has nothing to do with the issues. This is about control of the money, and money translates to power in the House."[89] It is much clearer that Hunter was able to call upon military commanders to support his position even when such actions brought them into direct conflict with their commander in chief's publicly announced position. Presumably, Hunter also had either the support or tacit acceptance of his party's leadership in the House. Certainly,

Democratic skeptics believed that Hunter's actions could have been overridden by a committed president or House speaker.

NOTES

1. The third incident site was in Shanksville, Pennsylvania, where the terrorists, under attack by the passengers, crashed a plane that was presumably on its way to Washington, D.C.

2. Testimony of Carol Ashley to the 9/11 Commission, 26 January 2004, Washington, D.C., <http://www.911independentcommission.org/pdf/CarolAshley_1_26_04.pdf> (17 June 2005).

3. For a more extensive discussion of law enforcement and intelligence organization, see chapter 5.

4. This position was taken on December 5, 2001, by the House-Senate conference committee on H.R. 2883, the FY 2002 intelligence authorization.

5. Chuck McCutcheon, "Former CIA Official to Head Hill Intelligence Probe of Sept. 11," *CQ Weekly*, 16 February 2002, 485.

6. Dan Eggen and Dana Priest, "Bush Aides Seek to Contain Furor," *Washington Post*, 17 May 2002, A1.

7. Chuck McCutcheon, "Sudden Departure of Staff Director Hampers Intelligence Investigation," *CQ Weekly*, 4 May 2002, 1174.

8. Dana Priest, "Staff Director Emerges as Key to 9/11 Probe," *Washington Post*, 25 September 2002, A25.

9. As reported in an appendix to the inquiry's final report. U.S. Congress, House, House Permanent Select Committee on Intelligence and the Senate Select Committee on Intelligence, *Report of the Joint Inquiry into the Terrorist Attacks of September 11, 2001*, H. Report 107-792, 107th Congress, 2nd Session; U.S. Congress, Senate, *Report of the Joint Inquiry into the Terrorist Attacks of September 11, 2001*, Final Appendix, "Access Limitations Encountered by the Joint Inquiry," S. Report No. 107-351 pp. 1–7, 107th Congress, 2nd Session.

10. U.S. Congress, House, House Permanent Select Committee on Intelligence and the Senate Select Committee on Intelligence, *Report of the Joint Inquiry into the Terrorist Attacks of September 11, 2001*, H. Report 107-792, 107th Congress, 2nd Session; U.S. Congress, Senate, *Report of the Joint Inquiry into the Terrorist Attacks of September 11, 2001*, Final Appendix, "Access Limitations Encountered by the Joint Inquiry," S. Report No. 107-351 pp. 1–7, 107th Congress, 2nd Session.

11. James Risen, "Threats and Responses: The Congressional Inquiry," *New York Times*, 11 September 2002, A1.

12. Eggen and Priest, "Bush Aides Seek to Contain Furor," A1.

13. Family Steering Committee for the 9/11 Independent Commission, "Commission Timeline," <http://911independentcommission.org/history.html> (11 October 2006). Later in the year, at a June 2002 rally sponsored by a coalition of victims' groups, Lieberman, Roemer, and Smith spoke as well as Senators Torricelli (D-NJ), Clinton (D-NY), Schumer (D-NY), and Representative Gephardt (D-MO).

14. Family Steering Committee, "Commission Timeline."

15. Chuck McCutcheon, "House-Passed Intelligence Bill Calls For Independent Probe of Sept. 11 Attacks," *CQ Weekly,* 27 July 2002, 2067.

16. Dana Milbank, "Two Mothers Helped Move Mountain on Post-9/11 Bill," *Washington Post,* 9 December 2004, A1.

17. Statement from FSC on October 4, 2003, "Response to the 9/11 Commission's Second Interim Report," <http://www.911independentcommission.org/oct42003.html> (15 July 2005).

18. <http://homepage.tinet.ie/~gulufuture/future/breitweiser.htm> (2 July 2005).

19. <http://www.911independentcommission.org/pdf/KristenBreitweiser_9_18_02.pdf> (2 July 2005).

20. <http://www.911independentcommission.org/pdf/KristenBreitweiser_9_18_02.pdf>, 3–4 (2 July 2005).

21. McCain and Lieberman proposed S. 1867 in December 2001, but it had languished. See a discussion by Niels C. Sorrells, "Intelligence Panel Says Probe into Failures Needs Independent Commission, More Time," *CQ Weekly,* 21 September 2002, 2468.

22. Niels C. Sorrells, "Goss Tries to Keep Intelligence Bill From Snagging on Sept. 11 Probe," *CQ Weekly,* 12 October 2002, 2683.

23. Niels C. Sorrells, "Battle Over Independent Sept. 11 Probe Keeps Intelligence Authorization in Limbo," *CQ Weekly,* 19 October 2002, 2759.

24. Carl Hulse, "How a Deal Creating an Independent Commission on September 11 Came Undone, " *New York Times,* 2 November 2002, A8; also see Niels C. Sorrells, "Intelligence Authorization Clears, Creating Independent Panel To Probe Sept. 11 Terrorist Attacks," *CQ Weekly,* 15 November 2002, 3040.

25. McCain and Shelby pushed for the selection of Warren Rudman, former Republican senator from New Hampshire, but incoming Majority Leader Trent Lott balked at the idea. Niels C. Sorrells, "For 9/11 Probe, Rudman's Style Loses Points with Lott," *CQ Weekly,* 7 December 2002, 3159.

26. Editorial, "Exit Henry Kissinger," *New York Times,* 14 December 2002, A24.

27. Editorial, "A New Chairman for 9/11 Review," *New York Times,* 17 December 2002, A34.

28. Barry S. Surman, "Conservatives Angry, Hint at Walkout: Keynoter Kean Appeals to GOP Moderates," *CQ Weekly,* 6 August 1988, 2177.

29. Rob Gurwitt, "Gubernatorial Election: Wide Lead for Kean in New Jersey Contest," *CQ Weekly,* 12 October 1985, 2054.

30. Surman, "Conservatives Angry, Hint at Walkout," 2177.

31. John Felton, "The House Committee: Well-Respected Hamilton Is Propelled Into the Limelight," *CQ Weekly,* 20 December 1986, 3100.

32. Felton, "The House Committee: Well-Respected Hamilton," 3100.

33. Carroll J. Doherty, "INVESTIGATIONS: 'October Surprise' Task Force Rejects Hostage Allegations," *CQ Weekly,* 16 January 1993, 137.

34. <http://9-11congress.netfirms.com/9-11committee.html> (12 July 2002).

35. Even before the report's release, Kerry had raised questions about other intelligence issues surrounding the invasion of Iraq.

36. Dana Milbank and Dan Eggen, "Bush Counsel Called 9/11 Panelist before Clarke Testified," *Washington Post*, 1 April 2004, A13.

37. Editorial, "Undercutting the 9/11 Inquiry," *New York Times*, 31 March 2003.

38. Tim Roemer quoted in Julian Borger, "9/11 Inquiry Alleges Witness Intimidation," *The Guardian*, 10 July 2003, < http://www.guardian.co.uk/september11/story/0,11209,994933,00.html> (23 July 2005).

39. Dan Eggen, "9/11 Panel Granted Look at Clinton Papers," *Washington Post*, 3 April 2004, A4.

40. Ned Zeman, David Wise, David Rose, and Bryan Burro, "The Path to 9/11," *Vanity Fair*, November 2004, 326.

41. Eleanor Clift, "The Wizard of Oz Letter: Bush Pulls Back the Curtain on Who Really Runs the White House," *Newsweek*, 2 April 2004, <http://www.msnbc.msn.com/id/4653858> (27 June 2005).

42. Richard A. Clarke, "Honorable Commission, Toothless Report," *New York Times*, 25 July 2004, A11.

43. Dana Milbank and Mike Allen, "For the Bush Camp, A Well-Cushioned Blow," *Washington Post*, 23 July 2004, A20.

44. Milbank and Allen, "For the Bush Camp, A Well-Cushioned Blow," A20.

45. Zeman, Wise, Rose, and Burro, "The Path to 9/11," 326.

46. Benjamin DeMott, "Whitewash as Public Service," *Harpers*, 12 November 2004, <http://www.harpers.org/WhitewashAsPublicService.html> (15 June 2005).

47. Martin Kady II, "Pentagon Wields an Iron Hand in National Director Debate," *CQ Weekly*, 2 October 2004, 2308.

48. Philip Shenon, "Senate Approves 9/11 Bill at Odds with House Version," *New York Times*, 7 October 2004, 22.

49. Kady, "Pentagon Wields an Iron Hand," 2308.

50. Amy Klamper, "Panel Rejects Contentious Amendments to Intelligence Reform Bill," *Congressional Daily*, 21 September 2004; "Senate Panel Fends off Challenges to Intelligence Overhaul," *Congressional Daily*, 22 September 2004.

51. "Senator Joe Lieberman," *Almanac of American Politics* (updated June 22, 2005) <http://nationaljournal.com/pubs/almanac/2006/people/ct/cts2.htm> (10 August 2005).

52. "Senator Susan Collins," *Almanac of American Politics*, National Journal, updated June 22, 2005, <http://nationaljournal.com/pubs/almanac/2006/people/me/mes2.htm> (10 August 2005).

53. Helen Fessenden, "House Leaders Take the Reins on Intelligence Overhaul," *CQ Weekly*, 2 October 2004, 2313.

54. Philip Shenon and Rachel L. Swarns, "House Approves Measure To Reorganize Intelligence," *New York Times*, 9 October 2004, A16.

55. Philip Shenon, "Partisan Split in the House May Slow a Final 9/11 Bill," *New York Times*, 6 October 2004, A19.

56. Shenon, "Senate Approves 9/11 Bill," 22.

57. Kady, "Pentagon Wields an Iron Hand," 2308.

58. "Representative Duncan Hunter," *Almanac of American Politics*, National Journal, <http://nationaljournal.com/pubs/almanac/2006/people/ca/rep_ca52.htm> (10 August 2005).

59. Niels C. Sorrells, "New House Armed Services Committee Chairman: Duncan Hunter, R-Calif.," *CQ Weekly,* 11 January 2003, 93.

60. John M. Donnelly, "Troop Safety at Heart of Debate Over Stalled Intelligence Bill," *CQ Weekly,* 27 November 2004, 2774.

61. Martin Kady II, "Uproar Over Intelligence Bill Puts Hunter in the Bull's-Eye," *CQ Weekly*, 27 November 2004, 2770.

62. Kady, "Uproar Over Intelligence Bill," 2770.

63. Philip Shenon, "Bush Asks Leaders of Congress To Pass a 9/11 Bill Quickly," *New York Times,* 25 October 2004, A18.

64. See our discussion in chapter 4.

65. George W. Bush, White House Press Conference, 4 November 2004, <http://www.whitehouse.gov/news/releases/2004/11/20041104-5.html> (23 June 2005).

66. Opening remarks, Press Conference, 4 November 2004, <http://www.whitehouse.gov/news/releases/2004/11/20041104-5.html> (23 June 2005).

67. Walter Pincus, "Bush Is Asked to Break Deadlock on Intelligence Reform," *Washington Post,* 11 November 2004, A10.

68. Martin Kady II, "Chances for Intelligence Rewrite Grow Slim as Pentagon Digs In," *CQ Weekly*, 13 November 2004, 2701.

69. "Congress Makes a Deal on Intel Overhaul," FoxNews.com, 20 November 2004, <http://www.foxnews.com/story/0,2933,139165,00.html> (24 June 2005).

70. Charles Babington and Walter Pincus, "Intelligence Overhaul Bill Blocked: House Conservatives Deal Blow to President, Speaker in Rejecting Compromise," *Washington Post,* 21 November 2004, A1.

71. Charles Babington, "Hastert Launches a Partisan Policy," *Washington Post,* 27 November 2004, A1.

72. Sheryl Gay Stolberg, "Republican Defiance on Intelligence Bill Is Surprising, or Is It?" *New York Times,* 21 November 2004, 18. Also see "Congress Fails to Pass Intelligence Overhaul," *FoxNews.com,* 21 November 2004, <http://www.foxnews>. com/story/0,2933,139174,00.html> (13 July 2005).

73. Thom Shander and Richard W. Stevenson, "White House Seeks Deal to Save Stalled Intelligence Bill," *New York Times,* 24 November 2004, A21.

74. "Lawmakers Say Intelligence Bill Not Dead," *FoxNews.com,* 22 November 2004, <http://www.foxnews.com/story/0,2933,139196,00.html> (19 June 2005); Stolberg, "Republican Defiance on Intelligence Bill."

75. Stolberg, "Republican Defiance on Intelligence Bill," 18.

76. Editorial, "A Truly Lame Duck," *New York Times,* 23 November 2004, 24.

77. "Dems, GOP Urge Bush to Champion Intel Bill," *FoxNews.com,* 29 November 2004, <http://www.foxnews.com/story/0,2933,139827,00.html> (24 June 2005).

78. Beverly Eckhert, quoted in "9/11 Families Urge Action," *FoxNews.com,* 6 December 2004, <http://www.foxnews.com/story/0,2933,140075,00.html> (15 July 2005).

79. Jessica Bruder, "At Ground Zero, Lawmakers Urge Passage of Intelligence Bill," *New York Times* December 4, 2004, p. 2.

80. Tony Blankley, "Misbegotten Intelligence Reform," *Townhall.com,* 1 December 2004, <http://www.townhall.com/columnists/tonyblankley/tb20041201.shtml> (14 July 2005).

81. Jonathan Allen with John M. Donnelly, "From Intelligence Overhaul Impasse to Enactment: How a Deal Is Brokered," *CQ* Weekly, 11 December 2004, 2938.

82. Martin Kady II, "Cleared Intelligence Rewrite Is Big Finish for the 108th," *CQ Weekly,* 11 December 2004, 2937; also see Philip Shenon, "Accord Reached on Overhauling U.S. Intelligence," *New York Times*, 7 December 2004, A1.

83. Kady, "Cleared Intelligence Rewrite Is Big Finish," 2937.

84. Kady, "Cleared Intelligence Rewrite Is Big Finish," 2937.

85. Spencer Ackerman, "Bush Won't Reform Intelligence: Small Change," *New Republic Online*, 2 December 2004, <http://www.tnr.com/ackerman121304> (12 July 2005).

86. Fred Kaplan, "You Call That a Reform Bill? The New National Intelligence Director Will Be a Toothless Figurehead," *Slate.com*, 7 December 2004, <http://slate.com/> (23 June 2005).

87. Helen Fessenden, "GOP Criticism of Gorelick's Participation on Sept. 11 Panel Could Have Fallout," *CQ Weekly*, 1 May 2004, 1038.

88. Philip Shenon, "9/11 Group Says White House Has Not Provided Files," *New York Times*, 7 August 2005, 18; Editorial, "Reliable Voices for Reform," *New York Times*, 9 June 2005, 22.

89. Donnelly, "Troop Safety at Heart of Debate," 2774.

4

Campaign Finance Reform

On January 3, 2006, Jack Abramoff pleaded guilty to fraud, tax evasion, and conspiracy in connection with a scheme to defraud Indian tribes of millions of dollars. Over the course of several years, Abramoff and business partner Michael Scanlon reportedly accepted $82 million in lobbying and public relations fees from Indian tribes and defrauded four of the tribes out of millions of dollars. The Abramoff story is particularly pertinent to the study of campaign finance because Abramoff then used this money to buy influence over Congress. As part of his plea bargain, Abramoff admitted that he had participated in many illegal activities. For example, he paid a congressional staffer's wife $50,000 to help kill an Internet gambling bill that would affect Abramoff's gambling interests. He also admitted to conspiring to bribe lawmakers by providing campaign contributions, all-expense-paid trips, and jobs for lawmakers' spouses.[1]

In addition, Representative Bob Ney (R-OH), identified as Representative #1 in the Abramoff indictment, was investigated for his connections with Abramoff, and other members of Congress were under investigation as well. Ney's former chief of staff, Neil Volz, pleaded guilty to a conspiracy with Abramoff to provide illegal gifts to Representative Ney in May 2006.[2] The investigations led to Representative Ney's decision to abandon reelection efforts in August 2006,[3] and Ney pleaded guilty to two criminal charges on October 13, 2006.[4]

Even the most novice political observer would recognize the Abramoff scandal as the worst-case example of how money can poison the political process. And while campaign finance reform was passed before details of the Abramoff scandal came to light, the scandal exemplifies why campaign finance reformers tried to secure revisions in the law that would both prevent malfeasance and

create a transparent campaign finance system that would assure the public that
money was not being used improperly within the system. Campaign finance
reform is an interesting issue area because it is one in which members police
their own behavior—and campaign finance laws can potentially improve or cur-
tail incumbents' chances of winning reelection.

The Bipartisan Campaign Reform Act of 2002 (BCRA) is a classic example of entrepreneurial leadership as it was primarily championed by four members of Congress: Representatives Shays and Meehan and Senators McCain and
Feingold. These four members of Congress built a coalition, continued building support through adversity and long odds, and ultimately prevailed over
opposition from the Republican Party leadership in the House and Senate and,
to a lesser extent, President Bush, by taking advantage of the prevailing political winds in the wake of the Enron collapse.

Over the last four decades, campaign finance reform has generally not been
a prominent issue on the national agenda. During the first Bush term, campaign
finance reform took a back seat to more critical legislation on homeland security and intelligence reform—only reemerging on the agenda through the sponsors' perseverance. Passing legislation in the face of opposition from the highest
leadership offices in Washington can be a daunting and often fruitless task. The
story of BCRA is one of failure, patience, and ultimately success through the
individual leadership of four members of Congress.

Without support in the key leadership positions in the Congress, BCRA did
not easily flow from one committee to the next or secure favorable treatment
on the House or Senate floors. BCRA's sponsors made use of uncommon legislative procedures to shepherd their bill through a gauntlet of procedural
obstacles designed by Republican leaders in Congress. As such, this chapter
highlights how leaders use rules and procedures to their advantage in passing
and defeating bills.

In this chapter we will assess the leadership roles BCRA's sponsors played
and how they provided direction, coherence, and energy to a lawmaking system that was not otherwise motivated to address campaign finance reform. We
will assess leadership in this case study by following BCRA's legislative history through the most relevant stages of the lawmaking process with a special
focus on the actions the sponsors took as individual leaders. First we provide a
brief history of campaign finance reform with an emphasis on the last major
revisions of campaign finance law passed in the 1970s under the Federal Election Campaign Act (FECA) and its amendments. We explore the problems
Congress addressed with FECA, the measures Congress passed to reform campaign finance, and the failures of those reforms in the eyes of BCRA's supporters. Following the legislative history we address how the 1996 presidential
election served as the motivation to begin the first substantial reform effort
since the 1970s. Finally, we explore BCRA's legislative history from initial

introduction in 1995 to passage in 2002 and the leadership roles played by BCRA's sponsors.

BACKGROUND: PREVIOUS CAMPAIGN
FINANCE REFORM EFFORTS

Congress last overhauled campaign finance law with passage of FECA in 1972 and its amendments in 1974 and 1979. Prior to these reforms, campaign finance was largely unregulated with little disclosure to the public.[5] While finances were supposed to be regulated under the Corrupt Practices Act, the law did not create an enforcement mechanism to ensure that candidates followed the law. Federal candidates routinely violated the spending cap, wealthy individuals funneled illegal money to candidates through family members, corporations made illegal donations through employees, and the public did not trust the system that allowed such corruption.[6]

Congress, therefore, had three goals in mind when working on FECA. First, Congress wanted to create a system that would place limits on the amount of money individuals and groups could contribute to any single candidate to limit the influence of wealthy contributors. Second, critics of the system often asked what wealthy contributors got in return for their extravagant contributions, suggesting a quid pro quo arrangement of selling congressional votes or other favors. Congress deemed that the appearance of corruption could be minimized by limiting contributions. Third, one of the biggest flaws of previous campaign finance reforms was that while the law limited contributions or spending, it did not make enforcement easy or demonstrate to the public that candidates were following the law. Congress intended to create a transparent system to force candidates to follow the law or risk public recrimination.

Congress addressed these goals through three changes in the law. First, Congress limited the amount of money contributed to and spent by candidates for federal office. The new law limited how much individuals could contribute to an individual federal campaign and capped the total amount an individual could contribute during an entire federal election cycle. Congress also established limits for how much a candidate for federal office could legally contribute to his or her own campaign. The law created caps for how much candidates for federal office could spend on their campaigns and for how much a candidate could spend on broadcast advertising. In 1974, Congress went even further by adding a new optional public financing system for presidential campaigns that provided federal matching dollars for money raised by a presidential candidate during the primary season and full public funding during the general election.[7]

Second, Congress established a new federal agency, the Federal Election Commission (FEC), to implement federal election law and act as an enforcement mechanism to make sure candidates and contributors followed the law. To this end, Congress gave the FEC the power to fine or incarcerate candidates or contributors who broke campaign finance laws. The FEC was also designed to provide public disclosure of campaign finance activities. Under FECA, candidates and organizations were required to file periodic reports on their financial receipts and expenditures, and the FEC made these reports available to the public.[8] Public disclosure of financial reports, and of candidates and organizations that broke the law, served as a way to ensure a transparent process that the voters could trust to prevent corruption.

Third, Congress created Political Action Committees (PACs) to regulate nonparty and noncandidate organizations. Organizations could register with the FEC to create a PAC, and just like candidates, PACs were required to file periodic financial reports, including itemized contributions to federal candidates.[9] These reports were made available to the public through the FEC with the intent of preventing organizations from pumping illegal contributions into the political system.

While FECA and its amendments initially transformed the campaign finance landscape, many of its requirements were struck down by the Supreme Court as unconstitutional, including mandatory limitations on spending for congressional candidates and limits on self-financing. Even after the Court decisions, FECA was a major step forward in meeting Congress's goals. The Supreme Court upheld voluntary spending limits, public funding for presidential elections, limits on contributions, and public disclosure of contributions and expenditures.[10]

The combination of contribution limits with an enforcement mechanism and public disclosure of finances met Congress's goals. FECA was seen by its contemporaries as a strong solution to many of the problems that plagued the pre-Watergate campaign finance system. After implementing the last of the FECA amendments, Congress had satisfied its goals of keeping wealthy contributors from dominating the system, significantly lowering the level of perceived corruption and making the system much more transparent.

THE 1996 PRESIDENTIAL ELECTION

The 1996 presidential election ushered in a new approach to financing presidential campaigns as both the Democratic and Republican National Committees began skirting the spending limits imposed on presidential campaigns with an increased reliance on the raising and spending of "soft money" for the benefit of presidential candidates.[11] The FEC defined *soft money* as nonfederal funds that were not regulated by FECA. Soft money referred to funds raised for traditional party-building purposes, including parties' organizational costs, voter registration, and turnout efforts but not for directly affecting the outcome of federal elections. Because the funds were not intended to directly affect federal elections, the FEC ruled that the funds could not be regulated by FECA.[12]

National party committees could therefore raise unlimited amounts of money from individuals, corporations, and unions for party-building efforts.

In addition to the FEC ruling on soft money, the Supreme Court widened the discretion parties had in spending soft money. The Court ruled that advertisements that did not include terms expressing advocacy for a *specific* candidate were not subject to FECA restrictions limiting party spending on a candidate. In practice, this decision meant that parties could use soft money to pay for advertising as long as the advertisements did not include key words like "elect," "support," or "oppose."[13] With the Supreme Court decision to allow soft money expenditures on advertising, the parties found an unquenchable thirst for soft money and the advertising it could buy. The parties took advantage of the Court decision by raising unprecedented amounts of money and spending it on advertisements featuring specific candidates' images and issue positions while avoiding the key words that advocated electoral support or opposition.[14]

During the 1996 election cycle, after the soft money rulings, the Democrats spent $124 million dollars in soft money with $40 million spent on advertising promoting President Clinton's reelection prior to the Democratic National Convention. In contrast, during the 1992 election cycle, before the soft money rulings, the Democrats spent a total of $36 million in soft money.[15] Likewise, the Republicans spent $138 million in soft money, spending $20 million to support its presidential candidate Senator Robert Dole. In the 1992 election cycle, the Republican Party spent only $50 million in soft money.[16]

This overwhelming demand for soft money led to a series of campaign finance scandals as the parties waged a full-scale campaign for soft money. The Clinton campaign in particular was found guilty of numerous campaign finance law violations, including acceptance of illegal contributions from foreign sources (about $3 million); privileged access for large soft money donors including invitations to the White House for coffee with the president or sleepovers in the White House; and illegal use of federal resources (phones and offices) for fundraising.[17] The Republicans also violated the law by illegally transferring money between party coffers and tax-exempt organizations and using private corporations to solicit contributions for organizations that engaged in issue advocacy.[18]

The increase in soft money contributions, advertising expenditures, and fundraising abuses served as the motivating factor for several members of Congress to attempt changing the campaign finance system to eliminate soft money.[19] This reform effort was led by four members of Congress: Representatives Chris Shays (R-CT) and Martin Meehan (D-MA) and Senators John McCain (R-AZ) and Russell Feingold (D-WI). Not all members of Congress wanted to stop soft money, and the opposition was led by Senator Mitch McConnell (R-KY) and Representative Tom DeLay (R-TX). These six members of Congress manipulated legislative hurdles and obstacles across a five-year period in a struggle over campaign finance reform.

THE BIPARTISAN CAMPAIGN REFORM ACT: 1997–2000

Campaign finance reform is one of the few areas in which elected federal officials regulate their own behavior. As such, it is an area that is generally handled very carefully as changes in campaign finance could have potentially devastating effects on a political career if unforeseen outcomes arise. As members of Congress have little incentive to change a system that helps them win reelection, and voters do not rank reform among their most important issues, long periods of inaction should be expected. So while Senators McCain and Feingold introduced their first campaign finance bill in 1995, it was not until the 1996 presidential election and public outrage over soft money that BCRA experienced its first jolt of legislative momentum in nearly thirty years.[20]

In 1997, McCain and Feingold introduced BCRA in the Senate as S. 25, the Bipartisan Campaign Reform Bill. It was a broad, comprehensive campaign finance reform bill that included many controversial points including mandates for free airtime for federal candidates on both television and radio and reducing the limits on PAC contributions. These controversial items were later dropped during negotiations to attract more support, but a ban on soft money was the heart of the bill and remained the central focus of debate throughout consideration.[21]

Senator John McCain (R-AZ)

On the Senate side, the figure most closely associated with campaign finance reform was BCRA's lead cosponsor, John McCain. When scholars describe the model of the new senator who is media- and public relations–savvy, they are describing Senator John McCain. Since McCain's arrival in the Senate in 1986, he has been perhaps the Senate's most visible member outside of the formal leadership. McCain's rise to national prominence is no accident as his personal story and personality scream star power. According to Senator Phil Gramm, McCain's personal history as a prisoner of war in Vietnam is so revered in the Senate that it seems that the words "war hero" are part of his official title.[22]

Senator McCain is a traditional maverick, eschewing partisan ties in favor of an individualized course in the Senate. He has followed the party's voting position on budget, defense, and social issues, and over his career he has been quite conservative. The qualities that have earned McCain personal disdain among his colleagues—the lack of deference to more senior senators and frank criticisms of the Senate and its members, especially on special interest relationships—seem to be the very qualities that the voters admire. Senator Mike DeWine (R-OH) said of McCain's temperament, "While senators may not like it, it's endearing to the public."[23]

McCain has spent considerable time building a national reputation as a media entrepreneur that allows him to carry out his maverick role without taking advantage of the party support other members enjoy. His maverick status allows him to tackle issues that others may find difficult. For example, each year McCain releases a report and maintains a website dedicated to the most egregious pork barrel projects in the federal budget. This is a bipartisan report in the sense that it annoys Democrats and Republicans alike as it includes projects supported by either or both parties. In addition to a focus on pork, McCain is also a fervent critic of the influence of special interests in politics.

McCain's critics point out that he takes just as many campaign contributions from these special interests as anyone else. In 1997 McCain rose to the chairmanship of the Senate Committee on Commerce, Science and Transportation, which is one of the most lucrative chairmanships as the committee legislates over corporate interests. A review of McCain's campaign finance records shows that McCain accepts contributions from the corporations he deals with on a daily basis in his committee work.

In 1991, McCain was rebuked by the Senate for his involvement in the Keating Five scandal. In 1987, McCain and four other senators intervened in a federal investigation into Charles Keating's failed savings and loan company. Some political observers claim that his involvement in cleaning up government through campaign finance reform is at least in part motivated by his desire to clean up his own image after the scandal—a claim McCain dismisses.[24] The scandal is now behind him after successful reelection to his Senate seat and an unsuccessful presidential run in 2000.

Early reform efforts followed investigations into campaign finance violations by the Democrats during the 1996 presidential election. While Republican congressional leaders liked the idea of using the investigations to highlight the unethical behavior of Democrats for partisan gain, they were uneasy about the effect the investigation would have on campaign finance reforms they opposed, a concern reflected in the narrow jurisdiction given to the Senate Committee on Governmental Affairs to investigate only illegal activities, not solutions.[25] But after several months of investigating Clinton, Senator Fred Thompson (R-TN), the chair of the committee, changed the focus of his committee's investigation from an inquiry into campaign finance abuses to an examination of how to fix the system's problems in late September 1997, with disregard for the leadership's concern.[26] BCRA's supporters hoped that the investigations would give added momentum to the legislation, and after the summer-long investigations, public support for campaign finance reform reached 77 percent.[27]

Senator Russell Feingold (D-WI)

John McCain's lesser-known cosponsor was Russell Feingold. Feingold operates further from the spotlight than his campaign finance partner John McCain, but his maverick streak runs just as deep. In 2001 Feingold was the only senator to vote against the PATRIOT Act, citing concerns over violations of the Bill of Rights. His refusal to yield to his party's demand that he support the bill is exemplary of the rest of his Senate career. Feingold drew harsh criticism from the Democratic Party leadership as well as from rank-and-file members for his vote against the PATRIOT Act, but Feingold's pride in this vote is evident as it is the second legislative accomplishment he discusses in his Senate webpage biography.[28]

His maverick style and personal commitment to campaign finance reform, however, nearly cost him his Senate seat. In 1998, Feingold faced a tough race with Representative Mark Neumann. Neumann, buoyed by more than $1 million in advertising paid for by the National Republican Senatorial Committee (chaired by Feingold's campaign finance reform opponent Senator Mitch McConnell), began closing in on the senator. Feingold, however, refused any similar soft money assistance from his Senate colleagues, demanding that they pull from the air independent ads calling for his reelection.[29] Feingold won reelection by two percentage points.

Soon after McCain and Feingold introduced their bill in the Senate, Representatives Shays and Meehan joined McCain and Feingold in a bicameral, bipartisan work group to develop a strategy to pass BCRA through both chambers and share information in an organized response to opponents.[30] This network proved to be important in the passage of the act by providing logistical support and information, coordinating responses to proposed amendments, and even handing out cue cards on the chamber floor instructing members how to vote.[31]

While the issue network included a wide variety of political actors including senators, representatives, and campaign finance reform interest groups, the absence of White House representation was quite conspicuous. President Clinton publicly supported campaign finance reform, and publicly endorsed BCRA, but there were questions about the sincerity of his commitment.[32] At the same time that Clinton was voicing support for BCRA, he was also under investigation for campaign finance irregularities, and it is possible that Clinton's support for BCRA was a convenient way to control damage from these investigations.[33]

This criticism is similar to the criticism levied at Senator McCain for potential damage control efforts following the Keating Five incident.

The president did not invest much political capital in campaign finance reform, choosing to spend his political capital elsewhere.[34] For example, President Clinton and Speaker Gingrich agreed to create a bipartisan commission to study the issue in 1995, but no such commission was ever created.[35] President Clinton also called on former Vice President Walter Mondale and former Senator Nancy Kassebaum-Baker (R-KS) to lead an effort to promote campaign finance reform,[36] but the White House failed to fund the effort and Mondale and Kassebaum-Baker were forced to rely on charitable trusts for support.[37] President Clinton did not actively promote BCRA, but the president's support changed the dynamic of consideration by ensuring that if the Congress passed BCRA, the president would sign the legislation.

Representative Christopher Shays (R-CT)

Chris Shays was the lead cosponsor of BCRA in the House. Shays was elected to the Connecticut state legislature in 1974, the year of the Watergate scandal. Shays has since seen his role in politics as cleaning up government. While serving in the Connecticut legislature, Shays began his first efforts to make the legislature live by the same rules it applies to others. These efforts continued in the U.S. House after his election in 1987.[38] Shays was a lead sponsor on the first bill the Republicans passed after taking over the House in 1994, the Congressional Accountability Act. The Act was an effort at reforming the internal behavior of the Congress and required that the Congress submit to some of the same labor, civil rights, and health laws that the private sector must follow. Shays was also a key figure in House passage of a ban on most gifts from lobbyists and the reform of rules requiring full disclosure of gifts and full disclosure of who lobbyists are, who pays them, and the issues on which they work.[39] Finally, Shays also supported the 1992 campaign reform bill that Congress passed but President George H. W. Bush vetoed.

Shays was in a unique position in the House because of his moderate issue positions and willingness to cooperate with the party leadership. He served as a bridge between the party leadership and moderate Republicans and was trusted as a mediator who would keep his word.[40] In his efforts to pull the party together on cleaning up government, Shays often referred to the Contract with America by saying, "When the Republicans took over, we said things were going to be different, but I have not seen that to be the case."[41]

While Shays was a unifying voice in the House, he was not averse to taking a stand. According to Shays, "Diplomacy is better than warfare. But whatever it takes."[42] Shays continued to fight for campaign finance reform after Speaker Gingrich warned that he might lose his committee assignments if he continued to pursue the issue.[43]

Representative Martin Meehan (D-MA)

Martin Meehan was first elected in 1992 in the most conservative district in Massachusetts. In Meehan's first congressional race, he challenged incumbent Representative Atkins in the Democratic primary election. Atkins was politically vulnerable for two reasons. First, Atkins's congressional district suffered an unfavorable redistricting effort that stripped Atkins's political base from the district. Second, Atkins had been stained by the House Bank overdraft scandal in which Atkins wrote 127 bad checks using his House bank account. Meehan ran against Atkins with a focus on the House Bank scandal, presenting himself as a reformer, and won the seat.

Once in office, Meehan's voting behavior in Congress has reflected his moderate constituency. While he ran for Congress as a reformer, his good government pedigree is not as well-developed as that of his cosponsor. Meehan's biggest claim to cleaning up government before campaign finance reform was his request that Attorney General Janet Reno start a criminal investigation of the tobacco industry for conspiracy to deceive the American government and people.

Meehan, as Shay's cosponsor, is perhaps the most overlooked of the lead sponsors for campaign finance reform. As a Democrat supporting a Democratic issue position, he did not attract the headlines and attention that his now more famous cosponsor attracted. While the national media showered Shays with attention for his David vs. Goliath image of taking on his party leaders over campaign finance reform, the national media largely ignored Meehan.

Meehan's role, however, was no less important. The Democratic Party leadership trusted Meehan to lead the party on campaign finance reform.[44] Meehan secured the Democratic leadership's support even though there was a very real possibility that the Democrats would lose some of their competitiveness if BCRA were to pass since the Democrats relied much more heavily on soft money than the Republican Party.

Early Consideration (1997–2000): Death by Filibuster

Both the Senate and House began consideration of campaign finance reform following the Thompson investigation in the Senate. The two chambers followed different legislative paths that resulted in different outcomes. In the House, where a majority of representatives supported some form of campaign finance reform, the Republican Party leadership used their majority control of the committee system and the speaker's scheduling power to prevent campaign finance reform from reaching the House floor for a majority vote. In each Congress between 1997 and 2000, after members began discharging petitions to circumvent the House leadership and bring campaign finance reform legislation to the floor, the House leadership attempted to derail campaign finance reform through manipulation of the rules of debate and use of killer amendments designed to fracture support for BCRA in 1998 and 1999. In both cases, however, BCRA's sponsors overcame the procedural obstacles and secured majority support.

In the Senate, where Republican Party leaders were confident that they had the votes to prevent cloture, the Republican leadership allowed debate on campaign finance reform in successive Congresses between 1997 and 2000. In each Congress, reformers failed to secure the sixty votes needed to invoke cloture and campaign finance reform died on the Senate floor.[45] While BCRA received majority support in both 1998 and 1999, BCRA's supporters could not prevent a filibuster, and the Senate proved to be the critical battleground in defeating BCRA. With McCain hitting the campaign trail to run for president in 2000, campaign finance reform would remain off the active congressional agenda until 2001 when the bill's sponsors would make another attempt at navigating the rough waters created by congressional leaders to stall and kill the bill.

Tom DeLay (R-TX)

The most important figure in opposition to campaign finance reform in the House was Tom Delay. Nicknamed "The Hammer" for his aggressive personality and leadership tactics, DeLay was the majority whip during consideration of BCRA before subsequently rising to majority leader. During his time as whip, DeLay kept a long leather bullwhip in his Capitol Hill office that was a symbol of his job and of Sugar Land, Texas, where he had been safely reelected since 1984. DeLay is fiercely partisan, and while holding the number three leadership position in his party, he may have been the most powerful individual in the House. In describing DeLay, Representative Peter King (R-NY) said, "If there is a power vacuum, he fills it."[46] Representative Steve Gunderson (R-WI) called DeLay the "ultimate political and power broker."[47]

DeLay's power was internal in the sense that he let other leaders be the public face of the leadership while he exerted his influence behind closed doors. Speaker Hastert relied on DeLay for strategizing against campaign finance reform and lining up the opposition. DeLay was a highly skilled partisan warrior and also happened to be a strong opponent of campaign finance reform and saw reform proposals as threats to free speech. As whip, he was in charge of blocking reform efforts from reaching the floor for consideration. After debate eventually began, he returned to the floor every day to lobby members for support on one amendment after another to derail the reform efforts.[48] While his name did not often appear in the headlines, his fingerprints were all over the process.

DeLay was also one of the Republican Party's most prolific fundraisers and has used the money almost entirely to expand Republican majorities in Congress. In describing the importance of campaign finance reform, DeLay said, "Money is not the root of all evil in politics. In fact, money is the lifeblood of politics."[49]

DeLay ultimately rose to the majority leader position but was forced to resign from his leadership position, and from the House, when he was indicted in Texas on a charge of conspiracy in fundraising. DeLay was charged with redirecting corporate money donated to a political action committee to the Republican National Committee which in turn contributed the money to candidates for office in Texas, where corporations are not permitted to make campaign contributions to candidates.

Senator Mitch McConnell (R-KY)

Mitch McConnell led the effort against campaign finance reform in the Senate. McConnell was elected to the Senate in 1984. In subsequent years, McConnell paid considerable attention to proving himself to his colleagues and party with the goal of moving up the party ladder. Unlike McCain and Feingold, McConnell is the picture of a loyal party member doing his best to assist the party and its leadership in reaching legislative and electoral goals. His efforts led to his selection as chairman of the National Republican Senatorial Committee (NRSC) for the 1998 and 2000 election cycles. As chairman, McConnell was the chief fundraiser for the party's Senate candidates. McConnell made his last moves up the party's ladder when he was elected whip for the 108th and 109th Congresses and became minority leader in the 110th.

Throughout his tenure in the Senate, McConnell has been a fervent defender of the First Amendment, and this has been reflected in his Senate voting record. He often cited his belief in free speech as a primary reason to vote against campaign finance reform. McConnell is consistent with this position as he also voted against an amendment that would have prohibited burning the American flag since he felt the amendment would have violated Americans' right to free speech even though his party was overwhelmingly in favor of the measure.[50]

McConnell was the Senate's most outspoken opponent to BCRA and campaign finance reform; he objected on both philosophical and practical grounds. Philosophically, McConnell argued that the limitation or elimination of soft money is akin to a limitation or elimination of freedom of expression. According to Senator Robert F. Bennett (R-UT), "The philosophical difference between Senator McConnell and Senator McCain is very deep and passionately held. We all want to get consensus but we are getting deeply held convictions. This isn't a matter of an appropriations bill where one is $7 million and the other is $6 million and we split the difference."[51]

McConnell also defended the status quo on practical grounds. In his first election to the Senate in 1984, McConnell relied on large amounts of money to defeat an incumbent and subsequently keep his Senate seat. According to McConnell, "Unless a conservative has an adequate amount of resources, he's going to lose and lose badly."[52] In 1999, McConnell was elevated to the chairmanship of the Committee on Rules and Administration, a key committee in the consideration of BCRA, giving him an institutional position with which he could block action on BCRA.

BCRA, PRESIDENT BUSH, AND ENRON: CHANGING THE POLITICAL ENVIRONMENT

President Bush's arrival in Washington, D.C., in 2001 fundamentally changed the campaign finance reform environment. Bush's position on reform during the 2000 campaign included a paycheck protection clause that would forbid unions from spending members' dues on political activity. Bush proposed that before spending dues money for political activities, unions would be required to obtain permission from each of its members. Bush also favored a ban on soft money contributions from corporations and unions, but not from wealthy individuals.[53] These principles were consistent with the Republican congressional leadership, and Bush pledged to veto BCRA.[54] Since President Clinton probably would have signed BCRA, Bush's election created another hurdle for BCRA's supporters.

Before campaign finance reform efforts could resume in the new Congress, the September 11 attacks in 2001 pushed campaign finance reform far down the list of pressing agenda items. With the nation and its government focused on homeland security, BCRA's supporters, even if they wanted to move forward with campaign finance reform, faced a legislative environment that would be impossible to navigate.

By spring 2002, however, the legislative environment was once again changing. In the wake of the collapse of Enron in one of the biggest corporate accountability scandals in history, the winds of change were beginning to blow. As public outrage increased over Enron's collapse, and the loss of billions of dollars in employee retirement accounts, the political heat was turned up under everyone in Washington. President Bush might have felt the heat a little more than others as he had accepted $114,000 from Enron's PAC and employees during his presidential campaign and $100,000 for his inaugural gala.[55] According to Representative James Greenwood (R-PA), "I don't think the President wants to appear to be against campaign finance reform. It's not a good climate for that, with Enron."[56] Since 1990, Enron had given $3.6 million in soft money contributions to the Democratic and Republican parties.[57] As the Enron scandal worsened, President Bush began sending signals that he could not be counted on to veto a campaign finance bill.[58] While Enron appeared to be an albatross around the opposition's necks, there were members who did not see it that way. Representative DeLay, who had received $28,900 from Enron since 1989, did not plan to give any of the money back and did not see anything wrong with the contributions. Of the contributions he said, "Their contribution means they supported us."[59]

So while the Republican leadership initially thought it would have an ally in the White House, the president's support, much like the limited support President Clinton gave Democratic leaders, was uncertain even before debate was rekindled. It is interesting that while both Clinton and Bush made limited attempts at providing support for their favored side, neither president took much interest in getting too personally involved in the campaign finance reform debate. This might in part be explained by the low priority the public traditionally placed on campaign finance reform. While Republican leaders in the Congress were forced to deal with the issue because of the coalition of support that had formed in the Congress, both presidents were more interested in using their political capital on issues at the top of their own agendas.

Passage in the Senate: 2001–2002

In 2001, the Senate took the lead in consideration of campaign finance reform with the House to follow. Similar to consideration during the 105th and 106th

Congresses, the House was embroiled in a battle over the rules of debate that pushed consideration back on the House agenda. While Shays and Meehan orchestrated support to bring the bill to the floor under more favorable rules, the Senate moved into debate in March with nine days of debate between March 20 and 30.

The year 2001 would be the first in which McCain and Feingold were able to overcome the Republican leadership's stall tactics and begin debate early in the Congress. There were three primary reasons for the early start in the Senate. First, pressure from voters over the Enron scandal forced the Senate into earlier action in an attempt to quell the rising storm of constituent anger. Second, new Senate Democrats supported the measure, increasing the demand for debate.[60] Finally, a series of amendments to the bill attracted some previous opponents, weakening the opposition. Among the amendments were a doubling of the amount of hard money candidates could collect (money donated for election purposes), an exemption to the soft money ban for state and local parties to collect $10,000 for get-out-the-vote and registration efforts, a millionaires' amendment that would allow opponents of wealthy self-financing candidates to raise more money from individuals and PACs, a guarantee of low broadcasting rates for candidates and parties, and a broadening of the restrictions on issue advocacy groups to include all nonprofit groups.[61]

Once debate began, opponents led by McConnell made various attempts at scuttling the bill by breaking up its coalition of support. First, they tried to amend the bill in ways that would make the final product unpalatable to its supporters, but like similar efforts in previous Congresses, the amendments were defeated. Opponents also tried to amend the bill with a nonseverability provision so that if the Supreme Court were to strike down one part of the law, the entire law would be struck down. Feingold characterized this provision as a "self-destruct mechanism" because the whole law would be invalidated if any part of it was found to be unconstitutional.[62] This amendment was a novel, indirect approach at defeating the bill. The brilliance of the nonseverability amendment was that the Senate might be able to defeat the bill after it had been passed by both chambers of Congress and signed into law by the president by filing suit in federal court. The nonseverability amendment would therefore serve as a self-destruct clause that proponents would have no way of stopping once it was added to the bill.

The nonseverability provision was the last credible attempt at defeating BCRA in the Senate. On the day of the vote on the nonseverability provision, McCain sent out e-mails to supporters asking them to lobby fence-sitting Democrats to vote against the provision. One line of the e-mail read, "Any senator who votes for this extremely rare non-severability provision is playing right into the opponent's strategy to preserve and protect the status quo and the corrupt soft-money system."[63] This provision failed to secure enough support when the Senate voted to table the measure in a 57–43 vote. The combination of public outrage over Enron and the changes McCain and Feingold made to the bill made invoking cloture a very real possibility for the first time in three Congresses. BCRA's opponents sensed that passage in the Senate may be inevitable and the Senate, that had been the chamber to defeat BCRA in the past, would have to rely on the House, the president, and the courts to defeat BCRA.

In a final attempt to scare reluctant Democrats away from the bill, McConnell referred to President Bush's intent to sign the bill when he told them, "Don't think there is anybody out there to save us from this."[64] McConnell was still holding out hope that some Democrats were only supporting the bill as a political weapon for use in reelection against the Republicans because they thought it would eventually be killed by the House or the president. This hope proved to be false as BCRA passed in the Senate in a 59–41 vote on April 2, 2001. For the first time, the Senate had passed BCRA.

Passage in the House: 2001–2002

With a victory in the Senate, reformers had high hope for success because the Senate had been the major stumbling block in the previous two Congresses. Shays and Meehan introduced BCRA on January 31, 2001, but there was a tacit understanding between the House and Senate that the Senate would consider BCRA first.[65] During the 107th Congress, therefore, BCRA's supporters in the House would face a tougher effort than in previous Congresses because the House opposition was the last line of defense. Once the Senate passed BCRA, Shays and Meehan wanted to bring BCRA to the House floor as soon as possible to build on the Senate's momentum. The Republican leadership, however, noted that they were more interested in scheduling items from the president's agenda, but allowed that they might schedule campaign finance reform for debate later in the year.[66] Debate over reform started with hearings in the House Administration Committee at a slow pace in May 2001. Republican Whip Tom Delay testified before the committee, saying, "We're hoping to get a bipartisan effort to kill it."[67]

Debate on the Rules Governing Debate

The Rules Committee did not produce a rule for consideration of BCRA until July 2001, and the proposed rule would help BCRA's opponents defeat the measure. The Rules Committee rule required that the Shays-Meehan bill be brought to the floor as fourteen separate amendments representing the fourteen changes Shays and Meehan wanted to make to their bill before consideration instead of using the typical single manager's amendment. This would make it easier for the leadership to break the supporting coalition along individual issue dimensions.

This was a well-designed strategy because BCRA's supporting coalition was a precarious collection of legislators interested in different parts of the bill. Shays and Meehan had attracted the support of several competing bill sponsors by amending their own legislation to co-opt parts of the competing legislation. If these co-opted pieces were removed one by one, BCRA would lose support from the initial sponsors of the co-opted sections. As an alternative to the Rules Committee rule, which Shays and Meehan strongly opposed, Hastert offered to package BCRA as one managers' amendment and make just one other amendment in order. The other amendment would be offered by Representative Ney (R-OH), but this amendment had not yet been written. This proposal was deemed too risky by BCRA's supporters because of the uncertainty surrounding an unwritten amendment, and Shays and Meehan rejected the offer.[68]

Before legislation can be debated under a Rules Committee rule, House rules require that a majority of members must approve of the rule with a vote on the House floor. As past House and Senate consideration of BCRA demonstrated, the rules of debate are often more important in deciding the final outcome than the text of the legislation. With strong objection to the Rules Committee's rule, and the vote on the rule uncertain, the House had developed a tense atmosphere. Both sets of party leaders were whipping members to toe the party line on the vote and looking for potential defectors from the other side. During a Republican meeting over the impasse on the proposed rule, Representative Shays was permitted to speak about his opposition to the rule and why he supported campaign finance reform so strongly. He explained his support for the bill and opposition to the rule with an emotional and heartfelt plea that led his colleagues to burst into applause when he was finished.[69]

The emotionally charged atmosphere was a result of more than just a disagreement over the rules of debate. The speaker largely controls the membership of the Rules Committee and has the power to pack the most powerful House committee with trusted allies. This power allows the speaker to control the terms of debate in all but the most unusual cases. Because the majority party has at least 218 votes, it can guarantee passage when its members toe the party line. As such, rules are rarely defeated because a significant number of majority party defectors must join a largely unified minority to reach 218 votes. Defecting from one's party on a procedural vote is considered to be one of the most treasonous activities in which a member can engage. Defeating a rule on the House floor is usually interpreted as a personal rebuke of the speaker and his leadership. Speaker Hastert had never been defeated on a procedural vote, and his leadership team was fully engaged in making sure that this would not be the first defeat.

When the vote on the rule commenced, 19 Republicans joined 208 Democrats and 1 Independent to defeat the rule on July 12.[70] With the defeat of the rule, the debate on campaign finance reform would not proceed. The vote on the floor turned out to be a referendum on how far the leadership should go to defeat a bill. The Rules Committee rule was so unusual, and designed such a difficult process for BCRA's supporters, that many members questioned the basic fairness of the rule. For example, one Republican who voted against the rule, Representative Greg Ganske (IA), said he voted against the rule in part because he thought the rule set bad precedent for future debate and that he feared the same tactic would be used against legislation he supported on a patients' bill of rights. While the rule created a debate process that heavily favored BCRA's defeat, it was the violation of the norm of a manager's amendment that sparked the most dissent to the rule.

Campaign finance reform was temporarily frozen because without an accepted rule, the debate could not begin. The two possible solutions were that the Rules Committee could produce a new set of rules subject to majority vote or the reformers could determine their own terms for debate by using a discharge petition. The rebuke of the speaker on the procedural vote on the rules, and the intense debate surrounding the rules, had a chilling effect on the congressional leadership. Speaker Hastert and Minority Leader Gephardt were no longer speaking and showed little willingness to break the impasse. This lack of communication made it unlikely that the bill would be rescheduled without a discharge petition. Representative Zach Wamp noted that, "It quickly became clear that scheduling another vote on campaign finance was not going to be an easy thing for [Hastert] to do even if he wanted to."[71]

Forcing Debate with a Discharge Petition

On July 19, the Blue Dog Coalition of conservative and moderate Democrats filed a rules proposal for floor debate as a prelude to a discharge petition. The difficulty of organizing a discharge petition was that it would once again ask Republican members to vote against their own leadership. Since 1967, only twelve discharge petitions have succeeded[72] and since discharge petitions were first adopted in 1910, only two discharged bills had become law.[73]

While the September 11 attacks brought consideration of BCRA to a halt for several months at the end of 2001, the Enron scandal was generating momentum behind campaign finance reform, and there was a connection in the public eye between a corrupt corporation that made contributions to the Congress and campaign finance reform.[74] Representative Shays claimed, "Enron is getting the signatures [on the petition], not me."[75] The Enron scandal probably made Shays's and Meehan's lobbying effort easier as members were likely to be looking ahead to the November elections with the fear of being labeled as not doing enough in response to Enron's collapse. Just hours before the final petition signature was secured, House and Senate committees began formal investigations into both Enron and Arthur Anderson LLP.

According to Representative Richard Neal (D-MA), "Enron will drive this issue. A tidal wave is coming."[76]

There was some concern within the ranks of Democrats supporting BCRA that they would be forfeiting their election chances to the Republicans because of the large advantage Republicans held in hard money contributions. According to a labor union lobbyist, "When you're inside a closed room, [Democrats] are very concerned about the bill, the great majority of them in terms of what it will do to Democrats. The disconnect between what goes on behind closed doors and public utterances—I've seen a lot of it in Washington, but this one just about reaches the zenith."[77]

Two Republicans, Representatives Charles Bass (NH) and Thomas Petri (WI), met with Speaker Hastert for thirty minutes on January 23 discussing their intention to support the discharge petition, and minutes before signing the petition, Hastert called them to his office for one last attempt at discouraging their participation. The hard sell was coming from both sides of the aisle. Representative Shays said that he became reluctant to lobby members on the floor because lobbying in public would trigger lobbying from the other side. He felt that speaking on the phone seemed to be a more effective tool.[78]

The reformers secured the 218th signature on their discharge petition to bring BCRA to the floor on January 24, 2002. It took supporters six months to collect the signatures and while they were elated to get another chance at passing the bill, there was still concern over whether they had the necessary votes to pass the bill.[79] Representative Corrine Brown (D-FL), the 218th to sign the petition noted, "I felt it was very important to get it up. But I have not committed to vote for it."[80] Representative Jim Turner (D-TX) who filed the discharge petition said, "This is just the first step. The battle is yet to be fought."[81]

The Final Showdown on the House Floor

Once Shays and Meehan got enough votes for the discharge petition, the Rules Committee began writing a rule to govern debate on campaign finance reform, identical to the rules described in the discharge petition.[82] The main alternative bill (H.R. 2360), sponsored by Representative Bob Ney (R-OH) and Representative Albert Wynn (D-MD), was designed to drive a wedge through the BCRA coalition by proposing to cap soft money contributions rather than ban them.[83] Under the rules of debate, Ney was permitted to present his bill as a substitute for BCRA on the floor during debate. Representative Wynn was a member of the Congressional Black Caucus (CBC) and there was concern among BCRA supporters that the Ney-Wynn bill would attract the support of other CBC members. Many CBC members were concerned about the effect BCRA might have on get-out-the-vote and registration drives that benefit their constituents.[84]

Representatives Shays and Meehan were personally calling members to drum up support for their bill, Minority Leader Gephardt was lobbying hard for the bill, and Whip Nancy Pelosi convened a special task force to respond to efforts to defeat the bill.[85] The Republican leadership was also mobilized. They made defeating Shays-Meehan their top legislative priority, and it was the only topic discussed at the House GOP caucus meeting on February 6. Some Republicans reported that they had never been lobbied so hard by the leadership.[86]

House floor consideration of BCRA got underway on February 13, 2002. In a double blow to the Republican leadership, President Bush first refused a personal request from Speaker Hastert to help defeat the measure and then announced through Press Secretary Ari Fleischer that he would sign any campaign finance bill that would help improve the system.[87] President Bush's reluctance to get involved in the debate or to provide a veto threat might have helped undercut efforts at defeating the bill on the House floor.

The Republican leadership's strategy was to saddle the bill with amendments the Senate would never accept in a conference committee, hence killing the bill. According to Representative Doolittle, "We're not going to defeat [Shays-Meehan]. The only question is can it be amended in such a fashion that it goes to conference. The master strategy is to get it to conference."[88] They had two substituting amendments offered by Representative Ney and Majority Leader Armey. The Ney substitute was Shays and Meehan's own 1999 version of BCRA. The substitute failed 53–377, and even Ney voted against it. The other Republican substitute was a stronger version of BCRA that would have banned all soft money at all political levels while BCRA would allow state parties to raise limited amounts of soft money for voter registration and mobilization. This substitute was also defeated with a final vote of 179–249. The final substitute, offered by Shays and Meehan, was a revised copy of BCRA, and it passed 240–191.

After passing several amendments that made the House bill consistent with the Senate version, the House passed BCRA 240–189 in the early hours of February 14, 2002. Despite the intense pressure the Republican leadership exerted on its members, forty-one Republicans crossed the aisle and voted to support final passage. The split in the party had caused bitter feelings within the caucus and between the caucus and the president.[89] The bitter feelings were summed up by Representative John Doolittle (R-CA) who cryptically said, "I can guarantee there will be consequences in the long term. I don't intend to let bygones be bygones."[90] Doolittle also suggested that, "We're going to have a hard and fast rule you don't sign discharge petitions. If it's a matter of conscience, you carry a price. The price is resignation from your chairmanship. People who were a part of this need to be remembered for a long time when out seeking favors. You've seen people off the reservation for years, slipping away over the years. People got used to putting selfish interest above the final good."[91]

The relationship between the White House and the Republican caucus became strained over BCRA. Many in the caucus felt abandoned on the issue by the president and thought that with a little more pressure from the White House, the bill may have been scuttled. According to Representative Cliff Stearns (R-FL), "I'm sorry we couldn't get the support of the White House on the hard work the Republicans did over a long period of time. All the White House had to do was press down on one or two members [to vote some amendments] and it would have gone to conference" such that the leadership would be able to kill the bill.[92] And Representative John Shadegg (R-AZ), chairman of the Republican Study Committee said, "I understand that the White House has to protect itself and chart its own course. The signals they sent that were ambiguous or made it clear they would sign it certainly didn't help."[93]

Many would-be opponents of BCRA were starting to feel heat from Enron and through voters in their districts. In order to vote against a very popular measure, they were in need of political cover. The White House could have provided that cover through President Bush's public threat to veto the bill. With the president on record against the bill, members would be able to vote against the bill and claim they were supporting the president. When the president did just the opposite and signaled that he would sign the bill, his action had just the opposite effect. Instead of providing political cover to potential opponents of BCRA, he lent political cover to potential supporters. Knowing that he would sign the bill, Republicans feeling heat from home to vote against the bill could claim that they voted for the bill to support the president.[94]

Final Senate Passage: March 20, 2002

Once the House passed BCRA on February 14, the Senate took up the legislation to pass the same version as the House. McCain said, "While I'm cautiously optimistic about the prospects of success, I don't underestimate the determination of the opponents of reform. I fully realize that we're trying to break both parties' addiction to soft money, and it will be a very difficult habit to kick."[95] But the Senate's strongest opponent to reform faced a dilemma. Senator McConnell was widely expected to run for whip as Senator Don Nickles (R-OK) was going to step down at the end of his term.[96] On the one hand, he very much wanted to defeat the bill at all costs, but on the other hand, the whip's job is to count votes for the leadership, and a failed filibuster would offer evidence to his caucus that he was not qualified for the job of counting votes.

Senator McConnell's strategy at this stage was to focus on amending a bill that was certain to pass rather than trying to defeat the bill outright.[97] Trying to defeat the bill outright would be impossible because it had already passed the Senate once, it had passed the House, the Republican leadership in the Senate had moved its efforts on to other agenda items, and the president had already signaled willingness to sign the bill. McConnell had simply run out of ammunition to kill the bill on the Senate floor. His only chance then, like in the House battle, was to send the bill to a conference committee where it could be killed by leadership-friendly conference members. This effort was not successful when on March 20, 2002, BCRA cleared its last legislative hurdle when the Senate voted 60–40 to invoke cloture, handing long-sought victory to McCain, Feingold, Shays, and Meehan.

THEMES OF INDIVIDUAL LEADERSHIP
ON CAMPAIGN FINANCE REFORM

BCRA's legislative odyssey demonstrates important lessons about individual leadership with regard to *direction, coherence*, and *energy*. BCRA languished for years suffering through filibuster after filibuster—but BCRA's sponsors had leadership skills that kept hope alive for passage and ultimately prevailed. The important question that we will now address is how leadership skills were necessary to reverse the tide and find enough support in the Congress to pass a comprehensive campaign finance reform bill.

Individual leadership contributed to passage in a number of important ways. First, Representatives Shays and Meehan and Senators McCain and Feingold deserve a good deal of the credit for passing BCRA. Passage of BCRA would not have occurred without the persistence of its sponsors across three Congresses. Senator Larry Craig (R-ID) pointed to the sponsors' tenacity in pushing the legislation onto the floor year after year as a reason why BCRA ultimately passed. Senator Craig said, "Sometimes even bad policy has a way of making it to the top. You just rub and rub and rub until people are sore. It's a wearing-down factor."[98] In part, their persistence was motivated by their personal interest in the policy. All four of the sponsors began work on BCRA because the issue was at the core of their personal legislative agendas. All four sponsors had significant interest in good government efforts, and the issue came to define their collective purpose in Congress. It was this persistence in keeping the issue on the agenda that demonstrated *energy* as a component of leadership. In this case, energy was provided by entrepreneurial leaders with a deep dedication to their cause, and their personal efforts led to floor consideration in multiple Congresses. Without the energy provided by the sponsors, campaign finance reform may not have been reincarnated after each successive death.

Considering how much each legislator cared about reform, it is not surprising that they continued to reintroduce the legislation in Congress after Congress even though most external observers felt that BCRA was essentially dead on arrival in the House, the Senate, or both. But the sponsors' persistence is all the more impressive in the face of substantial opposition from the Republican leadership in both the House and Senate and low public pressure to address the issue. Keeping the issue on the agenda over seven years was no easy feat but allowed the sponsors to take advantage of a changing issue environment. In the wake of Enron's collapse, the public became much more interested in campaign finance reform as many voters began to identify a link between corporate accountability and unregulated soft money. Without Enron's collapse, it is unclear if President Bush would have dropped his opposition to BCRA, and it was a lack of support from Bush that allowed the coalition in opposition to reform to quickly erode in 2001. The sponsors were also able to outlast retiring opponents of reform who were subsequently replaced by reform supporters.[99]

BCRA's sponsors also actively worked to expand the conflict at the grass roots by drawing attention to the problems in the campaign finance system and the need for solutions. The first example of this was when Senator Fred Thompson (R-TN) changed the focus of his committee's investigation from illegal fundraising during the 1996 presidential election to how to fix the problems in the future. This investigation and the parallel House investigation did not drive campaign finance to the top of the national agenda, but the investigations helped keep the issue in the headlines and helped give the reformers some momentum.

Finally, BCRA's sponsors often took advantage of a willing partner in the national press in publicizing their efforts to drum up more support. McCain and Shays in particular used their opposition to their own parties as a way to attract additional coverage of the issue to keep it alive after numerous failures. Thompson's investigation received more coverage once he turned to fixing the problems in the system. Outside pressure from the press also helped solidify the connection between Enron as a symbol of financial abuse and campaign finance reform.

Taking advantage of the Enron scandal demonstrates the sponsors' ability to provide *coherence* to reform. Rather than returning to each new Congress with the same bill that was defeated in the last, the sponsors crafted new legislation with each new Congress and made substantive changes during each Congress in an effort to balance their substantive concerns and the political reality of attracting enough support for passage. The sponsors used their political acumen and guile to read the political tea leaves and offer a bill that might maximize support in building a coalition without compromising on the central tenets. By finding the right political context and writing a bill that could take advantage of such an opening in the national agenda, BCRA found success.

Another example of coherence is the coordinated effort across the two chambers. In 2002, Shays and Meehan amended their House bill in ways that would make it more consistent with the already passed Senate version and make final passage easier as it would be fruitless for House supporters to maximize support in their own chamber if the resulting bill would be unacceptable to more than forty senators. Shays and Meehan decided to amend their bill to double the limit on hard money contributions in an effort to attract more Republican support in both the House and Senate even though this was not something that Shays and Meehan had originally intended to do with their bill.

The sponsors were also required to overcome Republican leaders' efforts to kill BCRA through unorthodox legislative procedures as BCRA's legislative history is a case study in unorthodox lawmaking.[100] Departing from the traditional path of how a bill becomes a law in which a bill follows a specific path from introduction through the committee system to a vote on the floor, BCRA's opponents tried to construct as many legislative hurdles as possible, and its supporters had to rely on their legislative acumen to overcome each hurdle through rarely used procedures and legislative techniques.

BCRA's legislative history includes many examples of these hurdles and evasive maneuvers. In the Senate the opposition's strategy relied on the use of the filibuster, which was once used only in the most extraordinary cases. Over time the filibuster has been used with increasing frequency over a wide range of bills. The House leadership employed various unorthodox hurdles, including the refusal to allow Shays and Meehan to amend their own bill with a single managers' amendment and the use of creative voting procedures. Republican leaders in both chambers used various forms of killer or poison pill amendments to fracture BCRA's support coalition as well as using their scheduling power to coordinate between the two chambers to delay scheduling BCRA for as long as possible.

The sponsors responded to the labyrinth designed to kill BCRA by leading with *direction.* The issue coalition kept reform supporters acting in unison under the direction of BCRA's sponsors as they navigated the morass of unorthodox procedural hurdles. With a unified coalition following their lead, BCRA's sponsors relied on their own unorthodox methods. The BCRA issue network was instrumental in serving as a coordinating force in researching competing legislative efforts, planning tactical responses to procedural hurdles, and negotiating compromises with potential allies. During the 105th Congress, the House leadership turned to a strategy of making twelve competing bills face off against each other and made hundreds of amendments in order. The strategy was intended to fracture the reform coalition among competing bills and drown the reform effort in a sea of paperwork. By allowing hundreds of amendments, the floor would be chaotic as members struggled to understand each amendment and differentiate between them. The value of the issue network was that it could coordinate efforts by researching each amendment and informing members what their vote on each amendment would mean. The network allowed supporters to cut through the poison pill amendments that might have otherwise brought the process to a halt.

The issue network also served as a valuable way to communicate ideas between competing bill sponsors and for BCRA's supporters to draw support by co-opting the ideas of others. With hundreds of campaign finance bills circulating the House and Senate, BCRA's sponsors had to narrow the field of competition to avoid losing their coalition of support. They used the issue network to open lines of communication with other bill sponsors and come to compromises that BCRA's sponsors incorporated into BCRA and to expand the coalition of support. Since Republican leaders opposed BCRA, the committee system did not serve as a very fertile ground for developing a bill that would attract majority support. By providing direction, McCain, Feingold, Shays, and Meehan kept the Congress focused on reform and kept their supporters in a unified effort.

An interesting lesson from BCRA's history is that no matter how creatively the opposition designs its defenses against a bill, or uses its power to manipulate the legislative process, nothing can stop a determined majority from passing a bill. Once a coalition has 60 votes in the Senate and 218 in the House, the Congress will pass a bill. While the leadership has many tools at its disposal, as long as the coalition is able to maintain its support, they will find ways around even the most complex procedural obstacles. BCRA's sponsors must be credited with maintaining their coalition of support over such a long period of time in the face of the highest pressure party leaders can apply. Because McCain, Feingold, Shays, and Meehan provided leadership in the form of energy, coherence, and direction, they were able to keep the bill alive through multiple failures, reach the forefront of the national agenda, and guide the bill to passage.

NOTES

1. Anne E. Kornblut, "Lobbyist Accepts Plea Deal and Becomes Star Witness in a Wider Case," *New York Times,* 4 January 2006, A1.

2. Philip Shenon, "Trial Is Expected to Bring New Scrutiny to Lawmaker," *New York Times,* 30 May 2006, A15.

3. Philip Shenon, "Ohio Republican Tied to Abramoff Abandons Re-election Bid," *New York Times,* 8 August 2006, A15.

4. Pete Yost, "Rep. Ney Pleads Guilty; GOP Vows Ouster," *Associated Press,* 13 October 2006.

5. Other early attempts at regulating campaign finance included the Pendleton Act (1883); the Tillman Act (1907); the Publicity Act (1910) and its extensions (1911); the Corrupt Practices Act (1925); the Wagner Act (1935); the Hatch Act (1939) and its revisions (1940); the Taft-Hartley Act (1947); and the Revenue Act (1971).

6. Anthony Corrado, "Money and Politics: A History of Federal Campaign Finance Law," in *Campaign Finance Reform: A Sourcebook*, ed. Anthony Corrado, Thomas E. Mann, Daniel R. Ortiz, Trevor Potter, and Frank J. Sorauf (Washington, DC: Brookings, 1997), 29.

7. Frank J. Sorauf, *Money in Elections* (Glenview, IL: Scott, Foresman and Company, 1988), 38–39.

8. Frank J. Sorauf, *Money in Elections*, 38–39.

9. Frank J. Sorauf, *Money in Elections*, 41.

10. See *Buckley v. Valeo* 424 U.S. 1 (1976).

11. Leslie Wayne, "'Soft-Money Far Outpaces Other Gifts in Presidential Race, U.S. Reports," *New York Times*, 25 October 2006, A28.

12. Soft money was created by two advisory opinions issued by the FEC. Advisory opinion 1976-72 allowed parties to use nonfederal money to pay for part of a party's overhead costs. Advisory opinion 1978-10 allowed parties to use nonfederal money for traditional party-building activities like get-out-the-vote efforts. See Diana Dwyre and Victoria A. Farrar-Myers, *Legislative Labyrinth: Congress and Campaign Finance Reform* (Washington, DC: CQ Press, 2001), 247.

13. Dwyre and Farrar-Myers, *Legislative Labyrinth*, 227.

14. Ruth Marcus and Charles R. Babcock, "Parties' National Committees Set Records for 'Soft Money'; Much Is Used for Ads Indirectly Promoting Candidates," *Washington Post,* 18 July 1996, A08.

15. Michael J. Malbin, *Life After Reform: When the Bipartisan Campaign Reform Act Meets Politics* (Lanham, MD: Rowman & Littlefield, 2003), 26.

16. Malbin, *Life After Reform.*

17. Malbin, *Life After Reform.*

18. Malbin, *Life After Reform.*

19. Sandy Hume, "Three House Members Propose Bill to Ban Fundraisers, 'Soft Money' Donations," *Hill*, 10 July 1996.

20. Ellen S. Miller, "Mission Impossible? Passing Real Campaign Reform," *Hill*, 12 June 1996.

21. Stuart Rothenberg, "There's a Little Life Left in McCain-Feingold's New, Improved Version," *Roll Call*, 16 October 1997.

22. Carroll Doherty, "McCain, McConnell Turn to Hardball as Campaign Finance Cools Camaraderie," *CQ Weekly*, 27 September 1997, 2280.

23. Karen Foerstal and Andrew Taylor, "Temperamental Journey: What Makes McCain Grate," *CQ Weekly*, 12 February 2000, 314.

24. Dwyre and Farrar-Myers, *Legislative Labyrinth*, 36; Donna Cassata, "Senators Give Voice to GOP Gap over Campaign Finance Overhaul," *CQ Weekly*, 28 February 1997, 520.

25. Carroll Doherty, "Inquiry on Campaign Finance: Burning with a Short Fuse," *CQ Weekly*, 5 April 1997, 767.

26. Mary Ann Akers, "Hearings Alter Focus to Advance Reform Bill; McCain, Feingold Drive Senate Shift," *Washington Times,* 19 September 1997, A12; Rebecca Carr, "Overhaul Bills Head to a Vote, But Obstacles Remain," *CQ Weekly*, 28 September 1997, 2279.

27. Doherty, "McCain, McConnell Turn to Hardball," 2280.

28. Feingold Senate website, <http://feingold.senate.gov/> (3 June 2005).

29. Emily Pierce, "Emerging Players: Sen. Russell D. Feingold, D-Wis.," *CQ Weekly,* 5 January 2002.

30. Dwyre and Farrar-Myers, *Legislative Labyrinth*, 115.

31. Dwyre and Farrar-Myers, *Legislative Labyrinth*, 129.

32. Paul Bedard, "President Promises to Push Finding Reforms," *Washington Post,* 7 August 1997, A1.

33. Dwyre and Farrar-Myers, *Legislative Labyrinth*, 164.

34. Dwyre and Farrar-Myers, *Legislative Labyrinth*, 162.

35. Holy Ramer, "Bradley Joins 89-Year-Old in Pitch for Campaign Finance Reform," *Associated Press*, 26 October 1999.

36. John F. Harris, "Mondale, Kassebaum-Baker to Tackle Campaign Reform," *Washington Post*, 18 March 1997, A04.

37. Dwyre and Farrar-Myers, *Legislative Labyrinth*, 163.

38. Michael Barrone and Grant Ujifusa, *The Almanac of American Politics* (Washington, DC: National Journal, 1995), 267.

39. Dwyre and Farrar-Myers, *Legislative Labyrinth*, 153.

40. Dwyre and Farrar-Myers, *Legislative Labyrinth*, 115.

41. Dwyre and Farrar-Myers, *Legislative Labyrinth*, 126.

42. John Cochran, "Backers Prepare Discharge Petition to End Shays-Meehan Bill Standoff," *CQ Weekly*, 21 July 2001, 1760.

43. Dwyre and Farrar-Myers, *Legislative Labyrinth*, 126.

44. Dwyre and Farrar-Myers, *Legislative Labyrinth*, 116.

45. Carr, "Overhaul Bills Head to a Vote," 2279.

46. Gebe Martinez and Jackie Koszczuk, "Tom DeLay: 'The Hammer' That Drives the House GOP," *CQ Weekly*, 5 June 1999, 1322.

47. Martinez and Koszczuk, "Tom DeLay: 'The Hammer,'" 1322.

48. Martinez and Koszczuk, "Tom DeLay: 'The Hammer,'" 1322.

49. Jeffrey Katz, "Dueling Campaign Finance Bills Threaten Overhaul's Chances," *CQ Weekly*, 16 May 1998, 1283.

50. Dwyre and Farrar-Myers, *Legislative Labyrinth*, 36.

51. Cassata, "Senators Give Voice to GOP Gap," 520.

52. Doherty, "McCain, McConnell Turn to Hardball," 2280.

53. Andrew Taylor and Derek Willis, "As Campaign Finance Debate Nears, Maneuvers and Worries Intensify," *CQ Weekly*, 17 March 2001, 591.

54. George Will interview of George W. Bush on ABC's *This Week*, 23 January 2000.

55. Karen Foerstal, "Campaign Finance Bill Finds New Energy in Enron," *CQ Weekly*, 19 January 2002, 168.

56. Karen Foerstal, "Mixed Signals, Hard Feelings," *CQ Weekly*, 16 February 2002, 443.

57. Karen Foerstal, "Campaign Finance Passage Ends a Political Odyssey," *CQ Weekly*, 23 March 2002, 799.

58. Ralph Z. Hallow, "McCain-Feingold Foe Says Senate Would Sustain Veto; Interest Groups Join Strategy Session," *Washington Times*, 5 April 2001, A5.

59. Foerstal, "Campaign Finance Bill Finds New Energy in Enron," 168.

60. Sarah Ovaska, "Feingold, McCain Reintroduce Campaign Finance Legislation," *States News Service*, 22 January 2001.

61. "Legislative Summary: Campaign Finance," *CQ Weekly*, 22 December 2001, 3033–34.

62. Andrew Taylor, Derek Willis, and John Cochran, "McCain-Feingold Survives Hard Fight Over Soft Money," *CQ Weekly*, 31 March 2001, 698.

63. Taylor, Willis, and Cochran, "McCain-Feingold Survives Hard Fight," 698.

64. Taylor, Willis, and Cochran, "McCain-Feingold Survives Hard Fight," 698.

65. Mary Shaffrey and Kerry Kantin, "House Coalition Seeks Reform Vote," *Hill*, 31 January 2001.

66. Helen Dewar, "McCain, Feingold Turn to House; Senate Campaign Finance Champions Push to Match Success," *Washington Post*, 4 April 2001, A04.

67. Juliet Eilperin, "House Tackles Campaign Reform; Representatives Remain Divided on McCain-Feingold Bill," *Washington Post,* 2 May 2001, A06.

68. Stephen Dinan, "Shays-Meehan Reform Bill Dies on Technicality; Backers Reject Rules for Vote," *Washington Times,* 13 July 2001, A1.

69. Karen Foerstal, "A Bitter Day for the GOP," *CQ Weekly,* 12 February 2001, 1676.

70. Dinan, "Shays-Meehan Reform Bill Dies on Technicality," A1.

71. John Cochran, "Backers Prepare Discharge Petition to End Shays-Meehan Bill Standoff," *CQ Weekly,* 21 July 2001, 1760.

72. Karen Foerstal, "Campaign Finance Bill Wins Its Day on the House Floor," *CQ Weekly,* 26 January 2002, 221.

73. Dwyre and Farrar-Myers, *Legislative Labyrinth,* 67.

74. Andrew Mollison, "Enron Collapse Improves Chances for Campaign Finance Reform," *Cox News Service,* 18 January 2002.

75. Foerstal, "Campaign Finance Bill Wins Its Day on the House Floor," 221.

76. Foerstal, "Campaign Finance Bill Finds New Energy in Enron," 168.

77. Taylor and Willis, "As Campaign Finance Debate Nears," 591.

78. Foerstal, "Mixed Signals, Hard Feelings," 443.

79. Stephen Dinan, "Backers of Campaign Reform Force a Vote; 218 Signatures Bring Bill to House Floor," *Washington Times,* 25 January 2002, A4.

80. Foerstal, "Campaign Finance Bill Wins Its Day on the House Floor," 221.

81. Foerstal, "Campaign Finance Bill Wins Its Day on the House Floor," 221.

82. John Bresnahan and Amy Keller, "Hastert Calls Vote Critical; Says Reform Outcome 'Life or Death' for GOP," *Roll Call,* 7 February 2002.

83. Bresnahan and Keller, "Hastert Calls Vote Critical."

84. Foerstal, "Campaign Finance Bill Wins Its Day on the House Floor," 221.

85. Foerstal, "Campaign Finance Bill Wins Its Day on the House Floor," 221.

86. Karen Foerstal, "Opponents of Shays-Meehan Bet It All on a Conference," *CQ Weekly,* 9 February 2002, 393.

87. Foerstal, "Mixed Signals, Hard Feelings," 443.

88. Foerstal, "Opponents of Shays-Meehan Bet It All," 393.

89. Foerstal, "Mixed Signals, Hard Feelings," 443.

90. Foerstal, "Mixed Signals, Hard Feelings," 443.

91. Foerstal, "Mixed Signals, Hard Feelings," 443.

92. Foerstal, "Mixed Signals, Hard Feelings," 443.

93. Foerstal, "Mixed Signals, Hard Feelings," 443.

94. Susan Benkelman, "Editor's Notebook: Under Cover," *CQ Weekly,* 16 February 2002, 434.

95. Foerstal, "Campaign Finance Bill Wins Its Day on the House Floor," 221.

96. David Nather, "Campaign Finance Finale Puts McConnell on the Spot," *CQ Weekly,* 23 February 2002, 527.

97. Nather, "Campaign Finance Finale Puts McConnell on the Spot," 527.

98. Karen Foerstal, "Campaign Finance Passage Ends a Political Odyssey," *CQ Weekly,* 23 March 2002, 799.

99. Foerstal, "Campaign Finance Passage Ends a Political Odyssey," 799.

100. Barbara Sinclair, *Unorthodox Lawmaking,* 2nd ed. (Washington, DC: CQ Press, 2000).

5

Creating the Department of Homeland Security

The Homeland Security Department rose out of the decimation of the United States civil defense network.[1] In the aftermath of the September 11 terrorist attacks in Washington, New York, and Pennsylvania, the American public was shaken by such a large-scale attack and fearful that the likelihood of subsequent attacks was high. The September 11 attacks exposed gaping holes in national security and changed the way Americans thought about the balance between personal liberty and security, with security weighing much more heavily. While some within the federal bureaucracy, the Congress, and the military had been trying to restructure homeland security for years, it took the complete failure of the system—and the single worst attack on American soil—to bring about the largest security overhaul in the nation's history.

Lawmakers faced two motivating factors in improving homeland defense as quickly as possible: overwhelming pressure from constituents to fix the nation's defenses and the fear that another attack might be imminent. In the months following the attacks the country experienced a rare period of unanimity, with the public and the government focused on correcting the security problems that allowed the September 11 attacks to occur. Americans rallied around President Bush, and his approval ratings hovered just under 90 percent (an all-time high), and the prevention of terrorism was the most important issue on the public agenda.[2] Given this overwhelming support for improving homeland security, it was clear to all that the government would make significant changes in homeland security.

With the administration and the Congress interested in playing an important role in redesigning homeland security, there was uncertainty over whether the two branches could redesign the system together by maintaining the spirit of unanimity that had developed on Capitol Hill or if the process would devolve into institutional and partisan squabbling. In the immediate aftermath of the September 11 attacks, Congress deferred to the president on homeland security, waiting in the wings as Bush pursued a unilateral strategy and created the White House Office of Homeland Security under the direction of Tom Ridge. Like czars before him who battled drugs or oversaw energy supplies, Tom Ridge was put in charge of coordinating the nation's homeland security efforts. But while the president was creating a new White House office, members of Congress began thinking about how they might create a new department that would give them more oversight of homeland security.

If the administration were to make the homeland security czar the permanent director of homeland security, it would mean that Congress would not have power to provide advice and consent to the director of homeland security or over the execution of policy; homeland security would be in the complete control of the president. The Congress largely preferred creating a new cabinet-level position to run a new Department of Homeland Security. Under the Congress's preferred course of action, the Senate would provide advice and consent to the president's appointees to the Department of Homeland Security, and Congress would have complete oversight over the new department and its budget.

Congress began laying the groundwork to create a new department and began pressuring the president to accept a department, but the president resisted. Ultimately, the president reversed his position and proposed a new department. As such, members of Congress initiated the policy debate and were ultimately successful in creating the new department. The department that Congress subsequently created was almost a carbon copy of the president's vision for the new department. It is notable that once the president acquiesced to Congress's insistence on a new department, one of the biggest reorganizations of the federal government took less than six months to bring from introduction of the president's plan in June 2001 to final passage in November 2001.[3]

In this chapter we will first describe the homeland security network in place on September 11, 2001, and explain where lawmakers perceived shortcomings in homeland security. We will then follow the lawmaking process through the creation and implementation of the White House Office of Homeland Security and the legislative history of the Homeland Security Act with special emphasis on how individual policymakers provided leadership during the process. We conclude with a section on individual themes of leadership, drawing themes from the process as a whole.

BACKGROUND: THE HOMELAND SECURITY NETWORK

On September 11, 2001, the nation's homeland security network was largely a piecemeal effort within, and across, each level of the government.[4] At the federal level, law enforcement duties were largely the responsibility of the agencies within the Department of Justice, including the Federal Bureau of Investigation (FBI), the U.S. Marshals Service, the Drug Enforcement Agency, and the Immigration and Naturalization Service. Within the Treasury Department, the Secret Service, the Bureau of Alcohol, Tobacco, and Firearms, and the U.S. Customs Service also shared law enforcement duties. Finally, the Federal Aviation Agency was housed in the Department of Transportation. While these federal agencies shared law enforcement responsibilities, there was not a great deal of coordination between agencies in combating terrorism. Antiterrorism efforts in one agency often went unnoticed in other agencies.[5]

Furthermore, within each individual agency, there was often not a great deal of coordination on combating terrorism. For example, the FBI was divided into fifty-six field offices with fifty-six separate agendas. Each field office was largely left to combat crime as a distinct unit, and the priorities were largely parochial. The field office system created a patchwork law enforcement effort where the antiterrorism efforts of one field office were not necessarily tied to the efforts of others.

In addition to the law enforcement agencies, the federal government also had multiple agencies involved in collecting intelligence. The intelligence community was led by the director of central intelligence (DCI) who provided intelligence to federal agencies. The intelligence community was widespread with intelligence collecting agencies in the Department of Defense, the Department of State, the Central Intelligence Agency (CIA), and the National Security Agency, and the White House and Congress shared oversight responsibilities on the intelligence agencies.[6]

The intelligence community suffered from many of the same problems as the law enforcement community. While many agencies shared intelligence responsibilities, they often failed to share information or keep each other apprised of their antiterrorism efforts. Compounding the communication and organizational problems in each community was that communication between the law enforcement and intelligence agencies was limited at best. In sum, the homeland security network at the federal level was fragmented by a lack of organization between the law enforcement and intelligence communities and the agencies in those communities. Given that federal law enforcement agencies were not fully coordinated in their antiterrorism efforts, it should not be surprising that the efforts of the national government were not coordinated with the efforts of state or local agencies.[7]

The lack of communication between agencies and levels of government was not intentional. The cause of disorganization started with the lack of a single authority managing all antiterrorism efforts but was exacerbated by several factors. First, each federal agency had developed its own protocols for how they carried out their responsibilities. Therefore, coordination between agencies became more difficult as different agencies implemented policy with different strategies and management techniques. Second, different cultures existed in the various agencies. The differences in cultures can best be explained by the difference between the CIA and FBI. While the FBI had a law enforcement culture, the CIA had a research culture, and individuals in each had difficulty sustaining interagency partnerships which led to less communication.[8] Finally, communication suffered because of modern day compatibility issues: different agencies used different computer systems, software, and communication devices. For example, the New York City Fire Department, Police Department, and Port Authority were having trouble with communication between the departments because each used different mobile communication systems that were not interoperable.[9]

THE SEPTEMBER 11 TERRORIST ATTACKS

In a matter of hours, the country had escalated from a nation at peace to a nation at war and the public was scared, shocked, and angry. The public was largely united behind the president, and it was clear to all involved that the security system had been exposed as flawed and something would have to be done to make the country more secure. The September 11 attack was not the first terrorist attack on American soil but had the biggest effect on the political landscape. Recent attacks included a 1993 bombing of the World Trade Center that killed six and injured more than a thousand; a bombing of the Murrah Federal Building in Oklahoma City in 1995 that destroyed the building and killed 168 people; a bomb detonated in a park at the 1996 Olympics in Atlanta; and a foiled bomb plot at the end of 1999 that was intended to occur with the new millennium. These earlier attacks, however, did not motivate the same massive reorganization of homeland security that followed the 2001 attack.

The attack on the World Trade Center in 1993, as explained by the 9/11 Commission, is exemplary of why there was a tepid reaction to reorganizing the government to address homeland security concerns prior to September 11, 2001.[10] In 1993, terrorists parked a Ryder rental van beneath the twin towers of the World Trade Center with the intent of killing thousands of Americans. While the attack injured more than one thousand, only six people were killed. Following the attack, the Clinton administration used the National Security Council to coordinate efforts to apprehend the terrorists. This effort was largely successful as within days the government started arresting suspects. The federal investigation moved forward quickly and effectively and following the

investigation, federal prosecutors successfully tried and convicted several suspects. While the success of the federal investigation and prosecution of suspects
was a successful use of the federal government's law enforcement capabilities,
the success overshadowed the significance of the new terrorist threat confronting
the United States.[11]

The response to the 1993 attack highlights the false sense of security that
had set in prior to the September 11 attack. The September 11 attack motivated a massive overhaul while these earlier events did not for two reasons.
First, the September 11 attack was on an entirely different scale than earlier
attacks with thousands dead and injured. Second, previous terrorist attacks
occurred on foreign soil or were carried out on a local scale. The September
11 attack, however, exposed the systemic failure of multiple *national* defense
systems on our own soil. In the weeks after the attacks, the public saw video
footage of the terrorists walking through security check points with ease, not
at one airport but at four, including two of the busiest airports in the country.
Furthermore, the terrorists lived in the United States for some time before the
attacks, taking flight lessons at U.S. flight schools without much notice from
the authorities.

If the September 11 attack was not enough to make the need for tighter
security obvious to Capitol Hill lawmakers, the subsequent anthrax attack that
targeted congressional offices certainly drove the point home. On Monday,
October 15, a staffer opened a letter addressed to Senator Tom Daschle (D-SD)
containing anthrax. On October 17, Speaker Hastert (R-IL) closed Congress
due to the presence of anthrax, and twenty-eight people in and out of Daschle's
office tested positive for exposure.[12] Members were forced out of their offices
as hazardous materials teams sealed off entire congressional office buildings
in response. While some members were forced into temporary office space,
and others worried about staff members who had tested positive for anthrax,
the Congress had intimate exposure to the failures in the national security system. National leaders also had only to look up to the sky, or to popular memorials outside their office windows, for a daily reminder of the problem at hand.
For months after the September 11 attack, Washington was protected by air
patrols over the city, and national memorials were defended by sand bags, bar-
ricades, armed soldiers, and anti-aircraft batteries.[13] Finally, on December 22,
2001, a flight from Paris to Miami was diverted to Boston when Richard Reid
tried to light the fuse for a bomb that was hidden in his shoe. The bomb was
large enough to drop the airplane from the sky by blowing a hole in the plane's
fuselage. Passengers and crew members managed to subdue Reid and detain
him until they could deliver him to authorities on the ground.[14] Again, the
nation was on alert as the fear of a terrorist attack continued to keep the country on edge.

THE DEBATE OVER DEPARTMENT STATUS

The central problem of homeland security is one of coordinating a federal system with multiple layers of authority. At the state and local levels, there are many different first responders from police and fire fighters to paramedics, hospitals, and emergency management teams. At the federal level, there are multiple agencies carrying out both intelligence and law enforcement activities. Administrators must coordinate the immediate response to emergencies and manage the sharing of information coming from different sources, each with different priorities and political cultures.

In the months following the September 11 attacks, Congress and the president worked in a bipartisan manner to diagnose and solve problems. As one might expect in a matter of national security, the Congress was somewhat deferential to the president in the months following the attacks, allowing the president to pursue a unilateral strategy for solving security problems without much interference. Both sides promised to keep the lines of communication open, and Bush even had weekly breakfast meetings with the top four congressional leaders to keep them abreast of developments and coordinate policy efforts.[15] With good communication between party and institution leaders, the president took the lead on the initial response to the attacks with strong support from congressional leaders.

The Office of Homeland Security

Nine days after the attacks, President Bush made a speech to a joint session of Congress and the nation. Bush delivered this speech in one of the most dramatic settings in American history. Outside the Capitol building the military created perhaps the most secure joint session in the history of the Congress: barbed wire was strung around the perimeter; buses were lined up to block access to the roads around the Capitol and to shield the building from car bombs; tanks and heavily armed soldiers patrolled the grounds; attack helicopters circled the building; and guests were thoroughly screened before entry.[16] In this speech, Bush announced that he had created a new Office of Homeland Security that would be charged with the strategic oversight of the nation's security. The president argued that appointing a director within the White House with a small staff to coordinate efforts among existing agencies and departments would provide the best security for the nation because the director would be in close proximity to the president with the authority to restructure or coordinate efforts as needed. President Bush also announced that he had selected Pennsylvania Governor Tom Ridge to run the new office.[17]

Secretary Tom Ridge (R-PA)

Tom Ridge has a long record of public service. Ridge enlisted in the Army in 1968 and was awarded the Bronze Star for valor in Vietnam. Ridge was first elected to the House of Representatives in 1984 and holds the distinction of being the first enlisted Vietnam veteran elected to Congress.[18]

Throughout Ridge's seven-term congressional career, he was a moderate Republican voting conservatively on some issues and liberally on others. A quick review of his interest group rating scores during his time in Congress reveals middle-of-the-road scores from nearly every group providing ratings. Ridge rose from the obscurity of a congressional district based in geographically distant Erie, Pennsylvania, which is quite far from the political centers of Harrisburg, Philadelphia, and Pittsburgh, to become governor in 1994 and was reelected in 1998.

Bush and Ridge first became friends when Ridge backed President George H. W. Bush's campaign in 1980, and as governor, Ridge worked closely with Texas Governor George W. Bush. In 2000 Ridge supported Bush's presidential candidacy, offered his fundraising skills to help the campaign raise money and became a close campaign advisor for Bush.[19] Ridge was on Bush's short list of potential running mates in 2000, but it was not until 2001 that Bush called upon Ridge—asking him to serve as the first Office of Homeland Security Advisor. Ridge oversaw initial efforts at reorganizing the government in the first year following the September 11 attacks, and in 2003, became the first secretary of Homeland Security.

President Bush cited Ridge's organizational skills as a primary reason for his selection. Ridge holds a reputation as a straight shooter with the ability to lock into a problem and solve it without falling victim to distraction.[20] Ridge's initial position as the Office of Homeland Security advisor required not only strong organizational skills but innate political ability to coordinate the efforts of elected and appointed officials. When appointed, no one questioned Ridge's political skill as he had never lost an election and built a political empire in Pennsylvania through the use of his deep understanding of state politics and his willingness to use his political power to forge coalitions.[21] One additional quality that made Ridge attractive was his popularity among his fellow governors and former colleagues in Congress—relationships that would serve him well in trying to coordinate homeland security across the fifty states.

This speech represented the beginning of the reorganization of homeland security efforts. President Bush signed an executive order on October 8 making the Office of Homeland Security an official unit within the Executive Office of the President. Creating a White House office to address a problem had been done before. During World War II, Harold Ickes served as the energy czar and William Jeffers served as the rubber czar. The Clinton administration employed Kristine Gebbie as its AIDs czar in 1993 and 1994. The nation also had a series of drug czars including Lee Brown, Bob Martinez, William Bennett, and Barry McCaffrey.

In the short term, Congress was willing to give Bush wide discretion in structuring a temporary solution. According to Senator Fred Thompson (R-TN), the ranking member of the Senate Governmental Affairs Committee, "The president has a lot to deal with lately; maybe after a while he'll have a different view as to what is appropriate, I don't see the need to rush into a major organizational change until we are all on the same page."[22] While members of Congress had introduced a handful of bills to restructure homeland security, the sponsors expected the bills to wait in a legislative holding pattern while the president took the lead. Senator Bob Graham (D- FL), the chair of the Senate Intelligence Committee, said of his bill, S. 1449, "I do not seek to compete with President Bush's plans for Governor Tom Ridge. Rather, I want to complement them."[23] In fact, Graham acknowledged that he held off pushing his bill at the White House's request.[24]

Federalizing Baggage Handlers

With President Bush in the lead, the federal government started to make changes to the homeland security system. One of the first changes was to close the holes in airport security that allowed terrorists to bring knives onboard four airplanes. The near unanimous solution was to change the baggage screening process at airports in an attempt to tighten security. Congress began consideration of legislation in October that would tighten security by requiring President Bush to federalize baggage screeners.[25] By federalizing baggage screeners, the federal government would have more control over the hiring and training of baggage screeners to serve the dual purpose of improving airport security and reassuring travelers that they would be safe.

The Senate voted on October 11 to unanimously support a bipartisan bill sponsored by Senators Ernest Hollings (D-SC) and John McCain (R-AZ) to require Bush to federalize baggage screeners. After the Senate vote, the president indicated that he would accept federalizing the baggage screeners, and with support from the speaker of the House and fourteen Republican cosponsors of the companion bill in the House, the bill seemed likely to pass into law. Shortly thereafter, however, President Bush changed his mind on the question of federalizing baggage screeners and decided to lobby the House to vote against the Senate bill. He instead put his support behind a Republican bill that would give the decision of federalizing screeners to the president. Following President Bush's lead, the House defeated the House version of the Senate bill 214–218 with eight Republican cosponsors voting against their own bill.[26]

The House subsequently voted 286–139 to give President Bush full discretion over whether to designate twenty-eight thousand baggage screeners as federal employees with union protection or as private contractors. This change of heart by the president was one of several signs that the cordial relationship between the president and Congress that developed in the aftermath of the September 11 attacks was starting to chill. Members of Congress, most notably the Democratic leadership, were beginning to feel more isolated from decision-making and were bristling at the president's choice of a unilateral strategy. According to Representative David Price (D-NC), "It's kind of a go-it-alone strategy on the part of the White House that's hard to understand . . . the administration is pushing the envelope dangerously."[27] Senator John Breaux (D-LA) insisted that the White House needed to keep the lines of communication open with Congress. He said, "If they don't, they'll probably find that Congress will be less cooperative in funding things they need."[28]

Congressional Leadership Emerges: The Congress–Tom Ridge Standoff

The flashpoint of disagreement between the Congress and the president in spring 2002 was when Ridge refused to testify before Congress about ongoing homeland security efforts.[29] On March 15, Senator Robert Byrd (D-WV), chair of the Senate Appropriations Committee, invited Ridge to testify before the committee as part of the appropriations process, but that invitation was immediately rejected, as were subsequent requests for testimony. The president argued that because Ridge was a political advisor serving in a position created by executive order, not congressional statute, Ridge was not required to testify before Congress. Bush argued that requiring his advisors to testify before Congress may cause his advisors to temper their advice out of fear that they would later face congressional inquiry, and tempering advice could weaken national security.[30]

The administration's insistence on keeping Ridge from testifying caused congressional tempers to flare, and even Republican lawmakers were starting to question the administration's position. According to Senator Larry Craig (R-ID), chairman of the Republican Policy Committee and Senator Ted Stevens (R-AK), if the president expected Congress to appropriate $38 billion for homeland defense, then the Congress should be allowed to ask the Homeland Security director about how the money would be spent.[31] In the House, more than fifty members signed a letter to President Bush demanding that Ridge appear before Congress. Representative Ernest Istook (R-OK), chair of the Treasury–Postal

Service Appropriations Subcommittee, was usually a bulwark of support for the president, but on this matter, he disagreed with the administration's refusal to let Ridge testify. He said, "In light of this, the chance of any big consolidation of the White House accounts falls between slim to none."[32]

This growing rift between Congress and the president was over more than just whether Ridge would testify before Congress—Ridge's testimony was symbolic of the battle for institutional power. Congress and the president have grappled over the distribution of power over the last two hundred years with the balance of power oscillating between the two branches over time.[33] The question of which branch would have authority over homeland security was paramount because billions of dollars were flowing into homeland security, and the branch winning this dispute would see a significant increase in relative power. The president was making an effort to put homeland security firmly in the executive branch, but Congress was starting to resist his effort. In addition to formalizing the Office of Homeland Security as a White House office through executive order, Bush signed a second executive order creating the Homeland Security Advisory Council that further entrenched homeland security authority within the White House.[34]

The standoff over Ridge's testimony continued into May. While Ridge had been giving private briefings to lawmakers since he was named the director of Homeland Security, these private meetings were not meeting legislators' expectations.[35] Senator Byrd called the meeting on May 2 a "sham" and a "stunt."[36] Democratic leaders argued that they would only get the answers to their questions, and feel like they were meeting their oversight obligations, if Ridge were to testify under oath.[37]

In addition to frustration over the standoff with the administration over Ridge's testimony, members of Congress had expressed concern over the direction homeland security was headed under White House authority. First, members of Congress were concerned that as a White House advisor, Ridge would not have the authority to enforce his decisions. The common perception of czar positions like director of Homeland Security was that such directors held no real budget authority and were therefore ineffective.[38] The Congress wanted to strengthen the Homeland Security director's position by making the director a department secretary. Second, lawmakers were also troubled by the widening authority Ridge would have. As director, Ridge would have influence over budgeted programs larger than those of six existing cabinet secretaries but without congressional oversight. By creating a Department of Homeland Security, the Senate would be responsible for confirming the secretary and could subsequently oversee the department and its budget. Third, Democrats in the Senate were questioning whether Bush's request of $37.7 billion for strengthening homeland security was enough to meet the growing challenges, and they began calling for increased spending.[39]

Representative William "Mac" Thornberry (R-TX)

Mac Thornberry was first elected in 1994 and serves the Texas 13th congressional district. In his first campaign he defeated an incumbent, Representative Bill Sarpalius, and has been easily reelected ever since, enjoying comfortable margins of victory. Thornberry holds a respected place in the Republican party. He signed the Contract with America in 1994 and while many of his colleagues from the class of 1994 joined the coup against Speaker Gingrich, Thornberry did not. His solid conservative record, strong national defense positions, and loyalty to the party have allowed Thornberry to hold powerful committee positions and become an influential member within the party.[40] Thornberry currently serves on the Armed Services Committee and on the Permanent Select Committee on Intelligence where he chairs the Oversight Committee.

Like many members of Congress, Thornberry identifies national defense as the first priority for the national government. With a seat on the Armed Services Committee, Thornberry is in good position to address his national defense concerns. Thornberry's biggest claim to fame before September 11, 2001, was his bill to improve security at the nation's nuclear weapons facilities. Thornberry's bill, passed in 1999, created the National Nuclear Security Administration that handed all oversight of nuclear weapons facilities to a single federal agency.[41] Thornberry was subsequently named the chairman of the Special Oversight Panel on Department of Energy Reorganization to implement the new law.

Thornberry's other claim to a national reputation was his insistence that the United States better organize its efforts at preventing and responding to terrorist attacks. In March 2001, Thornberry introduced legislation in the House to reorganize the federal government by transforming the Federal Emergency Management Agency (FEMA) into the National Homeland Security Agency. This agency would take the lead in securing America's borders from attack with authority over the Justice Department's Border Patrol, the Coast Guard, and the Customs Service. This legislation was based in part on the recommendations of the Hart-Rudman Commission that warned of dire consequences if the nation's security network was not reorganized. Thornberry's bill received a hearing with the House Government Reform Committee but attracted only one cosponsor and was destined to die without a vote on the House floor.[42]

> Shortly following the September 11 attacks, however, Thornberry's
> ideas on border security were embraced by the House as members added
> their names as cosponsors to Thornberry's legislation, and Thornberry
> became one of the resident experts on the most important topic on the
> national agenda. Thornberry's expertise on national security earned him a
> key role in creating the Department of Homeland Security.

A bipartisan group of lawmakers introduced legislation (S. 2452 and H.R.
4660) on May 2, 2002, that would create a new National Homeland Security
Department with a secretary who would face congressional approval and oversight. The bills were sponsored by Senators Joe Lieberman (D-CT), Arlen
Specter (R-PA), and Bob Graham (D-FL) and Representatives Jane Harman
(D-CA), Jim Gibbons (R-NV), and Mac Thornberry (R-TX). Thornberry said
of the effort, "The further away we get from September 11, the harder it is going
to be to make real change."[43] Lieberman added, "I think if we move this legislation ahead, we will strengthen Governor Ridge and the forces of reform."[44]

Congress's efforts to make Ridge a secretary were met with resistance from
the administration. Contrary to congressional opinion, Ridge indicated in his public remarks that statutory authority would not be necessary for him to carry out
his job. Instead, Ridge pointed to his close relationship with the president as a
source of political power and argued that the president's authority was sufficient.[45]

Despite Ridge's insistence that he could rely on the president's authority,
Congress feared that Ridge would not have enough authority to do his job,
and the fears seemed to be coming to fruition.[46] As an example, Ridge was
starting to lose battles with existing cabinet secretaries. When Ridge circu-
lated a plan to consolidate separate inspection services operated by the Border Patrol, Customs Service, Coast Guard, and the Department of Agriculture,
the plan was leaked to the press and subsequently scuttled due to administrative infighting.[47] He also lost a series of turf battles within the Bush administration, and state and local agencies with homeland security responsibilities
began questioning his approach.[48] President Bush created the Homeland Security Council with the intent of strengthening ties between homeland security
agencies and the White House but, once created, Bush decided to preside over
the meetings himself, and Ridge's role as the leader on homeland security
seemed to decrease.[49] Finally, after announcing the development of a color-
coded warning system, the president decided that Attorney General John
Ashcroft would also play a role in deciding when to increase or decrease the
alert levels. Ridge and Ashcroft often butted heads because their roles as the
nation's top law enforcement officer and head of homeland security often over-
lapped in jurisdiction.

For a number of reasons, Ridge was not able to develop as commanding a presence in the administration as he might have hoped. Senator Lieberman said of Ridge, "I don't mean to make it sound like I'm saying I told you so, but this is such a big and critical job and he has to oversee so many different agencies and offices of the government that I just think he needs the power to do that. So long as we don't give him that power, we're not doing as much as we should be doing to protect our homeland security."[50] While there were many detractors, Ridge continued to have supporters in Congress as well. Senator Pat Roberts (R-KS), a former House colleague and occasional basketball teammate said of Ridge's ability to get the job done, "He is a very determined rebounder, and this is a lot like rebounding. You've got to get position, you've got to go up and get the ball, bring it down, don't bring it down too far and pass it to somebody else, which he does to the president."[51]

As the standoff over Ridge continued, the Senate began considering more confrontational methods to compel Ridge and the president to comply with congressional invitations to testify. Some Democrats, including Senate Majority Leader Tom Daschle, called for a subpoena to force Ridge to testify, prompting the White House to express its surprise at Daschle's "vehemence."[52] Congressional Republicans, and some Democrats, joined the White House's objection to such an overt act, and sought a more subtle solution. Lawmakers on both the Senate Appropriations Committee and the Senate Governmental Affairs Committee were considering holding the president's legislative requests hostage until Ridge testified. By delaying legislation that the president wanted, their intent was to convince President Bush that the congressional requests for Ridge's testimony were not going away, and Ridge must eventually comply or risk sinking the president's agenda. While some lawmakers were steeling themselves for institutional conflict, others were trying to moderate Congress's position. Senator Fred Thompson (R-TN), ranking Republican on the Senate Governmental Affairs Committee, said, "I don't think you're going to be able to reorganize the executive branch without the cooperation of the executive branch. It's just not going to happen."[53]

Bush Makes a Proposal

After months of congressional requests for a new department to organize homeland security, the president suddenly announced a plan to do just that.[54] After trying to rely on a Homeland Security Office created by executive order, the president gave in to congressional demands and tried to reclaim the initiative of directing the redesign of homeland security.[55] The plan was formulated quickly and quietly and came as quite a surprise to lawmakers returning from their Memorial Day 2002 recess.[56] The Congress welcomed the president's proposal since it gave them virtually everything Congress wanted and then even more.[57]

Most importantly, the new proposal outlined a single department, subject to congressional oversight, with a secretary requiring Senate confirmation.[58]

Like previous practice in the Bush administration, the proposal to create a new department was formulated in near absolute secrecy. White House Chief of Staff Andrew Card was joined by Tom Ridge, White House Counsel Alberto Gonzalez, and Office of Management and Budget Director Mitchell E. Daniels Jr. in developing the proposal over ten days in late April and early May.[59] While the White House did not broadcast its intentions to Congress, out of fear of prematurely starting turf battles, the White House did inform Speaker Hastert and Majority Leader Armey of their intentions.[60] This secrecy was likely quite important in making sure that the bill would pass quickly because an administration analysis showed that eighty-eight congressional committees and subcommittees had some hand in the homeland security related agencies Bush wanted to move into the new department.[61] Eliminating advance warning allowed the president to introduce his proposal without allowing significant turf-based opposition to develop before congressional consideration.

President Bush introduced his plan in a televised speech to the nation on June 6 and said in the speech, "As we have learned more about the plans and capabilities of the terrorist network, we have concluded that our government must be reorganized to deal more effectively with the new threats of the 21st century."[62] President Bush proposed one of the most complex reorganizations of the federal government ever attempted. The new department would become the third largest department behind Defense and Veterans Affairs based on personnel. Bush's plan would combine border security and emergency response agencies, but the reorganization would exclude the intelligence gathering agencies. These agencies would later be addressed when Congress and the president created the director of national intelligence position discussed in chapter 3.

The president's plan called for Congress to organize the new department around four different areas: border and transportation security; emergency preparedness; countermeasures against chemical, biological, radiological, and nuclear weapons; and information analysis and infrastructure protection.[63]

Many observers were surprised to see the president embrace an idea that he had rebuffed only months earlier by remaining committed to the Homeland Security Office.[64] According to Senator Graham, "In this town, there's a lot of macho in never admitting that you learned something. President Bush should be commended for studying the issue closely . . . it's a sign of reassurance to the American people."[65] After the president's announcement, Senator Lieberman held what he called a victory press conference noting that the president's plan was close to his own. Lieberman also applauded the president in answering a question about why the president had reversed himself: "I don't know. I take it as a sign of strength when someone sees that something is not going as they wanted. I congratulate the administration."[66]

But not all members took a conciliatory approach in their reaction to Bush's sudden change of course. Senator Byrd said, "For many months, we have heard tales of little or no real direction from the federal government in assessing risk and pinpointing vulnerabilities. I hope that this new status for the Office of Homeland Security amounts to more than just reshuffling the deck chairs on the Titanic."[67]

After introducing his plan, President Bush invited Lieberman and Thornberry, along with some cosponsors to the White House for a breakfast meeting to discuss how Congress would attempt to overhaul homeland security. At this meeting Lieberman indicated that his committee would probably combine the president's proposal with his own bill and hold hearings while Thornberry stated that the president's plan was a better starting point than anything they had on hand and he would start work immediately to get it passed.[68] Thornberry testified at a National Security Subcommittee of the House Government Reform Committee hearing on June 11 and said of the plan, "The need for this kind of reorganization, I think, is beyond question. Everybody agrees a hundred different agencies scattered around the government is unacceptable. They can't be coordinated. They don't have the right focus. Homeland security is not the kind of priority that it needs to be."[69]

After unveiling his proposal for homeland security, the president set out to convince lawmakers to pass the legislation quickly. On June 12, Bush told his Homeland Security Council, "I'm also going to remind Congress, that I'm going to continue speaking with the American people about this issue. Once I proposed it, I'm going to take my case beyond Washington to the real influence-peddlers of America, and that's the American people."[70] Polling data suggested that Bush would not have to do much lobbying to get the public behind the reorganization as 72 percent of those polled in a June 7–8 CNN/USA Today/Gallup poll supported the idea of creating a new department.[71]

While the president submitted a proposal to Congress, he did not submit a bill. Bush tasked Congress to come up with a formalized product that met his organizational vision. So while there was widespread support in Congress for the idea of a new cabinet-level department, there remained a considerable amount of negotiation and maneuvering before a final product would be completed. According to Representative Thornberry, based on his personal contact with the president at strategy meetings after the plan was released, Bush was open to negotiation with the Congress on the proposal. Thornberry said, "He [Bush] did say that he does not expect his proposal to pass exactly as written. He's willing to have the legislative process work its will."[72] The details of how the new department would be constructed, however, would have to be added to the skeletal structure the president provided.

One motivating factor that kept dissent to a minimum was the continued specter of terrorism. On June 10, the administration announced that it had foiled a plan to explode a "dirty bomb," possibly in Washington.[73] This reinforced the feeling on the Hill that this legislation was vitally important and helped reinforce the personal link to the legislation for each member of Congress that was first made during the September 11 attack and the subsequent anthrax attack.

It was significant that the Bush administration had not really taken a firm position on the issue of creating a new department in the seven months following the September attacks. While the administration moved quickly to create a new Homeland Security Office and indicated that the Homeland Security Office would have enough authority to do the job, it never specifically rejected the idea of creating a new department. This lack of position taking left the door open for the president to later co-opt Congress's demand for a new department. While the president might have been happy to keep the Office of Homeland Security without congressional action, that position quickly became untenable. Congress was starting to apply pressure on the administration, and there were fears within the Republican Party that if there were another attack, the president might be accused of slowing or preventing the creation of a department that might have prevented such an attack.[74] The lack of earlier position taking allowed the president to concede without appearing to do so.

Furthermore, Bush was able to seize the momentum, and credit, for the new department by announcing his plan out of secrecy. As the small cadre of four senior White House officials developed the president's proposal, the group of those in the know expanded as other senior staffers were invited to help finalize details on specific parts of the proposal—not the entire proposal. One of Andrew Card's deputies, Joseph Hagin, served as the "enforcer" for the group, limiting the participation of other staffers to small pieces of the proposal and reminding the participants that the plan was being developed in secrecy. Hagin is quoted as telling participants, "This is the president's news to make."[75] In addition, the proposal booklet was printed overnight in the basement of the Eisenhower Executive Office Building the day before public release, and the White House released a calendar listing no public events to ensure the plan would not be leaked to the public and journalists would not start investigating.[76] Hagin's role in the process, and the perception that this was Bush's "news to make," emphasizes the strategic implications the Bush administration saw in developing the proposal in secrecy and announcing it with no forewarning to Congress. Secrecy allowed Bush to capture momentum behind his plan with no opportunity for committee chairmen or party leaders to build legislative roadblocks.

HOUSE PASSAGE

House consideration of the president's plan, H.R. 5005, followed a distinctive path. Rather than using the committee system to legislate on homeland security, the Republican leadership announced on June 13 that it had decided to establish the Select Committee on Homeland Security to help manage passage of the bill. Speaker Hastert outlined a legislative plan that included the use of ten authorizing committees that would write the House bill and a select committee, chaired by Majority Leader Armey (R-TX), that would serve the same purpose as the Rules committee in rewriting the bill and preparing it for the floor. The bill would then go to the floor with an open rule, where it could be amended by the membership.[77] According to Republican Conference Committee Chairman Representative J. C. Watts (R-OK), using a "leadership-driven" select committee made sense because the leadership would be better able to shepherd the bill through the House.[78]

Representative Dick Armey (R-TX)

Dick Armey had no previous political experience before challenging first-term incumbent Representative Tom Vandergriff in the 1984 general election to represent Texas's 26th district. Armey, a professor of economics, narrowly beat the incumbent while riding Ronald Reagan's coattails. His rise to power in the Republican Party started in 1987 when he earned national recognition for achieving the near impossible: closing military bases. For twelve years, the Congress had been stymied in efforts to close military bases that were protected by powerful members of Congress and military officers. Armey's bill proposed an independent base closing commission that would produce a list of bases to be closed and then require Congress to either accept or reject the entire list.[79]

Armey began his climb up the leadership ladder in 1993 when he was elected to the number three leadership position as the Republican conference chairman. As part of the leadership team, Armey championed Newt Gingrich's idea for a Contract with America, drumming up support among Republican House candidates.[80] Armey was subsequently elected as majority leader when the Republicans captured a majority in the House in 1994. He was quite effective in leading a party that had not been in the majority for forty years. While Armey rose to power quite swiftly, his tenure was somewhat rocky. Armey's blunt political persona often led him to say things that he wished he had not.[81] In addition to style concerns, many Republicans faulted him for his role in supporting the coup against Speaker Gingrich. Despite his uneven relationship with the Republican caucus, he remained the majority leader until he retired at the end of the 107th Congress in 2002.

Creation of a bipartisan select committee to oversee the creation of the Department of Homeland Security was no small task. Relying on goodwill remaining from the aftermath of the September 11 attacks, party leaders were able to come together and establish a system that satisfied both parties—an effort that failed at other points during the Bush administration (see chapter 6). Both Speaker Hastert and Minority Leader Gephardt applauded the bipartisan cooperation.[82] The Select Committee on Homeland Security would be chaired by Majority Leader Dick Armey with Minority Whip Nancy Pelosi as the ranking member. The other committee members were also party leaders. Republican members included Majority Whip Tom Delay; J .C. Watts, the Republican conference chair; Deborah Pryce, the vice chair of the Republican conference; and Rob Portman, the chairman of the House Republican leadership. The other Democrats included Martin Frost, the Democratic caucus chair; Robert Menendez, the vice chairman of the Democratic caucus; and Rosa DeLauro, the assistant to the minority leader. With this committee membership, the Republican and Democratic Party leadership teams would have direct control over the legislative process. Many House committee chairmen lobbied the leadership for inclusion on the Select Committee, including Representatives Tom Davis (R-VA) and David Dreier (R-CA), but the leadership denied these requests because they wanted to maintain strict control of the committee.[83]

If twelve House committees had considered H.R. 5005, the House may have developed different conceptions of what the new department should be as referring a bill to multiple committees generally increases the level of debate over an issue with many hands shaping the legislation. Multiple referral was not a good option in this situation, from the leadership's perspective, because the leadership of both parties wanted the Congress to move in the same direction with speed.

Setting a Deadline: September 11, 2002

When the House took up homeland security legislation in June, the November elections were starting to loom large. Both parties had an interest in deriving the maximum advantage from the passage of, or failure to pass, legislation. While the Democrats were insistent on reminding the public that they had been pushing for the Bush plan long before Bush, and had met resistance from the president, Democratic lawmakers had an interest in making the issue go away as soon as possible or to let consideration drag on through the election without passage. The Democrats could conceivably take advantage of quick passage by moving the focus of the agenda away from security issues that favored the Republicans to domestic issues that favored the Democrats. Alternatively, the Democrats could also use a long legislative process to their advantage by asking the public why a unified Republican government was not able to pass a homeland security bill that had bipartisan support in time for the first anniversary of the September 11 attacks.

Accordingly, the Republican Party also stood to benefit or suffer politically from the timing of passage. They felt that the longer the issue was at the forefront of the agenda, the better their chances of reelection as the majority party would become. But, they were mindful that if the process took too long, they might be blamed for an inability to pass crucial national security legislation.

Strategists on both sides of the aisle, therefore, tried to put their respective parties in the best electoral position by strategically expediting or obstructing passage. Democratic leaders made the first strategic move by asking the Republicans to join them in a bipartisan effort to quickly pass legislation before the first anniversary of the September 11 attacks in 2002. The Republican leadership was divided on the issue, but Speaker Hastert decided to accept Majority Leader Gephardt's challenge on June 11, 2002. This agreement meant that executing one of the largest governmental reorganizations in history would be compressed into a few short months. In order to meet this deadline, the House would have to pass the bill before its August recess. Majority Leader Armey said, "We will all have to work hard and somewhat double-time to get it done. But if we have the level of cooperation and commitment I perceived this morning, I think we can do that."[84] Under immense time pressure, the Republican leaders' lobbying efforts began to equate dissent with disloyalty.[85] By quashing dissent within the party, while reaching out across the partisan divide, the Republican leadership hoped they would be able to pass the president's plan quickly. Majority Leader Armey said, "We're rising above our politics and we'll rise above our parochial and our jurisdictional issues as well."[86]

To meet its September 11 deadline, the leadership imposed a July 12 deadline on the eleven authorizing committees to mark up their bills. Each of the eleven, including the Agriculture, Appropriations, Armed Services, Energy and Commerce, Financial Services, Government Reform, Intelligence, International Relations, Judiciary, Science, Transportation and Infrastructure, and Ways and Means Committees, marked up the portion of the Bush plan that was relevant to their committee's jurisdiction.[87] Throughout the mark-up process, Representative Armey made an effort to keep in contact with the committee chairmen as well as Senator Lieberman, who chaired the committee considering the legislation in the Senate, to discuss ideas and address concerns about the legislation. After the mark-up process, the five Republicans and four Democrats on the new Select Committee on Homeland Security would be tasked to assemble the final bill from the authorizing committees' contributions for debate on the House floor.

Authorizing Committee Action

The separate mark-up sessions in the House provided the first opportunity for meaningful consideration of the plan and its ramifications for congressional jurisdiction. At the same time that Congress welcomed the sweeping proposal from the president, individual committees were concerned about how their particular jurisdictions would be affected by the reorganization. The jurisdictional question became the biggest stumbling block in the House with powerful committee chairs lining up to defend their turf. Representative Don Young (R-AK), chairman of the House Transportation and Infrastructure Committee, met with President Bush about his homeland security proposal with regard to transferring the Coast Guard into Homeland Security. Representative Young was very blunt about his concern, saying, "This isn't about turf, Mr. President. This is personal."[88] Young's statement underscores the importance of jurisdiction to individual members, especially committee chairs. Jurisdiction over a policy area gives committee chairs significant personal power—power they are reluctant to surrender.

Young's committee followed Young on the Coast Guard question by voting to keep the Coast Guard out of the Department of Homeland Security.[89] The same concerns were raised and protected by other House committees. The House Judiciary Committee voted to make changes to the Bush proposal by placing the Secret Service in the Justice Department rather than in Homeland Security, splitting the Immigration and Naturalization Service into two pieces instead of transferring the agency intact to Homeland Security, and refusing to put the Federal Emergency Management Agency (FEMA) into the new department. The House Armed Services Committee rejected the transfer of the Lawrence Livermore National Laboratory's intelligence analysts to the new department.[90] Throughout the mark-up period, it became clear that each of the federal agencies the president wanted to move into the new Homeland Security Department had friends in the House who wanted to protect the agency and their committee's jurisdiction over the agency. The mark-up period exposed the jurisdiction battles the president wanted to avoid. Creating a select committee to oversee the process and make final changes before floor consideration proved to be a brilliant stroke by the House leadership because it gave the leadership the ability to intercede in matters of jurisdictional protection.

Another concern during the mark-ups was the sometimes blatant practice of adding pork projects to the bill in the name of homeland security. For example, in the House Science Committee mark-up, Representative Joe Barton (R-TX) successfully added an amendment with support from other Texas lawmakers that defined twenty-one criteria to establish research centers of excellence. Coincidentally, the criteria would make Texas A&M University eligible for the benefits of that special status. The chair of the committee, Representative Sherwood

Boehlert (R-NY), reacted by saying, "Members should use this process as a way of using science to win the war on terror, not carve out a new center or research facility for their district."[91]

President Bush's Lobbying Activity

President Bush took a personal role in lobbying for his proposal. On July 10, Bush visited with 3,700 federal workers from the Customs Service, the Immigration and Naturalization Service, and other agencies at a homeland security event. The employees would later become a part of the new department, and Bush lobbied them to support the homeland security bill.[92] Bush lobbied the workers in part to shore up support for his request for more flexibility in managing the federal workforce, which was part of the president's initial proposal. Some critics had complained that this proposal would strip workers of civil service protections and change their compensation rates. Bush said, "The new department must be able to get the right people in the right place at the right time, with the right pay. We need to be able to reward excellence and ensure accountability for individual performance."[93] The president also used the phrase "management flexibility" to describe these ideas, and management flexibility became the key phrase in selling his position on labor rules in the new department.

Using the term management flexibility allowed the president to describe a process by which the president would have the ability to shift resources when needed while obscuring the fact that those resources are employees who will be transferred or fired. By referring to the position with a more acceptable label, the president was able to sell the policy more easily to the public. Winning control over the terms of debate can only marginally affect the outcome, but when a policy faces an evenly divided Congress, a marginal advantage can make the difference between winning and losing.

The Select Committee on Homeland Security and Floor Consideration

The White House was willing to compromise with Congress by deferring to congressional concerns over certain parts of the plan in exchange for passing legislation that remained consistent with the main objectives of the president's plan.[94] Armey's interpretation of the Select Committee's role involved some deference to the president and some compromise with House committees, but he was quick to remind the House that the committee would not be a rubber stamp for others' ideas. Armey said that his committee would be "respectful" of others' concerns but also said, "We do not feel bound by the chapter-and-verse details of the president's proposal or of any of the committees. We think the committees' expertise is going to make the president's proposal an even better proposal."[95] While Armey and his staff refused to divulge how the Select

Committee would amend the Bush proposal to appease committee concerns, Armey did say that "most of the chairmen will be pleasantly surprised with what they see."[96] Furthermore, one of Armey's aides added that Armey would side with the White House on the most contentious disagreements.[97]

In the end, the president did not need to compromise on much. Representative Armey released his mark-up of Bush's homeland security proposal on July 18, revealing that he had sided with the president on most issues. Chief among them was moving both the Coast Guard and FEMA into Homeland Security despite strong reservations from Republican committee chairmen. Armey said of the bill, "The White House is going to have a bill that's about 80 percent of what they started with." He added that the House committees, "got something they can be happy with me for and something they can be unhappy about."[98] On other issues, Armey sided with his congressional colleagues. For instance, Armey split the INS as the House Judiciary Committee requested. Armey also removed some programs from the Bush proposal including a national ID card program and a tipster program that would rely on private citizens like postal or utilities workers to provide tips to the federal government about suspicious behavior. In both cases, Armey cited concern over privacy as driving his decision. Armey also sought compromise in some areas. Some House members were reluctant to let the head of the new department redirect up to 5 percent of the department's spending without asking Congress for permission. Armey took these concerns into account when he reduced the permissible redirect from 5 percent to 2 percent, which pleased members who had voiced such concern.[99]

The House Select Committee on Homeland Security passed H.R. 5005 on a party line vote 5–4 with Democratic leaders pledging to fight the bill on the House floor over labor rules. Democrats on the Select Committee wanted stronger civil service protections and collective bargaining for homeland security employees while Republicans argued that the increased protections would lessen the president's ability to manage the department and protect the country. According to Representative Martin Frost, "They [homeland security employees] should have the same protection that everyone else in the federal government now has."[100]

The president praised the House legislation as crafted by Representative Armey and urged lawmakers to pass the House version, while threatening to veto the Senate version that did not give the president as much flexibility in managing employees.[101] Once the legislation made it to the floor, the House debated the bill and made changes by amendment. The House passed amendments that directed federal agencies to share intelligence information with one another and with state and local authorities; gave unions "consultation rights" in homeland security labor matters; prohibited the department from doing business with any U.S. company with a headquarters located in a foreign country with the purpose of avoiding corporate taxes; and gave immunity to private companies that create and sell antiterrorism technology. The House also rejected proposals to keep FEMA and the Customs Service independent of the new department; strike a one-year extension to the deadline for airports to have baggage screening systems in place; loosen the Freedom of Information Act (FOIA), exempting companies holding information deemed to be sensitive to national security from reporting the information; and transfer visa issuance authority from the State Department to the Homeland Security Department.[102] After debating and amending the bill long into the night, the House passed Bush's plan on July 26, 2002, by a vote of 295–132.

SENATE PASSAGE

With swift passage in the House, the Senate became the legislative stumbling block for Bush's proposal. Majority Leader Daschle decided to give committee jurisdiction over the bill to Joe Lieberman and his Governmental Affairs Committee, with Lieberman using his own bill (S. 2452) as the starting point for consideration.[103] Daschle's decision to use Lieberman's bill as the starting point reflected his desire to remind everyone that the idea to create a new department was on the Democratic agenda before Bush co-opted the issue. Daschle said, "This is something we called for. This is something we reported out of the [Governmental] Affairs Committee on our side."[104] He also said, "This was on our agenda, not theirs."[105]

Senate Committee on Governmental Affairs

While the House leadership forced homeland security through the House quickly by using a select committee staffed by party leaders, the Senate moved more slowly by relying on the committee system. The Governmental Affairs Committee managed the legislative process and chose to include time-consuming steps like formal hearings. It was during these hearings, on June 20, that the Governmental Affairs Committee finally heard testimony from Tom Ridge when the Bush administration sent Ridge to the Senate as an advocate for the Bush proposal. The committee focused its questions for Ridge on the Bush plan's emphasis on management flexibility.[106] Just like the House, the Senate had concerns about stripping civil service protections from federal employees in the Department of Homeland Security.

The Governmental Affairs Committee agreed with much of the Bush proposal, even with a sticking point in the House to move twenty-two agencies into the new department. Lieberman estimated that his bill, after committee consideration, was consistent with about 90 percent of the president's proposal.[107] The Senate bill would have given a higher profile to a new intelligence unit inside the department and would have extended civil service protections and collective bargaining rights to the department's employees.[108] Lieberman also made some concessions from his original bill to make it more consistent with the

Bush proposal. For example, Lieberman originally wanted to give the Department of Homeland Security the authority to direct the FBI and CIA in information-gathering on domestic and foreign terrorism, but after consideration in committee, this power was dropped from the Senate bill.[109]

On July 25, the Senate Governmental Affairs Committee passed their homeland security bill (S. 2452) with a final vote of 12–5. On July 26, during a meeting with Senator Lieberman and other congressional leaders working on homeland security, President Bush voiced his opposition to any bill that would limit the president's flexibility in responding to terrorist threats. During a White House appearance with lawmakers, Bush said, "I'm not going to accept any legislation that limits or weakens the president's well-established authorities—authorities to exempt parts of the government from federal labor management relations statutes—when it serves our national interest."[110] Lieberman responded by saying, "We have some disagreements. We will continue to work on them. I can't believe, frankly, that the president would veto the bill over this."[111]

The Senate Battlefield: Labor Management

The marginal matters to which Lieberman referred included the possibility of giving the president discretion to exempt the government from the Freedom of Information Act and the Federal Advisory Committee Act. These acts require the government to relinquish information to the public and to include open meetings of advisory groups, respectively. In addition, labor unions and public employees feared that if the president were given the authority to create a flexible personnel system, the administration would have the power to easily fire workers and weaken their rights to appeal. More specifically, the administration wanted to have broad discretion in setting pay scales, job classifications, and evaluation methods, and in firing inefficient workers. The new department was estimated to include fifty thousand federal workers. While the House bill largely gave the president what he wanted on labor issues (for example, the power to exempt federal employees from union representation), the Senate bill maintained union representation for any employee whose job was not changed after transfer to the new department.[112] While Senate Democrats felt this language was necessary to protect workers' rights, the administration and its supporters felt that the labor rules would undermine national security.

Questions over union representation and management flexibility turned out to be the most contentious issues facing the Senate.[113] One of the most paralyzing factors in the debate over labor rules was the November 5 election as both the Democratic and Republican leadership were interested in delaying final decisions until after the election to use the bill in their election strategies.[114] In addition, the Democratic leadership was unlikely to concede on labor rules and offend a large constituency immediately before an election.

With the Governmental Affairs Committee passing its bill on July 25 and the summer recess on the near horizon, it became increasingly clear that the Congress would not be able to meet its September 11 deadline. The Senate Democratic leadership announced on July 29 that it would bring homeland security to the floor after the Labor Day recess, meaning that there would be little chance of finishing before the 11th. Daschle's decision to delay consideration sparked criticism from the White House and congressional Republicans.[115] Majority Leader Daschle indicated that while he would have liked to schedule homeland security for debate before the recess, the Senate had lingering legislation including a bill to add a prescription drug benefit to Medicare, appropriations measures, and a House-Senate compromise on legislation to expand the president's trade negotiating authority.[116] Daschle's decision to delay consideration was also influenced by a filibuster threat from Senator Byrd, who, as we discuss next, was concerned that the Senate was moving too quickly.

Obstruction Politics: Senator Byrd and the Legislative Pace

Senator Byrd was concerned that the pace of the legislative process was too fast to fully deliberate over the content of the legislation. By rushing to pass the bill by the first anniversary of the September 11 attacks, the Congress might compromise security by passing a poorly constructed bill that would, in turn, produce a poorly constructed department. Byrd described his obstructionism by saying, "If ever there was a need for the Senate to throw a bucket of cold water on an overheated legislative process that is spinning out of control it is now." He added, "With the level of endorsement the Congress has given to this idea, you would think that the proposal for a new Homeland Security Department had been engraved in the stone tablets that were handed down to Moses at Mount Sinai. But in reality, the idea was developed by four presidential staffers in the basement of the White House. For all we know, it could have been drafted on the back of a cocktail napkin."[117] Senator Thompson echoed Senator Byrd's concern saying, "I'd like to see the whole process slow down . . . and hear more expertise about how some of the agencies are going to be combined. But the train is moving forward, so we have to get on it."[118]

Senator Robert Byrd (D-WV)

Senator Byrd, the son of a coal miner, and eight-term U.S. senator, was first elected to the Senate in 1958 after serving in the West Virginia House of Delegates and the West Virginia Senate. During his first term in office,

Byrd was assigned to serve on the powerful Senate Appropriations Committee, a committee he continues to serve with today as chairman.

His dedication to the Democratic Party was recognized in 1967 when Byrd advanced into the party leadership as secretary of the Democratic conference. He continued his ascent, winning election to the whip's office in 1971 when he forced Senator Ted Kennedy from the post in the aftermath of the Chappaquiddick scandal, winning election with the deathbed vote of Senator Richard Russell.[119] Byrd was elevated to Democratic leader in 1977 and served as the majority leader from 1977 to 1980 and from 1987 to 1988 and as the minority leader in the six intervening years. Finally, from 1989 to 1994 and from 2001 through 2002, and 2007, Byrd was elected president pro tempore, standing fourth in succession to the presidency. Byrd's deep resumé of leadership experience gives him the distinction of holding more leadership posts than any other senator in the history of the chamber.[120]

In 1989, Byrd stepped aside from party leadership when he was finally named chair of the Appropriations Committee. Outside of his long tenure, considerable prowess on the Appropriations Committee, and formal leadership pedigree, Byrd also derives power from his status as the most respected parliamentarian in the Senate. After serving in the Senate for almost fifty years, Byrd has seen more Senate history firsthand than most senators have read, and he is a master of the Senate rules and procedures. It is a well-known fact that the Senate usually operates under unanimous consent, but there are thousands of technical points of order and procedures that keep the Senate moving smoothly. Senator Byrd is recognized as the master of this game with the ability to outmaneuver his opponents with arcane rules and procedures.

Senator Byrd is at heart a legislative historian, having written the definitive work on the Senate's history, a four volume text, *The Senate 1789–1989*, and *The Senate of the Roman Republic: Addresses on the History of the Roman Constitutionalism*. It is this love of the Senate's history and institutional pride that make Byrd a key player in the debate over homeland security. Byrd plays the role of defender of the institution.

Senator Byrd was also concerned with whether Congress would have budgetary control over the new department. Byrd and others wanted to tightly control funds in the new department to guarantee that the Congress would have enough influence over homeland security policy to counterbalance the president. Senator Byrd said, "Control of the purse is one of the most effective bulwarks ever constructed to repel a despot, control a tyrant or shackle the hands of an overreaching executive."[121] Byrd's concern reflected earlier debate in the House over the president's request for the power to redirect up to 5 percent of the funding for the agencies moved to the new department without congressional approval. Senator Byrd perceived the new department as a power grab by the administration and moving so quickly to give the president what he asked for might relinquish too much power to the president.

Senator Byrd was so troubled by his concerns over the budgetary issues and the speed with which the Senate was moving that he considered a filibuster to slow the Senate process and potentially win more control over homeland security for the Congress. If Senator Byrd had announced his intentions to filibuster the bill, there would not likely have been enough votes on the floor to invoke cloture.[122] A filibuster would have brought consideration of homeland security to a grinding halt, and the Senate, like the House, was facing a tight schedule after pledging to pass the bill by the first anniversary of the September 11 attack. As discussed earlier, Majority Leader Daschle decided to delay bringing up the homeland security bill from the week of July 29 until after the Senate returned on September 3 from its summer recess in part to satiate Senator Byrd. Therefore, Daschle prevented a possible filibuster with the delay by giving Byrd and others more time to carefully consider the legislation and potential amendments.

Bipartisanship and Elections

Before Congress could pass a homeland security bill, the labor issues had to be ironed out, and a bipartisan group was formed to end the disagreement between Senate Democrats and the president over labor rules, comprising Senators Nelson (D-NE), Breaux (D-LA), Collins (R-ME), Voinovich (R-OH), and Snowe (R-ME). This group included moderate senators who were willing to address the concerns of their more liberal and conservative colleagues and the president but also willing to make reasonable compromises from those positions. The group eventually accepted a compromise amendment written by Breaux and Nelson that included a provision that would preserve current union protections for workers moving into the new Department of Homeland Security unless their agency's purpose had "materially changed" and their new jobs were centered on intelligence, counterintelligence, or terrorism.[123] This amendment also included a mechanism for appeals regarding labor grievances. Similar language was used in the version passed in the House and was acceptable to the president. This compromise gave Democrats union protection for many in the new department and gave the president flexibility in reorganizing the labor force on terrorism-related issues.

An alternative compromise emerged when Senators Miller (D-GA) and Gramm (R-TX) coauthored a substituting amendment similar to the Nelson-Breaux amendment with the exception of a labor appeal. Both the Miller-Gramm and Nelson-Breaux amendments provided more flexibility to the president than the Lieberman bill.

After two weeks of debate, on September 19, 2002, the Senate rejected a Democratic cloture motion intended to end debate on Lieberman's homeland security bill. This vote was important because of its long term strategic implications: Democrats wanted to end debate and take a vote on the bill in order to pass legislation that was significantly different from the House version so they would be in a better bargaining position during the necessary conference with the House, while the Senate Republicans instead wanted to pass a bill similar to the House version so a conference would not be necessary and the president would get more of what he wanted.

The Miller-Gramm amendment was central in the Republican effort because the disagreement over labor rules was emerging as the biggest obstacle in passing a bill that reflected the president's vision for the new department. Miller and Gramm were actively lobbying twenty undecided senators, and the administration was directly involved in attracting moderates to the Miller-Gramm amendment. According to Senator Collins, the administration won her support by assuring her that federal employees would have access to an appeals process when disciplined or fired. In addition, she cited a letter from White House Homeland Security Director Ridge promising that the president would not remove all homeland security workers from their union contracts.[124] Senator Miller also tried to apply pressure to his party leadership. He said of his amendment and the Democratic leadership's opposition, "If we don't accept this substitute, and somehow, some way, the Democratic leadership is successful in defeating or even weakening the president's national security legislation, we will be slitting our own throats."[125]

Negotiation on labor rules continued through September and, as predicted on July 29, the Senate missed its self-imposed deadline of September 11. The administration and its allies in the Senate leadership played a key role in these negotiations. Breaux and Nelson met with President Bush at the White House on September 18 to discuss their amendment while Miller and Gramm met with Bush on September 20. Breaux said of the meeting, "They're listening, but haven't agreed to it."[126] Senate Minority Leader Trent Lott, during floor debate over labor rules, held negotiation sessions in his office with Breaux, Nelson, Chafee, Lieberman, and Bush administration aides.[127] While the meeting with President Bush and Senator Lott did not lead to a consensus that the Democratic leadership would agree to, the meetings reflected the importance of the moderate senators in securing victory.

Intense negotiation continued over the next two weeks but ended in failure. Senate leaders made last-ditch efforts at ending the standoff by taking a vote on each amendment on the Senate floor. Daschle felt confident that there was majority support for his preferred option, the Nelson-Breaux amendment, so he proposed a unanimous consent agreement that would schedule a vote on the Miller-Gramm amendment first and then on the Nelson-Breaux amendment. Senator Gramm objected, however, acknowledging that he did not have majority support for his measure. Subsequently, Gramm tried several parliamentary delaying maneuvers but each was blocked by the Democrats' majority whip, Senator Reid.[128] On October 1, the Senate rejected a fifth cloture attempt 45–52, and by October 17, it was clear that the Senate would not pass legislation before the midterm elections because leaders could not agree on personnel rules.

During consideration of the homeland security bill, both party leadership teams seemed determined to let the bill languish until after the midterm election; voters would be able to lay blame for the delay on one party or the other. In the 2002 election, Republicans gained three seats in the House and two seats in the Senate, returning the Senate majority to the Republicans. President Bush aggressively promoted his party's candidates, and the president's stump speech on behalf of Senate candidates made support for Bush's homeland security positions a central campaign issue. With a strong Republican showing in the 2002 election and a new Republican majority in the Senate, while homeland security differences had been highlighted in several campaigns, the Congress was now ready to move on homeland security, and the Republican leadership would get the bill President Bush asked for in June 2002.

FINAL PASSAGE

With Republican majorities in both chambers and a strong mandate from the election, passing a homeland security bill was relatively easy and orderly. The Republican leadership dictated terms to the vanquished Democrats who were deeply stung by their electoral defeat. The only sticking point was that several moderate Republicans still held reservations about the bill. Among these reservations were provisions that would give the new secretary the ability to ignore a ban in the bill against granting federal contracts to companies moving offshore to avoid U.S. taxes and a pharmaceutical provision that would end ongoing litigation against drug companies making mercury-based vaccine additives.

Senators Snowe, Chafee, and Collins declared they would defect from the party leadership's position and vote with the Democratic leadership, handing victory to the Democrats, if their concerns over these issues were not addressed. While a roll call vote was taking place on a Democratic amendment on the Senate floor during final Senate consideration, Snowe, Chafee, and Collins remained in the Republican cloakroom with Minority Leader Lott working out an agreement that these provisions and others would be revisited during the omnibus appropriations process. Snowe, Chafee, and Collins were satisfied after

Republican leaders in both the Senate and House promised that their concerns would be addressed, and they dropped their defection threat.[129]

On November 13, the House passed a new compromise bill (H.R. 5710) to accelerate the process. The Senate substituted the text of H.R. 5710 to H.R. 5005 and approved the bill 90–9 on November 19. The House approved the Senate version of the homeland security bill in a voice vote on November 22, 2002.

The outcome of the midterm election had a direct effect on the design of the Homeland Security Department. Had the Democrats picked up seats, or even maintained their majority status in the Senate, it is possible that the eventual compromise may have looked more like the vision described in the Nelson-Breaux amendment on labor rules, which probably had majority support in the Senate before the 2002 election. Thus, the importance of election outcomes cannot be overstated in policy decision-making. The winner, based on the perceived mandate, can redirect ongoing negotiations or jump-start a stalled process. The 2002 midterm elections were interpreted as support for the president and Republican Party leadership, and they leveraged their electoral success and support into a new winning coalition on homeland security. In this instance, language for which Miller and Gramm could not attract majority support just one month earlier was included in the final version of the bill. According to Senator Breaux, "It's not a compromise. It's only an agreement to get this bill passed. It's the best we could get. It's not what I would have written."[130]

The final bill gave the president nearly everything he wanted and defined the balance of power between the Congress and the White House, with the White House holding the upper hand. The bill required the president to submit a transition plan for reorganizing the government to Congress, but the president would not need congressional approval to act on the plan. Furthermore, the new secretary of Homeland Security would be allowed to reorganize the department with sixty days' notice to Congress. Congressional oversight was limited by changes in the Freedom of Information Act disclosure rules and advisory committee rules for the new department. The final agreement on labor rules gave labor unions two months to review new labor rules, but the Homeland Security Department could still impose the new rules even if the unions objected. After opposing the creation of a new department, President Bush worked with his allies in the Republican congressional leadership to ultimately create a department that met President Bush's vision.

THEMES OF INDIVIDUAL LEADERSHIP
ON HOMELAND SECURITY

Creation of the Homeland Security Department followed a very different path than the other cases in this book and provides different examples of how leaders used *direction, coherence,* and *energy* to shape the lawmaking process and pass legislation. Because of the time-critical nature of homeland security, the process was relatively streamlined—especially in the House—and passage relied more on the formal leadership in each chamber than on typical agenda items.

The tidal wave of support from the public for significant changes in homeland security made homeland security a top agenda item. The central question facing lawmakers was how they would make changes to the existing homeland security system to improve security. Overwhelming support for immediate action on homeland security affected the process in two ways. First, public pressure unified the Congress behind an agenda with homeland security at the top. Second, public pressure acted as a constraint on the lawmaking process because the president and party leaders immediately took control of the issue to move quickly in repairing the system, locking the rank and file largely out of leadership roles. Congress initially deferred to the president during the national emergency, which meant that President Bush had an even more prominent role than usual in agenda setting, and it was Bush who first provided *direction*. With the president making many of the changes to homeland security through executive order, there was a reduced role played by individual members of Congress or by administration officials in public settings. Most of the early policy decisions were made behind closed doors at the White House by the president in consultation with his national security advisors and congressional party leaders. For the first few months after the attacks, members of Congress interested in participating in the process were only passively involved when briefed by the administration or their party leaders. Homeland security legislation, while introduced in the Congress, was held from committee consideration until the president had time to decide how he wanted to proceed.

Members of Congress, led by Senate Majority Leader Daschle and Senator Leiberman, chair of the Government Affairs Committee, were responsible for providing *energy* behind the idea of creating a Homeland Security Department. President Bush was content to rely on the Office of Homeland Security as an adequate change in the homeland security system, but the more the administration and Tom Ridge resisted congressional involvement in decision-making and the more they insisted that a new department was not necessary, the more Congress pressed for inclusion. The initial pressure from Daschle and Leiberman grew into pressure from many Democrats and Republicans alike for a greater congressional role and a new department. In this case, energy was not needed to sustain the idea of a new department for very long because the idea quickly gained steam with the president signing on after just a few months of pressure from the Congress.

After the president changed his position to supporting a new department, Congress began acting immediately. Congressional party leaders dominated congressional consideration from the start because homeland security was such a high-profile issue, and the party leaders wanted personal control from introduction to final passage. Party leaders generally do not get personally involved in most legislation, instead allowing the committee system to produce legislation. In this case Senators Daschle and Lott and Representatives Hastert, Armey, and Gephardt were the critical players in deciding how the two chambers would consider homeland security legislation and how the bill would be written. In the House, Speaker Hastert created a special process that would give final authority over the bill to a Select Committee on Homeland Security chaired by Majority Leader Dick Armey with Minority Whip Nancy Pelosi as the ranking member. The other Republicans and Democrats serving on the committee were prominent members of their party and its leadership. Republican members included Majority Whip Delay; Representative Watts, the Republican conference chair; Representative Pryce, the vice chairman of the Republican conference; and Representative Portman, the chairman of the leadership. The other Democrats included Representative Frost, the Democratic caucus chair; Representative Menendez, the vice chairman of the Democratic caucus; and Representative DeLauro, the assistant to the minority leader. Although creating a bipartisan leadership group signaled the potential for a widely supported final product, the final vote was a party line vote with support from the Republicans and opposition from the Democrats.

The House Select Committee on Homeland Security produced the final text of H.R. 5005 after the eleven authorizing committees made amendments. By staffing this committee with members of the party leadership, the parties would be certain that the party line would be toed in final production of the bill. The majority Republicans dominated this committee, reversing most amendments made by the authorizing committees to produce a final bill that came very close to President Bush's proposal.[131] Since the party leadership had such tight control over production of the House bill, the rank-and-file members of the House were largely excluded from the process.

In the Senate, where the party leadership cannot control the legislative process as tightly, rank-and-file members had more opportunities to exert leadership, but Majority Leader Daschle handed control of the process to Senator Lieberman and the Senate Governmental Affairs Committee. Even in the Senate where Senate rules make it harder for the party leadership to control the legislative process, the party leadership played a larger role than normal in guiding the legislation to passage.

In sum, with the party leadership in both the House and Senate working hard to pass the legislation, there was not as much room for other members of Congress to get involved. The only opening for others to get involved was for those members who had developed expertise on homeland security before the September 11 attacks. Senator Lieberman and Representative Thornberry, for example, were identified by the party leadership and by their colleagues as important players in writing homeland security legislation because they had been working on the issue of homeland security reorganization before the attacks. In fact, it was Lieberman and Thornberry who provided substantial *coherence* throughout the debate over department status, and bill consideration, through their homeland security bills. President Bush's proposal borrowed heavily from both bills and once Congress began consideration, Lieberman continued to use his own bill as the base bill for consideration in the Senate. Recognized unique experience paid a direct dividend to Lieberman, Thornberry, and others for opening the door to participation, and their involvement provided the necessary coherence to pass a bill.

Throughout the process, and especially in the first few months of the process, lawmakers were under intense time pressure because it was unknown when the next terrorist attack might occur, and lawmakers were fearful that changes would not be made in time to prevent those attacks—or, more cynically, to avoid the blame for such attacks. The public expected the federal government to quickly secure the borders and prevent terrorism. Most federal laws are the product of years of research and labor by the sponsoring members to navigate the congressional labyrinth and collect majority support in both chambers. In the creation of the Homeland Security Department, however, leaders provided direction, coherence, and energy to move quickly and solve the problem without falling victim to many of the turf battles and partisan standoffs that can cripple the legislative process.

NOTES

1. For a detailed discussion of the September 11 attacks, see chapter 3.

2. Pollingreport.com, <http://www.pollingreport.com/BushJob1.htm> (8 September 2006).

3. The relative size of this reorganization compared with others is debatable, and experts seem to agree that the size of a reorganization is in the eye of the beholder. See Brian Faler, "Doing the Cabinet Shuffle; Experts Debate Homeland Plan's Rank Among Reorganizations," *Washington Post,* A17. The Bush administration indicated that this would be the biggest reorganization since President Truman asked Congress to merge the Army and Navy in the Defense Department. See Rebecca Carr, "Chambliss Plays Key Role in Creation of New Homeland Department," *Cox News Service,* 6 June 2002.

4. For a more in-depth review of the nation's homeland security network, see Donald F. Kettl, *System Under Stress: Homeland Security and American Politics* (Washington, DC: CQ Press, 2004); and National Commission on Terrorist Attacks Upon the United States, *The 9/11 Commission Report* (Washington, DC: U.S. Government Printing Office, 2004).

5. Donald F. Kettl, *System Under Stress,* 31.

6. See chapter 3 for more detail on national intelligence.

7. Donald F. Kettl, *System Under Stress,* 43.

8. Donald F. Kettl, *System Under Stress,* 39.

9. National Commission on Terrorist Attacks Upon the United States, *The 9/11 Commission Report,* 321–23; and Donald F. Kettl, *System Under Stress,* 30.

10. National Commission on Terrorist Attacks Upon the United States, *The 9/11 Commission Report*, 72.

11. National Commission on Terrorist Attacks Upon the United States, *The 9/11 Commission Report*, 72.

12. Karen Foerstel and Gebe Martinez, "Fog of War Comes to the Hill," *CQ Weekly,* 20 October 2001, 2458.

13. Bradley Graham, "For Patrol Pilots a Nightmare Scenario," *Washington Post,* 29 September 2001, A17.

14. Kate Zernike, "A Nation Challenged: The Thwarted Attack; Passenger with Shoe Bombs First Raised Only Eyebrows," *New York Times,* 27 December 2001, A1.

15. Foerstel and Martinez, "Fog of War Comes to the Hill," 2458.

16. Dana Milbank, "On Fortress Capital Hill, United Roars of Approval," *Washington Post,* 21 September 2001, A22.

17. George W. Bush, Address to a Joint Session of Congress and the American People, 20 September 2001, <http://www.whitehouse.gov/news/releases/2001/09/20010920-8.html> (8 September 2006).

18. Michael Barone and Grant Ujifusa, *The Almanac of American Politics* (Washington, DC: National Journal, 1997), 1197–1202.

19. Eric Pianin, "Ridge Backed by Bush Friendship in New Role; Organizing Skill Seen as Helping Former Pa. Governor in Counter-Terrorism Plot," *Washington Post,* 7 October 2001, A10.

20. Pianin, "Ridge Backed by Bush Friendship in New Role," A10.

21. Pianin, "Ridge Backed by Bush Friendship in New Role," A10.

22. Adriel Bettelheim and Chuck McCutcheon, "Lawmakers Struggle to Define New Office of Homeland Security without Appearing Confrontational," *CQ Weekly,* 13 October 2001, 2406.

23. Bettelheim and McCutcheon, "Lawmakers Struggle to Define New Office of Homeland Security," 2406.

24. Adriel Bettelheim, "Ridge Rebuffs Congressional Efforts to Gain Departmental Oversight," *CQ Weekly,* 2 March 2002, 558.

25. Juliet Eilperin and Greg Schneider, "House GOP Refines Air Security Bill; Vote Set for Today in Fight Over Whether to Federalize Screening of Baggage," *Washington Post,* 1 November 2001, A04.

26. David Rapp, "Advantage: Congress," *CQ Weekly,* 3 November 2001, 2578.

27. David Nather and Jill Barshay, "Hill Warning: Respect Level from White House Too Low," *CQ Weekly,* 9 March 2002, 630.

28. Nather and Barshay, "Hill Warning: Respect Level from White House Too Low," 630.

29. Dave Boyer, "Ridge Reluctant to Testify in Senate; Precedent Feared by White House," *Washington Times,* 27 February 2002, A04.

30. Stephen Dinan, "Ridge Briefing Called 'Stunt'; Democrats Introduce Bill for Congressional Oversight," *Washington Times,* 3 May 2002, A09.

31. Jill Barshay, "Lawmakers Might Put Some Muscle Behind Call for Ridge Testimony," *CQ Weekly,* 23 March 2002, 816.

32. Barshay, "Lawmakers Might Put Some Muscle," 816.

33. See our discussion of institutional power in chapter 1.

34. George W. Bush, Executive Order Establishing the President's Homeland Security Advisory Council and Senior Advisory Committees for Homeland Security, 21 March 2002, http://www.whitehouse.gov/news/releases/2002/03/20020321-9.html (8 September 2006).

35. Dinan, "Ridge Briefing Called 'Stunt,'" A09.

36. Adriel Bettelheim, "Cabinet-Level Status for Security Office Gets Push from Bipartisan Measure," *CQ Weekly,* 4 May 2002, 1159.

37. Alison Mitchell, "A Nation Challenged: Congressional Hearings; Letter to Ridge is Latest Jab in Fight over Balance of Powers," *New York Times,* 5 March 2002, A8.

38. Ellen Nakashima and Bradley Graham, "Direct Authority Called Key in Homeland Agency; Analysts Say Ridge Needs Budget, Coordination Powers," *Washington Post,* 22 September 2001, A07.

39. Mary Lynn F. Jones and Allison Stevens, "Senate GOP Divided Over Ridge Testimony," *Hill,* 20 March 2002, 1.

40. Barone and Ujifusa, *The Almanac of American Politics,* 1368–70.

41. David Mark, "Emerging Players: Representative William 'Mac' Thornberry, R-Texas," *CQ Weekly,* 5 January 2002.

42. Mark, "Emerging Players: Representative William 'Mac' Thornberry."

43. Bettelheim, "Cabinet-Level Status for Security Office Gets Push," 1159.

44. Adriel Bettelheim, "Impatient Senate Drafts Its Own Homeland Security Plan," *CQ Weekly,* 25 May 2002, 1387.

45. Melanie Eversley, "Homeland Security Office Has the Proper Power, Bush Says," *Cox New Service,* 24 October 2001.

46. Eric Pianin and Bill Miller, "For Ridge, Ambition and Realities Clash; Homeland Security Chief May Lack Means to Implement Major Initiatives," *Washington Post,* 23 January 2002, A01.

47. Bettelheim, "Impatient Senate Drafts Its Own Homeland Security Plan," 1387.

48. Daniel J. Parks and Mary Dalrymple, "New Pot of Federal Dollars Has Admirers From All Over," *CQ Weekly,* 27 April 2002, 1066.

49. Adriel Bettelheim, "Turf Wars Take Toll on Ridge," *CQ Weekly,* 27 April 2002, 1071.

50. Bettelheim, "Turf Wars Take Toll on Ridge," 1071.

51. Bettelheim, "Turf Wars Take Toll on Ridge," 1071.

52. Bill Sammon, "Daschle 'Vehemence' on Ridge Irks White House," *Washington Times,* 19 March 2002, A03.

53. Bettelheim, "Impatient Senate Drafts Its Own Homeland Security Plan," 1387.

54. Alison Mitchell, "Traces of Terror: Congress; Plan for Security Agency Draws Bipartisan, but not Unconditional Support," *New York Times,* 7 June 2002, A21.

55. Tom Raum, "Bush Abruptly Shifts Strategy," *Associated Press State and Local Wire,* 7 June 2002.

56. There was some speculation in the press and among lawmakers that the timing of the announcement, during a period of particularly inflammatory testimony over intelligence failures and the September 11 attacks, was meant to preempt unfavorable coverage on intelligence failures. See Elisabeth Bumiller and David E. Sanger, "Bush, As Terror Inquiry Swirls, Seeks Cabinet Post on Security," *New York Times,* 7 June 2002, A1.

57. Mitchell, "Traces of Terror: Congress; Plan for Security Agency," A21.

58. Bumiller and Sanger, "Bush, As Terror Inquiry Swirls," A1.

59. Dana Milbank, "Plan Was Formed in Utmost Secrecy; Final Proposal Came from 4 Top Aides; Most Others out of Loop," *Washington Post,* 7 June 2002, A01.

60. Adriel Bettelheim and Jill Barshay, "Bush's Swift, Sweeping Plan is Work Order for Congress," *CQ Weekly,* 8 June 2002, 1498.

61. Joseph Curl, "Bush Proposes New Security Agency; Asks Hill to Quickly Make Place in Cabinet," *Washington Times,* 7 June 2002, A01.

62. Bettelheim and Barshay, "Bush's Swift, Sweeping Plan," 1498.

63. Bettelheim and Barshay, "Bush's Swift, Sweeping Plan," 1498.

64. Raum, "Bush Abruptly Shifts Strategy."

65. Bettelheim and Barshay, "Bush's Swift, Sweeping Plan," 1498.

66. Bettelheim and Barshay, "Bush's Swift, Sweeping Plan," 1498.

67. Bettelheim and Barshay, "Bush's Swift, Sweeping Plan," 1498.

68. Bettelheim and Barshay, "Bush's Swift, Sweeping Plan," 1498.

69. Joanna Cattanach and David Enrich, "Thornberry Urges Congress to Create New Homeland Security Dept.," *States News Service,* 11 June 2002.

70. Adriel Bettelheim, "Security Plan Gets Solid Backing But No Rubber Stamps on Hill," *CQ Weekly,* 25 May 2002, 1577.

71. Bettelheim, "Security Plan Gets Solid Backing," 1577.

72. Cattanach and Enrich, "Thornberry Urges Congress."

73. Dan Eggen and Susan Schmidt, "'Dirty Bomb' Plot Uncovered, U.S. Says; Suspected Al Qaeda Operative Held as 'Enemy Combatant,'" *Washington Post,* 11 June 2002, A01.

74. Tom Raum, "Bush Abruptly Shifts Strategy."

75. Milbank, "Plan Was Formed in Utmost Secrecy," A01.

76. Milbank, "Plan Was Formed in Utmost Secrecy," A01.

77. Bettelheim, "Security Plan Gets Solid Backing," 1577. Ultimately, eleven authorizing committees would be used.

78. Bill Miller and Juliet Eilperin, "Party Leaders Favor Security Agency; Goal Is to Create Department by Anniversary of September 11 Attacks," *Washington Post,* 12 June 2002, A19.

79. Barone and Ujifusa, *The Almanac of American Politics,* 1399–1402.

80. Gebe Martinez, "GOP Pick: An Armey of One," *CQ Weekly,* 22 June 2002, 1650.

81. Martinez, "GOP Pick: An Armey of One," 1650.

82. Susan Crabtree, "House Creates Panel," *Roll Call,* 20 June 2002.

83. Crabtree, "House Creates Panel."

84. Miller and Eilperin, "Party Leaders Favor Security Agency," A19.

85. Adriel Bettelheim, "House Homeland Security Bill Bends Strongly Bush's Way," *CQ Weekly,* 20 July 2002, 1927.

86. Susan Crabtree, "Armey Readies for His Last Act," *Roll Call,* 24 June 2002.

87. Kerry Kantin, "Homeland Security Bill Placed on Fast Track," *Hill,* 26 June 2002, 4.

88. Juliet Eilperin and Bill Miller, "Turf Battles Loom over Bush Security Plan; Powerful House Republicans Stubbornly Resist Proposed Homeland Department," *Washington Post,* 18 July 2002, A05.

89. Eilperin and Miller, "Turf Battles Loom over Bush Security Plan," A05.

90. Walter Pincus, Juliet Eilperin, and Bill Miller, "Details of Homeland Plan Assailed; House Panels Vote to Block Transfers of Some Agencies," *Washington Post,* 11 July 2002, A01.

91. Adriel Bettelheim, "Gauntlet of House Committees Greets Homeland Security Plan," *CQ Weekly,* 13 July 2002, 1858.

92. Ellen Nakashima and Bill Miller, "Bush to Ask Workers for Flexibility on Homeland Security; President's Pep Talk to 3,000 Employees To Include Appeal on Civil Service Rules," *Washington Post,* 10 July 2002, A15; Joseph Curl, "President Urges Concerted Voice on Security," *Washington Times,* 11 July 2002, A04.

93. Bettelheim, "Gauntlet of House Committees," 1858.

94. Bettelheim, "Gauntlet of House Committees," 1858.

95. Pincus, Eilperin, and Miller, "Details of Homeland Plan Assailed," A01.

96. Eilperin and Miller, "Turf Battles Loom over Bush Security Plan," A05.

97. Eilperin and Miller, "Turf Battles Loom over Bush Security Plan," A05.

98. Bill Miller and Juliet Eilperin, "GOP Leaders Unveil Homeland Bill; Armey Proposal for New Department Is Close To Bush Plans; Some Concessions Are Made," *Washington Post,* 19 July 2002, A04.

99. Miller and Eilperin, "GOP Leaders Unveil Homeland Bill," A04.

100. Bill Miller and Juliet Eilperin, "Panel Approves New U.S. Department; Homeland Security Reorganization Wins First Vote in House," *Washington Post,* 20 July 2002, A12.

101. Cynthia Kopkowski, "House Passes Legislation Creating Homeland Defense Department," *Cox News Service,* 26 July 2002.

102. Kopkowski, "House Passes Legislation."

103. Bettelheim, "Security Plan Gets Solid Backing," 1577.

104. Jill Barshay and Gebe Martinez, "Democrats Embrace Homeland Security While Working on Separate Political Persona," *CQ Weekly,* 15 June 2002, 1586.

105. Bettelheim, "Security Plan Gets Solid Backing," 1577.

106. Amy Hudson, "Ridge Defends Hiring Proposal," *Washington Times,* 21 June 2002, A14.

107. Stephen Dinan, "Senate Panel OKs Homeland Security Bill," *Washington Times,* 26 July 2002, A01.

108. Bill Miller and Walter Pincus, "Senate Panel Shapes Homeland Dept. Bill; Intelligence Unit, Worker Rights Stressed," *Washington Post,* 25 July 2002, A14.

109. Miller and Pincus, "Senate Panel Shapes Homeland Dept. Bill," A14.

110. Stephen Dinan and Joseph Curl, "House OKs New Security Agency; Bill Gives Bush Powers He Sought," *Washington Times,* 27 July 2002, A01.

111. Scott Shepard and Cynthia Kopkowski, "White House Threatens Veto of Senate Version of Homeland Security Bill," *Cox News Service,* 25 July 2002.

112. Adriel Bettelheim, "Homeland Security's Big Hurdle: Ceding Power to White House," *CQ Weekly,* 27 July 2002, 2028.

113. Bill Miller and Juliet Eilperin, "Obscure Labor Issues Block Homeland Security Agency; Moderates to Decide Outcome of Democrats' Tangle with Bush," *Washington Post,* 23 September 2002, A08.

114. For a more in-depth discussion of the 2002 election dynamics, see chapter 1.

115. Cynthia Kopkowski, "Homeland Security Bill Won't See Senate Floor Until Fall," *Cox News Service,* 1 August 2002.

116. Bill Miller and Helen Dewar, "Senate to Delay Voting On Homeland Department; Goal of Passing Bill by Sept. 11 Unlikely to Be Met," *Washington Post,* 30 July 2002, A02.

117. Adriel Bettelheim, "Byrd Prepared to Slow Bill," *CQ Weekly,* 3 August 2002, 2103.

118. Bettelheim, "Gauntlet of House Committees," 1858.

119. Barone and Ujifusa, *The Almanac of American Politics,* 1506–8.

120. Senator Byrd's Senate webpage.

121. Bettelheim, "Homeland Security's Big Hurdle," 2028.

122. Bettelheim, "Homeland Security's Big Hurdle," 2028.

123. Adriel Bettelheim, "Senators Band Together to Reconcile Labor Rules and Homeland Security," *CQ Weekly,* 5 October 2002, 2368.

124. Adriel Bettelheim and Mary Dalrymple, "Chafee Holds Key to Decision on Union Rights for Homeland Staff," *CQ Weekly,* 21 Sept 2002, 2441.

125. Bettelheim and Dalrymple, "Chafee Holds Key to Decision," 2441.

126. Bettelheim and Dalrymple, "Chafee Holds Key to Decision," 2441.

127. Adriel Bettelheim, "Moderates Vow to Keep Working on Homeland Security Deal," *CQ Weekly,* 5 October 2002, 2577.

128. Adriel Bettelheim, "Senate's Failure to Resolve Personnel Management Issue Stalls Homeland Security Bill," *CQ Weekly,* 19 October 2002, 2741.

129. Mary Dalrymple, "Department's Blueprint Approved, Final Plan Far From Complete," *CQ Weekly,* 23 November 2002, 3072.

130. Mary Dalrymple, "Homeland Security Department Another Victory for Administration," *CQ Weekly,* 16 November 2002, 3002.

131. Most of the recorded votes by the House Select Committee on Homeland Security on H.R. 5005 were party line votes.

6

Hurricane Katrina

On Tuesday, August 23, 2006, Tropical Depression 12 formed two hundred miles southeast of Nassau. By Thursday, August 25, the storm strengthened and forecasters designated the storm as Hurricane Katrina, a Category 1 hurricane, as it moved toward Florida. Unlike most hurricanes, as Katrina swept across Florida, it gained rather than lost strength as it fed on the warm marshes that make up Florida's Everglades. The storm continued to gain strength as it crossed the Gulf of Mexico ultimately reaching Category 5 status. Initial projections predicted that Katrina might make a second landfall on the Florida panhandle, but the storm changed course and headed on a path toward New Orleans and the Gulf Coast. Katrina stretched 230 miles from the eye, large enough to cover the distance between Boston and Washington, D.C. Katrina's eye made landfall on August 29 at approximately 6:10 a.m. with sustained winds of 127 miles per hour. Katrina brought storm surges of between eighteen and twenty-seven feet that flooded coastal communities in Alabama, Mississippi, and Louisiana; the storm decimated ninety thousand square miles, left thousands displaced, and more than fifteen hundred dead.[1]

Katrina, and the subsequent flooding, left thousands stranded and in need of assistance. In the hours after landfall, there were many acts of heroism by first responders in state and local emergency services agencies and the U.S. Coast Guard who were charged with rescuing the victims. Almost six thousand members of the Coast Guard helped rescue more than thirty-three thousand people along the Gulf Coast.[2] As reported by the White House:

Having evacuated with boats on trailers prior to the storm, Petty Officer Jessica Guidroz, a coxswain at the Coast Guard Station New Orleans, could not return to the station by road after the hurricane passed. She and her crew launched their boat and headed toward the station. Finding the station occupied by rescued victims already, she established order at the station and then piloted a twenty-five foot boat through Metairie and Lakeview, banging on roofs and yelling, scanning for open attic windows, and convincing reluctant evacuees to leave. Learning of a large number of trapped residents, she proceeded to lead a squadron of eight boats and crews in the evacuation of approximately 2,000 people from the campus of the University of New Orleans. Like most of the station crew, she lived nearby and lost all her personal possessions to the storm, yet put her duty first. After several days piloting a boat into devastated neighborhoods, ferrying thousands of people to safety, and seeing destruction on a scale so vast that it seemed surreal, Guidroz was moved when she saw an image on television. She had been haunted by the memory of a young mother who had almost been trampled during the evacuation. She remembered how "the baby was wearing this diaper that you know hadn't been changed in days." That night, a news channel showed images from the Houston Astrodome, and there she was—the lady with the baby. "She was in Houston now, and she looked like she'd showered and her kid had on clean clothes. That moment is when it clicked," Guidroz said. "Here was someone we had actually helped, and it fell into place that we were doing something that really mattered, something really good."[3]

As heroically as search and rescue personnel acted in saving lives, other parts of the response to Hurricane Katrina failed to live up to expectations. While investigations into the response to Hurricane Katrina roundly applauded rescue workers on the ground, the White House, the Senate, and the House each found overwhelming failure in the nation's response to Katrina. After the storm dissipated, many important questions remained, including: Why were so many citizens left at risk instead of evacuated? Why were emergency response teams not given the necessary resources and equipment to respond faster to those in need? How could a government that put so much emphasis on emergency preparedness after the September 11 attacks fail so miserably to respond better? Three investigations—by the White House, the Senate, and the House—would later answer these questions and others and suggest changes that might improve future responses.

In chapter 5, we explored the creation of the new Department of Homeland Security following the process from the September 11 attacks through passage of the Homeland Security Act in late 2002. Much of the debate about a new department was understandably about how the nation could best prevent terrorist attacks. In this effort, the Congress and administration sought to design a structure that would put the nation's homeland defense resources under a single authority, the secretary of Homeland Security. Included in this new department, however, were many offices and agencies charged with protecting the country from dangers outside of terrorism, including the Coast Guard, the Border Patrol, and the Federal Emergency Management Agency (FEMA).

In this chapter, we will begin with a brief discussion of the nation's emergency response system prior to the September 11 attacks with respect to natural disasters. We will then explore how the government created a new structure to improve response and how the new department began to carry out its emergency response mission over the next three years. Finally, we will explore the system's failure during its first test—the response to Hurricane Katrina—and efforts to redesign the system in 2006.

BACKGROUND: THE EMERGENCY MANAGEMENT SYSTEM

Emergency preparedness is a quintessential example of federalism as local and state governments share responsibility with the federal government. Traditionally, local and state governments are responsible for preparing for, and responding to, emergencies without help from the federal government. In fact, the federal government did not have a formal and active presence in emergency preparedness until the Flood Control Act of 1936 and the Disaster Relief Act of 1950. Until 1936, the only federal role in emergency management came in the form of an emergency congressional appropriation passed on a disaster-by-disaster basis to support recovery. This tradition of local and state governments holding primary responsibility continues today, but the federal government has a much higher profile in emergency preparedness and response with respect to coordination and support of local and state efforts.[4]

Emergency Management under FEMA: 1979–1992

The Federal Emergency Management Agency (FEMA) has been the public face of federal emergency management since President Carter created the agency in 1979 to consolidate federal emergency preparedness and response. FEMA and the federal government provide assistance to the states in emergency preparedness, response, and recovery. Over the course of FEMA's existence, it has offered many different types of mitigation programs and training exercises to help states prepare for disaster and train state emergency agencies to work with each other and federal agencies, helping states identify areas susceptible to natural disaster and either correct problems or prepare for specific disasters. In addition to mitigation and training, the federal government also provided emergency funding and support during and after a disaster. Because multiple levels of government share responsibility, the governments and agencies constituting the emergency management system put considerable effort into coordination through communication, holding joint training exercises, and clarifying before an emergency which government or agency will perform each task. The federal government also provides low interest loans for agricultural and urban disaster victims, as well as helping states pay for federal intervention during a disaster.

While local and state governments are primarily responsible for their own emergency response, major disasters such as hurricanes, floods, or earthquakes often bring devastation beyond the capacity of a city or state government. In such cases, the federal government usually takes charge in the response. The federal government has many more resources at its disposal and a much more in-depth and diverse record of disaster experience. Therefore, while the state and local governments take primary responsibility for dealing with most emergencies, the federal government moves from a support role to a lead role on most large-scale natural disasters.

Since 1979, FEMA has struggled to meet congressional, presidential, and state-level demands, and its reputation as an effective agency has fluctuated wildly. FEMA has often been called the worst performing federal agency throughout its existence, and for a short time, the best.[5] For much of its history, FEMA has suffered with a reputation as an ineffective agency due in large part to FEMA's status as a dumping ground for political appointees; the overwhelming majority of FEMA directors and upper-level executives have come to FEMA with little or no emergency management experience.[6] In 2003, the Partnership for Public Service, a nonprofit group that promotes careers in federal government, released a ranking of the best federal agencies for which to work, and FEMA ranked as the worst of twenty-eight agencies.[7] According to emergency management experts like former FEMA director James Lee Witt and I. M. Mac Destler, a professor at the University of Maryland School of Public Policy, during the five years before Hurricane Katrina, FEMA was an agency drained of the necessary resources, leadership, and institutional power to adequately respond to major disasters.[8]

FEMA's Golden Years

FEMA did not, however, always have the reputation of an underperforming federal agency. Following one of its worst performances in a failed response to Hurricane Andrew in 1992, which was shockingly similar to the failed response to Katrina in 2005, FEMA was in danger of being scuttled by Congress.[9] Congressional committees with oversight responsibility for FEMA threatened extreme action if FEMA could not fix the problems that were keeping it from responding to disaster in a timely and effective manner.[10] Though the Congress rarely goes as far as dismantling agencies, some members suggested that since FEMA could not be trusted to do its job as an independent agency, it should be moved under the jurisdiction of the Department of Defense that has experience coordinating large scale operations.

In 1993, however, President Clinton appointed James Lee Witt as FEMA's new director. Witt, unlike most former FEMA directors, had emergency management experience—he served as the Arkansas emergency manager while Clinton was governor. Clinton, with Witt's advice, appointed a highly experienced team of upper-level administrators to reform FEMA under Witt's direction. Witt's team quickly changed FEMA's disaster response operation with an emphasis on arriving at a disaster scene as quickly as possible and offering help to local and state officials whether it was asked for or not, and in less than a year, FEMA had earned a reputation as one of the most effective federal agencies.[11] Witt and FEMA were given high marks for their response to Midwest flooding in 1993 and to a 6.3 magnitude earthquake in Los Angeles in 1994.[12] As a reward for his success, Witt was given unofficial cabinet status which helped him better coordinate with other cabinet secretaries running departments with critical emergency roles, like the departments of Health and Human Services and Defense.[13]

Witt's success was in part due to his attention to mitigation programs designed to help local and state officials design emergency systems that could prevent costly damage in areas at risk for disaster. These programs were also designed to increase communication and coordination between FEMA and state emergency agencies so when disaster struck, the agencies could work together more seamlessly. One of the most highly touted mitigation programs, Project Impact, provided seed money to communities to make disaster readiness improvements with FEMA acting as an advisor on emergency management. Through Project Impact, FEMA gave local communities between $500,000 and $1 million to help defray the cost of improvements that would minimize losses due to flooding, fire, earthquakes, and other disasters.[14] Project Impact was credited with saving taxpayers millions of dollars by preventing major losses. For example, Seattle, Washington, was one of the first communities to join Project Impact and received $1 million to retrofit bridges, homes, and schools to help protect the city from earthquake damage. On February 28, 2001, a 6.8 magnitude earthquake shook Seattle, but only 250 people were injured with only one fatality from a heart attack. Emergency management officials indicated that improvements made under Project Impact prevented more extensive damage and limited injuries and loss of life.[15]

Bush, Allbaugh, and Changes at FEMA

Clinton and Witt markedly improved FEMA, but since the changes were made by executive action, rather than congressional statute, the changes were not permanent. When President Bush assumed power in 2001, he made his own changes at FEMA. According to Bush's first FEMA director, Joe Allbaugh, FEMA was an "oversized entitlement program."[16] President Bush's first budget proposed cuts in emergency management by ending FEMA's mitigation programs and redirecting FEMA's full effort to providing support to local and state officials after a disaster. The president's budget proposed to save $25 million by eliminating Project Impact because it had not proven its effectiveness.[17] The budget also eliminated the recently enacted Fire Grant Program that provided money to fire departments to pay for new equipment and training. The budget indicated that the Fire Grant Program did "not represent an appropriate responsibility of the federal government."[18]

Bush also proposed to save $12 million by requiring some homeowners who had been flooded repeatedly in low lying areas to pay high-risk premiums instead of paying for normal coverage under the National Flood Insurance Program, and the budget proposed $83 million in savings by requiring public buildings like hospitals, schools, and community centers to buy their own disaster insurance and free the federal government from the responsibility.[19]

FEMA Director Joe Allbaugh

Joe Allbaugh has a long resume as a political operative starting with a position with Senator Henry Bellmon (R-OK) in 1974. Allbaugh went on to work on the field staff for the 1984 Reagan-Bush campaign before going back to Bellmon to help him run for governor of Oklahoma in 1986. He later served as Oklahoma's deputy secretary of transportation for three years before leaving to manage George W. Bush's successful 1994 campaign for governor.[20] Allbaugh next served as Bush's chief of staff joining Karl Rove and Karen Hughes as Bush's most trusted advisors. As chief of staff, Allbaugh gained limited experience with disaster management when Governor Bush made Allbaugh his point man in coordinating federal and state disaster assistance.[21] Allbaugh next served as Bush's national campaign manager helping Bush win the presidential election in 2000.

Once Bush arrived in Washington, he appointed Allbaugh as FEMA's director, saying that "During the course of the campaign much was made of the so-called Texas iron triangle," referring to Hughes, Rove, and Allbaugh.[22] Bush noted that, "FEMA is an incredibly important part of a president's team. The person who runs FEMA is someone who must have the trust of the president. Because the person who runs FEMA is the first voice, oftentimes, someone whose life has been turned upside down hears from."[23] After working with Bush for seven years as his campaign manager and chief of staff, it is safe to say that Allbaugh had earned the president's trust.

It is important to remember that during Bush's first year, the administration was intent on finding budget offsets to help pay for a proposed $1.6 trillion tax cut. According to White House spokesman Scott Stanzel, "There's an effort to reduce programs that are seen as redundant or not effective, and that's occurring all across the budget. There's an ongoing effort to shift control and responsibility to the states and give them more flexibility."[24]

Many local and state officials, as well as members of Congress, feared that the changes Bush proposed for FEMA signaled a shift in philosophy from mitigation to recovery—that instead of taking an active role in preventing disaster, FEMA and the federal government would dedicate all of its attention and funding to disaster relief. Former FEMA director Witt, concerned that FEMA would no longer provide mitigation programs, met with current FEMA director Allbaugh and encouraged him to maintain the programs.[25]

Changes in FEMA's budget were not the only changes that concerned state and local emergency management officials. Unlike Clinton's FEMA director, James Lee Witt, Bush's first FEMA director was a political operative with little emergency preparedness experience. Allbaugh's appointment signaled a change from the previous administration in the type of officials who would run FEMA. By the time Katrina made landfall in August of 2005, five of FEMA's top eight officials had no previous experience in disaster management but were Republican political operatives, three of whom worked for President Bush's 2000 presidential campaign.[26] In addition to concern over a lack of experience at the highest levels of FEMA, state-level officials were concerned with the Bush administration's intent to add a new component to FEMA's mission: coordinating the nation's defenses against terrorism. The shift in FEMA's mission from primarily preparing for natural disaster to more responsibility for protecting against terrorism led to widespread resignations among high-ranking career FEMA employees who left for the private sector or other public emergency management jobs.[27] Combined, these factors signaled that FEMA was headed in a new direction with less attention to disaster preparedness.

PREPARING FOR AND RESPONDING TO HURRICANE KATRINA

Building the Department of Homeland Security

The story behind the response to Hurricane Katrina begins with the Homeland Security Act of 2002 (HSA). Following the structural outline provided in the HSA, the Bush administration began building the department Bush and Congress envisioned. Congress created DHS not as an entirely new structure, but one that would co-opt existing homeland security related agencies including FEMA. As such, FEMA lost its independent status with its director reporting to the secretary of Homeland Security. Moving into the DHS had advantages and disadvantages. On the one hand, inclusion in a department with many resources at its disposal and a director reporting directly to the secretary of DHS, an official member of the cabinet, were advantages. On the other hand, losing independent status meant that FEMA's mission and organization could be shifted by executives outside the agency more easily, there was an extra level of bureaucracy between FEMA's director and the president, and FEMA would face problems, at least initially, in finding its place in the new department as its responsibilities were divided into two directorates within the new department.

Before moving to the DHS, FEMA operated under an all-hazards approach, meaning that FEMA responded to a wide range of disasters, including natural disasters like floods, hurricanes, or earthquakes as well as human-caused disasters like chemical spills or terrorism. After moving to DHS, however, FEMA's responsibilities were divided between two separate directorates: responsibility for preparedness for terrorism was assigned to the department's Border and Transportation Security Directorate; while other disaster preparedness and response responsibilities were transferred with FEMA to the department's Emergency Preparedness and Response Directorate (EPR).[28]

With the move, over six thousand FEMA employees were transferred to the DHS along with FEMA's budgetary authority of roughly $12 billion based on FEMA's 2002 budget.[29] The total value of FEMA's budget, however, was variable from year to year depending on the severity of disasters and the associated costs. The challenge facing DHS was integrating multiple agencies involving the transfer of an additional twenty-one agencies and thousands of employees into an integrated and smoothly functioning department. This was a problem that FEMA would not be able to solve in the nearly three years between incorporation into DHS and Katrina.

Secretary of Homeland Security Michael Chertoff

Michael Chertoff began his legal career with a law degree from Harvard Law School in 1978 and served as a clerk for U.S. Supreme Court Justice William Brennan Jr. from 1978 to 1980. Following his clerkship, Chertoff worked in private practice before serving as a federal prosecutor for more than a decade, including positions as U.S. attorney for the District of New Jersey, first assistant U.S. attorney for the District of New Jersey, and assistant U.S. attorney for the District of New York under Rudi Giuliani before taking a partnership in a private firm. From 1994 to 1996 Chertoff served as special counsel for the U.S. Senate Whitewater Committee investigating President Clinton—the investigation that ultimately led to impeachment on December 19, 1998.

President Bush nominated Chertoff for a number of positions in the next few years. He began his service as the assistant attorney general for the Criminal Division at the Department of Justice. In this capacity, Chertoff was involved in many high profile endeavors, including serving as the lead prosecutor of suspected terrorist Zacarias Moussaoui, coauthoring the USA PATRIOT Act, and advising the Bush administration and CIA on how far they could go in detaining and coercing terror suspects and enemy combatants. In March 2003, President Bush nominated Chertoff for a seat on the Third Circuit Court of Appeals, and he was confirmed in an 88–1 vote in June. The lone vote against Chertoff, cast by Senator Hillary Clinton (D-NY), was reportedly a protest vote for Chertoff's involvement in the Whitewater investigation.[30]

After Bush's original choice to replace Secretary Ridge at DHS, Bernard Kerik, was forced to withdraw his nomination, Bush nominated Chertoff in January of 2005. Chertoff was approved unanimously for the position in February 2005.

Hurricane Katrina Arrives with Devastating Consequences

Hurricane Katrina approached the U.S. coastline as a Category 5 hurricane, one of the largest and strongest hurricanes on record. As it churned across the Gulf, local, state, and federal emergency management officials began preparations for landfall. FEMA undertook an unprecedented effort to preposition resources in anticipation of landfall, including more than eleven million liters of water, almost nineteen million pounds of ice, and six million ready-to-eat meals. FEMA also staged disaster medical teams, Rapid Needs Assessment Teams, and Mobile Emergency Response detachments.[31] FEMA put a substantial support structure in place before landfall, but the preparation seemingly came to naught as Katrina devastated Alabama, Louisiana, and Mississippi, and the demand for emergency supplies exhausted the available resources.

Katrina made landfall as a Category 3 hurricane and became the most destructive hurricane in U.S. history with damage spread across ninety thousand square miles of the Gulf Coast leaving more than fifteen hundred people dead.[32] The biggest tragedy of Katrina, however, was not the damage caused by the storm, but the delayed response, particularly in New Orleans, leaving thousands of people stranded without the basic necessities of food, water, and shelter. Millions of Americans watched events unfold live on television over Labor Day weekend. The images broadcast from the Gulf Coast were striking and devastatingly powerful—babies crying, bodies floating through city streets, people huddled on highway overpasses awaiting rescue for days, and a lack of law enforcement or emergency management officials to help those in need.

With tens of thousands stranded in New Orleans alone, frightening stories began to emerge from the survivors. For example, as reported by the Senate Committee on Homeland Security and Governmental Affairs:

Bobbie Moreau, a legal secretary in Nairn, a small town in Plaquemines Parish, stayed at home because she didn't have the means to evacuate. She was with her daughter Tasha and Tasha's four-month-old daughter, who was born prematurely and required a heart monitor. Moreau woke up at 4 a.m. on Monday, just as the wind and storm surge preceding Katrina's eye were reaching shore. "The pressure was so bad in the house, I opened a crack in the living room window," she recalled. When she walked into the den, she saw water pouring through the grout in the marble tile that lined a part of the wall. By the time she had climbed to the second floor, the water had risen halfway up the stairs. Moreau could see her living-room furniture floating.

"I shut the door upstairs, I guess thinking I could shut the water out," she said. "From then it was a nightmare. I held the baby at the foot of the bed fanning her. The pressure was awful; we thought the windows were going to pop. We got on our knees and prayed and begged God to save us. Then I felt the water under me on the second floor. . . . I got up and walked to the window and the water was right under the window. My legs felt like Jell-O, I staggered. My daughter screamed, 'Mama, what's wrong?' I knew at that moment we were going to die."

But "in an instant, survival kicked in." Moreau tore the canopy from the bed and tied knots so that she and Tasha could hold on to each other. She used a belt to create a makeshift life jacket for the baby. With the water halfway up the bed, they climbed out onto the roof, managing to take along Moreau's three dogs. "The eye of the hurricane was on us," Moreau recalled. "I told my daughter, you will have to swim and get a boat, I am too weak. She said, 'Mama, I'm scared.' There was dead animals floating by, snakes, debris, oil. I told her, 'We will die if you don't.' She handed me the baby and slipped into the water. . . . Then I lost sight of her and called and called because the wind was picking up. And then I knew it was the eye. Nothing but silence. I thought she had drowned. I was crying and praying. And then I heard an outboard motor start up. And I knew she was alive.

"Where she pulled [up] the boat, the power lines to the house was between us," Moreau continued. "I had to drop the baby through the power lines to her and the dogs and then myself. By then, the wind was so hard, we could not control the boat with the motors. . . . We came to a stop in the top of some little trees. We huddled under the steering wheel with the baby because a window was broke out of the cabin. We stayed there for about six to seven hours. The wind would almost turn the boat over and we sang and prayed . . . It was so weird. Felt like we were the only people left in the world, everything covered by water."[33]

As for many survivors of Katrina, the rescue hardly brought Moreau's ordeal to a close. The Coast Guard crew dropped off her and her family at West Jefferson Hospital in Jefferson Parish. "Barefoot, no purse, no money, no shoes," Moreau recalled. "My daughter went in with the baby. I sat on the curb crying." Soon, they were moved to a shelter. "There was over one hundred people in one room. The heat was incredible, could not go outside with the baby for mosquitoes. We fanned her all night." Moreau appealed to a National Guardsman, but she said he told her they would be at the shelter for another week. "My daughter said, 'I am not going to let my baby die. We are going to walk out of here and get help.'"

According to Moreau, Jefferson Police tried to prevent her from leaving, presumably for her safety, but "I said, 'Do what you want to do, I have nothing left anyway.'" Moreau and her family snuck out when the police were distracted by a scuffle and hitched a ride to Westwego, on the west bank of the Mississippi River, where a friend lived. He had evacuated. "I broke into his house, cooled the baby off, we took a shower and ate can food," Moreau said. "He had left his truck in the driveway. . . . [It] had no gas in it, and there was nowhere to buy gas, so I siphoned gas out of his boat, two gallons at a time, and put [it] into his truck. I left him a letter with my nephew's phone number [in Arkansas]. The only clothes he had that would fit us was boxer shorts and t-shirt, so that is what we left in. . . . We went across the Sunshine Bridge [across the Mississippi River], got to Prairieville, and my nephew picked us up. We had a hard time since then, but we made it."[34]

The twenty-five thousand people who took refuge from the storm in the New Orleans Superdome, designated by local and state officials as a shelter of last resort on Sunday, August 28, survived the storm but faced a trying experience in the days after the storm passed. Those stranded at the Superdome became symbolic of the failed response to Katrina and the epicenter of national news coverage. Dorothy Stukes was one of the people stranded at the Superdome and her story, describing conditions, was recorded by the Senate Committee on Homeland Security and Governmental Affairs:

"A female officer searched us before we went inside," she recalled. "She took some medicine I had, but she also took some insulin from an elderly woman behind me because it was not in its proper box. I don't know how they expected her to make it without her insulin. When we got in, we found a chair and just sat there. All I could think about was my daughter. The last time I talked to her, water was coming through the walls and roof of her house. I didn't know if she was dead or alive.

"The Dome was horrible; it was like jail or something," she went on. "One guy jumped from a balcony and committed suicide. We saw some people having sex under a blanket. There were kids all around. Some kids found where they were hiding the ice and stole some of it and started selling it. Most of the supplies were going to the people [special needs patients] up in the suites. Some folks found a newborn baby in a trashcan; they ended up taking care of it. People were sleeping in the halls on cardboard boxes in the middle of all that waste. And it stank; it was past stink due to all the urine and feces all over the floor. We just sat there and put our shirts over our face to mask the smell. We used an empty MRE bag and a box to go in. We would try to hide ourselves but you couldn't really get away. They wouldn't open any extra doors to let us get fresh air."[35]

Survivors at the Superdome waited for evacuation for at least two days with buses evacuating special needs patients on Wednesday, August 30. The general population started evacuating on Thursday, August 31 with the last evacuees leaving on Saturday, September 3.[36] With each passing day, television cameras captured the increasing despair at the Superdome, and anger began to rise among the public.

The Immediate Fallout

Rising anger was directed at those officials responsible for what the public deemed a failed response to Hurricane Katrina, and while there was plenty of blame to share among public officials at the federal, state, and local levels, the biggest target of criticism was FEMA's director, Michael Brown. During his first visit to the disaster area on September 2, President Bush thanked his FEMA director, appearing before the press with Brown and telling Brown, "Brownie, you're doing a heck of a job."[37] Over the next several days, however, pressure began to mount over the failed response and for the president to take action. On September 6, the president indicated that the immediate focus should be on recovery, not what he called the "blame game." He went on to say, "We've got to solve problems; we're problem solvers. There will be ample time for people to figure out what went right and what went wrong. What I'm interested in is helping save lives."[38]

Michael D. Brown

Michael Brown first began work at FEMA as the general counsel in 2001, hired by FEMA director Joe Allbaugh, his college roommate. After the September 11 attacks, Brown was named to the Consequence Management Principals' Committee and later led the Consequence Management Working Group, both of which assisted the White House in coordinating the domestic response to the attacks.

According to the *Washington Post*, the Congress engaged in very little oversight of Michael Brown's appointments in FEMA. When named deputy director of FEMA in 2002 Brown's Senate hearing lasted forty-two minutes, with only four senators in attendance, and no one questioned his lack of experience in emergency management. Before taking the job with DHS and FEMA, Brown had never worked in the emergency management field, and the only related experience on his resumé was from 1975–1978 while he served as an administrative assistant to the city manager of Edmond, OK. His White House biography indicated that Brown had oversight responsibility in this capacity but that responsibility came into question when *Time* reported that, "According to his bio posted on FEMA's website, [Brown] was 'serving as an assistant city manager with emergency services oversight' and that a White House press release indicated that Brown was responsible for 'overseeing the emergency services division.' "[39] *Time Magazine*, however, quoted the city's head of public relations as saying that Brown's position was similar to an internship. Brown disputed the article's conclusion that he lied in his bio about his responsibilities in Edmond and about other parts of the bio *Time* found misleading or incorrect.

When Bush promoted Brown to head FEMA, he had no confirmation hearing because of a DHS rule, written by Congress, waiving reconfirmation for DHS employees whose job description would not substantially change when transferred to DHS.[40]

By September 9, however, President Bush changed his mind and removed Brown from his post overseeing the disaster response, reassigning him back to Washington. President Bush named Coast Guard Vice Admiral Thad W. Allen as Brown's replacement in directing the federal response. Most members of Congress were happy to see Brown leave the disaster area, but pressure remained for Bush to fire Brown. Senator Harry Reid, minority leader, and three other Democrats sent a letter to President Bush stating that, "It is not enough to remove Mr. Brown from the disaster scene." They added that he "simply does not have the ability or the experience to oversee a coordinated federal response of this magnitude."[41] Once relieved of his duties directing the disaster response, Brown resigned from his post at FEMA on September 12, 2005.

Removing Brown from his post is a fairly extraordinary event because during his tenure in the White House, the president has demonstrated extreme loyalty to those who are loyal to him by publicly defending his staff. For example, President Bush resolutely stood by Secretary of Defense Donald Rumsfeld for years, despite intense public pressure to replace the secretary, press reports that he was unpopular with military commanders and the intelligence communities, opposition from Democratic and Republican members of Congress, and two offers from Rumsfeld to resign during the Abu Ghraib scandal.[42] Throughout his presidency Bush has chosen to avoid public reprimands of his staff or administration, preferring private communication.

Brown's demotion, and subsequent resignation, was a turning point in the response to Hurricane Katrina. By September 12 the response to Katrina was over and recovery had begun. Federal resources had begun flowing to the disaster area, and the victims were by and large evacuated, leaving behind miles and miles of destruction. Members of Congress, who had called for Brown's resignation and an investigation into the response, were chomping at the bit to begin their oversight work.

THE KATRINA INVESTIGATION

The Rising Political Storm

It is widely accepted that the U.S. government failed in its response to Hurricane Katrina with politicians on both sides of the ideological divide acknowledging that the emergency management system was dreadfully slow in acting to prevent further loss after the storm's landfall.[43] While there was widespread, bipartisan support for President Bush's request for substantial and immediate emergency aid, criticism over who was at fault for the disaster began to break along party lines with many Republicans leveling harsh criticism at the bureaucracy while many Democrats felt the blame was also shared by President Bush.[44]

Most Republicans were careful to insulate the president from their criticism. For example, Senator Trent Lott (R-MS), who lost a home in Pascagoula, Mississippi during the hurricane, blasted FEMA for its role in the response but thanked President Bush for his efforts.[45] Senator Norm Coleman (R-MN) said, "I'm a former mayor. The leadership starts at the local level. I didn't see the local mayor. I didn't hear from the mayor."[46] Other Republicans could see the connections between FEMA and Congress when it came to blame. Representative Mark Foley (R-FL) noted, "There'll be a lot of blame to go around, and we can all reasonably take a share of it."[47] After several days of sluggish reaction by emergency management officials, the president said, "The results are not acceptable," walking a fine line between criticizing the results of the response and the actions of the responders. He later clarified his statement by saying, "I am satisfied with the response. I'm not satisfied with the results." Bush also remarked that, "If it's not going exactly right, we're going to make it go exactly right." He continued, "If there's problems, we're going to address the problems. And that's what I've come down to assure people of."[48]

Hurricane Katrina quickly became a political problem for the Bush administration and Congress because unlike earthquakes or terrorist attacks, that occur with little or no warning, Hurricane Katrina blew across the Gulf of Mexico for days before landfall. The warnings from meteorologists about the severity of the storm led the public to find the government negligent in its failure to adequately respond, and policymakers in Washington realized quite quickly that the disaster could cost them their jobs as the level of criticism of the bureaucracy and president reveal. According to Senator Susan Collins (R-ME), chair of the Homeland Security and Governmental Affairs Committee, "It is difficult to understand the lack of preparedness and the ineffective initial response to a disaster that had been predicted for years and for which specific dire warnings had been given for days."[49]

Highlighting the extreme reactions Katrina induced, during an interview on ABC's *This Week*, Senator Landrieu (D-LA), responding to hearing that Bush administration officials were laying heavy criticism on the local response, said, "One more word about it after this show airs and I might have to punch him [Bush]. Literally."[50] The problem the Bush administration faced was that the public was looking to blame someone for the travesty it witnessed in the days following landfall, and the administration did not want the president to be the target of the blame—which had the potential to stop all momentum on other initiatives in the second term. This was a valid concern as the administration was already feeling pressure from the public on long-term issues like continued dissatisfaction with the course of the Iraq war and short-term issues like high gasoline prices. Criticism over a bungled disaster response would only add to the distraction and further reduce the president's public support. The first evidence of distraction came in the form of a reordering of the congressional agenda: the John Roberts nomination hearing was postponed; a Republican effort to repeal the estate tax was sidelined in the Senate; a reconciliation bill that would require cuts in health care and education spending was delayed; and a major Bush initiative, Social Security reform, was dropped from the congressional agenda.[51] Referring to the reconciliation bill, the Democratic leadership, including Senator Reid and Representative Pelosi, sent a letter to the Republican leadership on September 7 stating that, "It would be misguided to proceed with fast-track consideration of legislation that would place at risk services to those in need and divert resources that are necessary to fund the federal response to this tragedy."[52]

Fast-Track Appropriations and the High Cost of Recovery

With so much at stake for the president and Congress in terms of political blame and the national agenda, both the president and lawmakers were highly motivated to move as quickly as possible on three fronts: appropriating emergency aid to the disaster region; investigating the failed response to assess what went wrong; and implementing new policies that would improve future responses. The emergency aid, while delayed for several days by confusion in the federal emergency management system, began to arrive in earnest by the end of the weekend after landfall. The president proposed an initial aid package of $10.5 billion, and Congress moved quickly to pass the president's proposal to pay for the beginning of the recovery.[53]

In the following week, the president asked Congress for an additional $51.8 billion to support FEMA, which was spending $2 billion a day on the recovery, and that package was passed on September 8.[54] Later in September, the Congress passed by voice vote a $5 billion tax-cut package for hurricane survivors and those who housed the displaced.[55]

While there was overwhelming support for hurricane relief spending, especially early in the crisis, Congress was soon facing a $200 billion estimate for the total cost of the hurricane and began looking for ways to pay for continued expenditures. Many lawmakers favored budget offsets in which the Congress would cut spending in other areas and redirect the money to hurricane recovery. The House Republican Study Committee (RSC), a group of conservative lawmakers, proposed $1 trillion of cuts to one hundred federal programs, and some Senate Republicans released their own list of cuts.[56] But the RSC list faced immediate opposition from Speaker Hastert who objected to the inclusion of two of the biggest items on the list—the elimination of six thousand special projects included in the recently passed highway bill, with a $24 billion price tag, and delaying the Medicare prescription drug benefit, saving $31 billion.[57] Hastert said, "We are willing to look at offsets, if there are viable offsets. I don't think it would be prudent at this point to say we are going to stop our Medicare program. We need to have that. It is something seniors across the country look forward to." Of the highway bill, Hastert said, "It is exactly the highway bill we need." House Majority Leader Tom DeLay also noted that the president opposed delaying the introduction of the Medicare drug benefit, so the idea was "a nonstarter."[58]

So while finding offsets was a popular idea to pay for hurricane relief, the idea became less tenable once specific programs, with staunch support among individual members, were identified for possible cuts. Perhaps the best-known example was Congress's plan to cut funding for a bridge in Alaska, popularly known as "The Bridge to Nowhere," that would connect Ketchikan (population 8,000) with Gravina Island (population 50). An amendment to the 2006 transportation appropriations bill by Senator Tom Coburn (R-OK) would have diverted $223 million dollars from this bridge project and $231 million from another bridge project in Alaska, connecting two more areas with small populations, to Louisiana to rebuild Interstate 10. Senator Ted Stevens (R-AK) vehemently objected to the measure saying that, "If the Senate decides to discriminate against our state . . . I will resign from this body." With Stevens's objection fueling opposition, the amendment was defeated 82–15.[59] Later, under pressure from his party, Stevens agreed to drop the earmark spending for the bridges from the transportation bill—but the money was still given to Alaska as general transportation funding. Alaska's governor, Frank Murkowski, indicated that he would spend the money on the bridges.[60]

With money pouring into the hurricane-affected region, Congress began to debate how to make additional funds available for long-term recovery. On the one hand, Democratic leaders were pushing for immediate action including large expenditures on social services such as health care and housing for the displaced. On the other hand, Republican leaders argued for caution by scheduling hearings to investigate how much money would be needed for the recovery and how Congress could best spend the money.[61] In the week following landfall, there were countless proposals from members of Congress for how the government should appropriate recovery funds.

Negotiation on Investigation

The initial aid proposals were accompanied by proposals on how to address the failed response and make changes in the emergency response system. Senator Reid, the minority leader, proposed a 9/11 Commission–style independent, bipartisan investigation into the catastrophe, and Senator Hillary Clinton announced that she would be introducing legislation to create such a commission.[62] While Reid's proposal called for a bipartisan commission, his proposal was colored by his belief that the president was largely responsible for the failed response. Reid was quoted as saying, "The buck stops at 1600 Pennsylvania Avenue."[63] The House minority leader, Representative Pelosi, also supported a bipartisan, independent investigation into the response.

Chairs of various House and Senate committees began discussing and scheduling investigations without coordination with their party leadership, leading Speaker Hastert to attempt to reel in control of the investigations. He said, "What we don't want to have happen is the people who are on the ground in the Gulf States have to come up here to talk to 13 or 14 different groups."[64]

The White House Takes a Unilateral Approach

As early as September 6 it became clear that both the House and Senate would investigate the response and that the investigations would commence as soon as possible with the relevant committee chairs suggesting that they would begin their inquiries during the following week. What also became apparent was that the Congress wanted to investigate much sooner than the president. For his part, President Bush said, "What I intend to do is lead an investigation to find out what went wrong."[65] He also stressed that this investigation would take place after the recovery was fully underway when an investigation would not get in the way of recovery or bleed resources away from helping those in immediate need. The president announced that his homeland security advisor, Frances Fragos Townsend, would direct the administration's internal investigation into the Hurricane Katrina response.[66]

The president's preference for a unilateral approach is consistent with his approach in other areas like creating a federal stem cell program through executive order, developing the nation's energy policy without congressional input, initially favoring a White House Office to coordinate homeland security rather than creating the Department of Homeland Security with Congress, or prosecuting the wars in Afghanistan and Iraq with the bare minimum of communication with Congress.

The Hurricane Joint Review Committee

Facing a recalcitrant White House, Republican leaders in Congress moved forward with a plan for a House-Senate bipartisan investigative committee by announcing the creation of the Hurricane Joint Review Committee on September 7. While the White House signaled that it would not participate in a multibranch investigation, or approve of an independent panel, the White House gave its approval to the Republican leadership's plan. The Republican leadership announced that the committee would supercede individual standing committee investigations in the House and Senate and that while the Hurricane Joint Review Committee's size was not finalized, party ratios would reflect the ratios in Congress. In addition, the committee would have the power to issue subpoenas if both cochairs agreed or by majority vote of the committee. Both mechanisms for issuing subpoenas would therefore be controlled by Republicans who would hold both chair positions and a majority on the committee. The Republican Senate leadership appointed Senator Collins, chair of the Homeland Security and Governmental Affairs Committee, to cochair the Hurricane Joint Review Committee. Republican leaders announced that appointment of the House Republican cochair would follow, along with Democratic membership.[67]

The initial reaction to the Hurricane Joint Review Committee from the Democratic leadership, who were absent from the announcement, was negative. Both Representative Pelosi and Senator Reid indicated that they would not be willing to accept such a committee and both indicated that they would not appoint Democratic members. Both leaders called the Republicans' proposal, which was developed without Democratic input, a "charade" and again pressed for a 9/11-style commission.[68] Democratic leaders argued that if Congress used a joint congressional committee, an equal number of Democrats and Republicans should serve on the committee and both parties' committee members should have subpoena powers.[69] The Democrats' calls for an independent commission were echoed by many of the members of the 9/11 Commission who were still waiting for Congress to fully implement the recommendations included in their report on the September 11 attacks. According to Commissioner Slade Gorton (R-WA), "In Congress, this issue has already become a political football. If we're really going to learn anything from this new catastrophe, that's much more likely going to happen through an objective look. An independent commission is something that ought to be seriously considered."[70] Republicans in Congress, however, argued that the appointment of a joint committee was consistent with eleven previous congressional investigations since 1973.[71]

Interestingly, while the Hurricane Joint Review Committee was intended to supersede other congressional committees, two individual investigations proceeded with the blessing of Republican leaders. The House Government Reform Committee and the Senate Homeland Security and Governmental Affairs Committee proceeded with their own investigations with the understanding that these investigations would not interfere with the bicameral investigation of the hurricane response—though it was unclear how these individual investigations could go forward without overlapping, at least to some extent, with the bicameral investigation. Representative Davis, chair of the House Governmental Reform Committee, indicated that his committee would investigate response issues that could be examined without interfering with recovery efforts, such as examining emergency plans in other cities or information sharing capability between the local, state, and federal levels.[72]

Representative Thomas Davis III (R-VA)

Tom Davis was first elected to Congress in 1994 as part of the large freshman class of Republicans who gave the Republican Party a House majority for the first time in forty years. Davis won in his first congressional election by defeating first-term incumbent Democrat Leslie Byrne (50 percent to 45 percent). Since his first election, Davis has won easy reelection.

During Davis's freshman term, Speaker Gingrich gave him the chairmanship of the House Government Reform and Oversight Committee's District of Columbia Subcommittee. Davis has a moderate voting record in the House—he was one of only three House Republicans to vote against the Contract with America tax cut in 1995 citing his support for government employees, who make up a large constituency in Davis's northern Virginia district, and who would be hit with higher pension payments if the tax cut were passed.[73] Though a moderate in the House, Davis also served as the chairman of the Republican National Congressional Committee (NRCC) from 1998–2000, a position dedicated to raising money for and supporting Republican candidates in congressional elections.

Davis is also known as an advocate for good government reform. He was recognized by Public Citizen, a public interest group, as a "True Blue Reformer." In 2001, Davis was named chairman of the new Government Reform Subcommittee on Technology and Procurement Policy. In 2003 Davis was elected the chairman of the House Government Reform Committee, and in 2005 he was appointed to the Homeland Security Committee. Though he holds good government credentials, Davis has been criticized by Democrats for abusing his position as chairman of the Government Reform Committee—refusing to launch investigations the Democrats called for. Also, much of the activity in question during the congressional Jack Abramoff influence scandal took place while Davis chaired the NRCC.

While the party leadership experienced extreme partisan strife during the weeks after Katrina, there was bipartisanship among some of the representatives and senators from the afflicted states. For example, Louisiana's two senators, David Vitter (R) and Mary Landrieu (D), understood that they were in the crisis together and composed a joint letter to their respective leaders calling for bipartisanship in addressing recovery. Representative Jindal (R-LA), representing a district that was half underwater said, "On the ground there are no Democrats or Republicans."[74] The White House, at least publicly, embraced the idea of working with Democrats. When asked about why the administration had not created a "War Room" for dealing with the Katrina response like it had for John Roberts's nomination to the Supreme Court, White House Spokesman Trent Duffy replied, "We're all in this together. War rooms are designed to fight partisan battles. We're not fighting a partisan battle on this."[75]

This public embrace of bipartisanship was not, however, reflected in the administration's actions. Not only did the White House fail to embrace bipartisanship, its unilateral approach was seen as dismissive even by Republican lawmakers. The relationship between Republican lawmakers in Congress and the president was frayed by a combination of the White House's unilateral approach and the criticism of the administration by the public. Throughout the response and recovery period, congressional leaders felt the administration failed to provide sufficient communication on political or policy details, and the lack of communication made the party leaders' job more difficult because they wanted to maintain a cohesive front with the administration. Lawmakers were most concerned with this lack of communication early in the response and were increasingly disappointed with the administration's inability to explain how the billions of dollars Congress appropriated for Katrina would be spent. In response, the administration tried to provide better communication by granting the leadership's request for regular conference calls with House and Senate leadership and committee aides.[76] In addition, the administration decided to make frequent use of legislative affairs staffers to keep lawmakers informed—though informed at a distance.[77]

The House and Senate Choose to Go It Alone

With Democratic leaders continuing to oppose the Hurricane Joint Review Committee unless it included an equal number of Democrats and Republicans and gave subpoena power to Democrats as well as Republicans, the early hope for a bipartisan, bicameral investigation looked increasingly unlikely. Senator Reid proposed the creation of an independent commission on the Senate floor as an amendment to an appropriations bill, and as an amendment to a bill in the Homeland Security and Government Affairs Committee, but it was defeated on both occasions.[78] Republican leaders in the Senate, who wanted a bipartisan investigation, decided to abandon the joint committee unless it was a bipartisan effort—but the Republican leadership in the House refused to negotiate on the committee's makeup. With no agreement likely with House leaders, Senate leaders formed their own bipartisan investigation by the Homeland Security and Government Affairs Committee under the direction of the committee chair, Senator Susan Collins. Senator Collins repeatedly indicated that she would not cooperate with the House investigation unless it was bipartisan, so the Senate investigation moved forward without the House.[79]

Representative Davis announced that his committee would start hearings immediately by creating a timeline of events establishing who knew what, and when. Davis said the committee would begin by holding hearings on September 21 with testimony from the National Weather Service and the National Hurricane Service.[80]

The division between the House and Senate leadership over how to proceed with the investigation combined with internal disagreement within the

Republican Party over how to pay for the recovery led to a party with mixed messages coming out of Washington. The Democrats, however, were unified behind three positions: the federal government should move quickly to begin the recovery process and make the expenditures necessary for rebuilding; the administration, including President Bush, should be held accountable for the failed response; and the investigation into the response should be bipartisan and independent. The Democratic Party's unity allowed them to win the battle for public support—with Republicans earning most of the blame for the failed attempt at reaching a bipartisan agreement on how to proceed. The Republicans' inability to find common ground within the party also inhibited their ability to deflect blame for the response from the president and his administration.[81]

In addition to the debate over how to investigate the hurricane response, there was discussion in the Congress about how best to oversee the billions of dollars appropriated for recovery with the Senate and the House disagreeing on the best approach to spending oversight. Republican leaders in the House wanted to keep oversight responsibility within Congress. According to Speaker Hastert, "It is our responsibility to take a look at this money."[82] Others in the House, like the Republican Main Street Partnership, a group of moderate Republicans, supported using an inspector general to oversee the funds instead of Congress.

In the Senate, the Homeland Security and Governmental Affairs Committee voted on September 22 to support two bills that would create external oversight of Katrina spending: a bill (S. 1700) sponsored by Senators Tom Coburn (R-OK), Thomas Carper (D-DE), and Barack Obama (D-IL) that would create a chief financial officer to oversee Katrina spending; and a bill (S. 1738) sponsored by Senators Collins and Lieberman that would empower the special Iraq reconstruction inspector to oversee Katrina spending as well.[83] On October 11 Senators Collins, Lieberman, Coburn, and Carper sent a letter to Majority Leader Frist and Minority Leader Reid, with the support of committee members, calling for floor consideration of S. 1700 and S. 1738. Both Frist and Reid were cosponsors of S. 1738 but the bill, according to Coburn, was opposed by President Bush.[84]

By late November, just three months after Katrina, momentum behind legislation to help disaster victims recover was stalled in Congress as the national focus shifted to several other high-profile issues including the war in Iraq, the CIA leak investigation, and two Supreme Court confirmation hearings.[85]

Institutional Conflict

The Bush administration, while giving its consent to the creation of a tightly controlled congressional investigation into the Katrina response, was not willing to fully cooperate with the investigating committees. On Tuesday, January 24, 2006, the White House announced that it would not release some documents requested by Congress and would not make senior White House officials available for sworn testimony, citing confidentiality of executive branch communication.[86] This refusal was reminiscent of the Bush administration's response to similar requests from the joint House-Senate intelligence inquiry, and its refusal to allow Tom Ridge to testify before Congress on homeland security efforts. In addition, executive agencies were slow in responding or gave incomplete responses to investigators. Democrats, and some Republicans in the Senate, were especially critical of the administration for its lack of cooperation with their investigation.[87] According to Senator Lieberman, "There has been a near total lack of cooperation that has made it impossible, in my opinion, for us to do the thorough investigation that we have a responsibility to do."[88] He also threatened to subpoena any documents or testimony the White House refused to produce. Republican Senator Collins also complained that officials who were not part of the president's staff were refusing to testify about their communication with the White House during the Katrina response.

White House spokesman Trent Duffy argued that "The White House and the administration are cooperating with both the House and the Senate. But we have also maintained the president's ability to get advice and have conversations with his top advisors that remain confidential."[89] While the administration was less than forthcoming in some respects, they cooperated with the investigations on other matters. For example, the Department of Homeland Security turned over three hundred thousand pages of documents and provided sixty officials as witnesses. The Department of Defense turned over two hundred forty thousand pages of documents, made eighteen officials available for sworn testimony, and made fifty-seven other officials available for interviews. But Secretary of Defense Donald Rumsfeld, who was the target of the only subpoena, did not testify despite months of requests.[90] President Bush, commenting on his decision to restrict access to high-level officials, said, "If people give me advice and they're forced to disclose that advice, it means the next time an issue comes up I might not be able to get unvarnished advice from my advisors. It will have a chilling effect on future advisors if the precedent is such that when they give me advice it's going to be subject to scrutiny."[91]

One of the central figures of interest, former FEMA director Michael Brown, refused to discuss his communication with the president, the vice president, or any high-level White House official, citing advice from agency lawyers.[92] Once Brown left government service, however, he obliged Congress by testifying before the Senate Homeland Security and Governmental Affairs Committee on February 10, 2006, about his communication with White House officials. Brown said of his impending testimony, "The public needs to know the entire picture of what was going on."[93] In his testimony Brown defended himself by saying that senior White House officials, including President Bush, were aware of the severity of the problem in New Orleans from the outset, and changes in the organization of FEMA under the Department of Homeland Security kept him, and FEMA, from acting as effectively as he and they would have liked. He said, "Its [FEMA's] mission had been marginalized. Its response capability had been diminished. There's the whole clash of cultures between DHS's mission to prevent terrorism and FEMA's mission to respond to and to prepare for responding to disasters of whatever nature. The policies and decisions implemented by the DHS put FEMA on a path to failure."[94]

Secretary Chertoff also appeared before the congressional investigatory panels to answer questions about the response, defend himself and his department, and explain what he planned to do about fixing the problems at hand. On October 19, Chertoff pledged to rebuild FEMA so that it would be better prepared to respond to future disasters. Chertoff cited many areas he wished to improve and defended FEMA's inclusion in his department.[95] During his testimony before the House and Senate committees, Chertoff, like FEMA director Brown, received heavy personal criticism for DHS failures during the storm response.[96]

Having secured testimony from many of the principals in the federal, state, and local agencies and governments, and having reviewed millions of documents, each investigation came to a close. While the House focused on documenting failures, the Senate and White House investigations provided a long list of suggestions about how to fix the broken emergency management system.

Redesigning the Emergency Management System

The redesign of the emergency management system continues and will continue for some time after this book has been published. Since the investigations concluded, Congress and the administration have been contemplating how best to fix the emergency management system and FEMA. The Senate Homeland Security and Government Affairs Committee identified five broad issues as the causes for the failed Katrina response:

1. Long-term warnings went unheeded, and government officials neglected their duties to prepare for a forewarned catastrophe;
2. Government officials took insufficient actions or made poor decisions in the days immediately before and after landfall;
3. Systems on which officials relied to support their response efforts failed; and
4. Government officials at all levels failed to provide effective leadership.

The fifth issue, according to the committee, was that "These individual failures, moreover, occurred against a backdrop of failure, over time, to develop the capacity for a coordinated, national response to a truly catastrophic event, whether caused by nature or man-made."[97] The broad issues identified by the Senate were consistent with the House and White House investigations' conclusions.[98]

The three federal investigations came up with a combined 211 suggested improvements for the emergency management system.[99] As lawmakers and administrators digested the reports and their suggestions for improvements, much of the debate over where to start began with the controversial idea of removing FEMA from the DHS and returning it to independent status. In the House, two committees passed bills arguing for each arrangement. The House Transportation and Government Reform Committee passed H.R. 5316 that would move FEMA out of DHS, granting independent, cabinet-level status to the agency. The Homeland Security Committee passed its own bill (H.R. 5351) that would leave FEMA in the DHS but would allow FEMA to report directly to the president during a crisis. Despite differences in where FEMA would be housed, both bills would give FEMA control over disaster preparedness and response. This was an important difference from Chertoff's DHS reorganization that gave FEMA responsibility for disaster response but not disaster preparedness.[100] Neither of the House bills had strong support among the Republican leadership. Without a strong preference, the Republican leadership proposed to allow their membership to decide which course of action seemed most reasonable.[101]

Senate committees did not move as quickly as their House counterparts in passing legislation, but key senators began positioning themselves and their committees to win control over FEMA's fate. Senators Collins and Lieberman voiced their support for leaving FEMA in DHS and announced plans to begin consideration of legislation in the Homeland Security Committee to that effect. Other senators, like Lott and Clinton, have expressed support for cutting FEMA from DHS.[102]

While House leaders were not expressing a preference for either bill in May, the Bush administration expressed its preference that FEMA be left in DHS.[103] Continuing with a unilateral strategy, the administration began retooling the DHS to better respond to emergencies while the Congress continued to legislate. The administration moved quickly to change how the emergency response system would respond to future disasters. President Bush asked DHS Secretary Chertoff to implement changes in DHS structure and protocol in time for the 2006 hurricane season, using the White House report, which made 125 recommendations for changing the emergency response system as a starting point. Secretary Chertoff indicated that the DHS would meet the president's deadline of June 1, 2006, the official beginning of hurricane season, to implement eleven top-priority initiatives.[104]

By June, DHS reported that it had made substantial improvements to its disaster preparedness. The DHS carried out many different preparedness activities: conducting five regional hurricane preparedness exercises in the Gulf Coast area before the start of the 2006 hurricane season; making visits to all fifty states, six territories, and seventy-five urban areas to review preparedness plans for each; predesignating federal incident commanders to work with federal, state, and local officials to coordinate emergency response before disasters strike; creating a National Operations Center to coordinate emergency response and improve situational awareness; and updating the National Response Plan to clarify roles and responsibilities and improve performance.[105] In addition, the DHS improved FEMA's capacity for providing assistance during a disaster.

According to FEMA, the agency has improved its response effectiveness in multiple ways, such as improving the capacity to track supplies with a state-of-the-art tracking system, improving the ability to handle requests for assistance, and developing better plans for long-term housing. FEMA points to its integration of operations with the DHS as the most important step in the right direction. FEMA also claims to have improved its coordination with other departments; improved its communication systems and interoperability capacity; enhanced its supply system to provide disaster supplies like water, food, and ice for one million people through better use of predisaster contracts with contractors; improved its capacity to register storm victims to two hundred thousand people per day in order to process victims faster and expedite assistance; and doubled the number of disaster assistance employees.[106]

Congressional action moved more slowly than executive action, but Congress ultimately made statutory changes to the emergency management system. Senators Collins and Lieberman, chair and ranking member of the Senate Homeland Security and Governmental Affairs Committee, coauthored a bill to repair FEMA, DHS, and the rest of the emergency management system. The Collins-Lieberman bill strengthened FEMA by giving it special status in the DHS, returned to FEMA the preparedness responsibilities removed by Secretary Chertoff when FEMA moved to DHS, required that FEMA's executives have emergency management experience, and protected FEMA from future reorganization by the executive branch that might reduce its budget. The committee passed the bill on July 27, 2006, and Senator Collins said that "Our bill puts forth a careful and comprehensive program for improvement of our emergency management system. This is no academic exercise; it is a concrete, nuts and bolts plan designed to rebuild and strengthen a broken system."[107]

Collins and Lieberman began negotiations with the House over their bill and announced on September 15 that they had reached an agreement on a tentative deal that would allow an emergency management system overhaul through the Homeland Security Appropriations Bill. The compromise dictated that FEMA would remain within DHS but FEMA's director would have direct access to the president during a crisis and would implement many of the eighty-eight recommendations made in the Senate report on Katrina. The agreement mirrored the Collins-Lieberman bill quite closely and included several important measures to improve the emergency management system. The *States News Service* summarized the compromise as:

1. FEMA becomes a distinct entity within DHS as are the U.S. Coast Guard and the Secret Service—and is therefore protected from future reorganizations by DHS.
2. The Administrator of FEMA is the principal advisor to the President for emergency management. The language is modeled after the Joint Chiefs of Staff language.
3. The Administrator has authority to report directly to Congress and may be designated as Cabinet level at the President's discretion during disasters.
4. Reunites preparedness and response with FEMA so that the Administrator is responsible for all phases of emergency management (preparedness, response, recovery, and mitigation).
5. Stricter qualification requirements for Administrator of FEMA.
6. Stronger regional focus whereby FEMA would work closely and consistently with appropriate state and local governments, as well as private sector and non-governmental entities for planning emergency operations
7. Requires the Administrator to appoint a Disability Coordinator to ensure that the needs of the disabled are taken into account in emergency planning and operations.
8. It strengthens personnel at FEMA by enabling the organization to recruit and retain skilled employees.
9. Strengthens programs within FEMA, for example, by requiring FEMA to improve its information technology systems and requiring FEMA to provide technical assistance for evacuation to state and local governments.
10. It creates a system for ensuring that FEMA is engaged in appropriate planning, training and exercise programs with its counterparts at the federal, state and local levels. It also requires that FEMA establish specific performance measurements against which to measure progress in planning, training and exercises toward establishing readiness.
11. Establishes a national disaster recovery strategy to assist with the recovery from future catastrophes such as Hurricane Katrina.
12. Requires the FEMA Administrator to appoint a Disability Coordinator to ensure that individuals with disabilities are properly addressed in emergency preparedness and disaster relief.
13. Establishes within the National Center for Missing and Exploited Children a center for locating children separated from their families after a disaster.
14. Establishes a voluntary registry to help reunite families separated by a disaster.
15. Requires a number of provisions that will help prevent waste, fraud, and abuse.[108]

The Congress subsequently passed the compromise version of Collins-Lieberman as part of the Homeland Security Appropriations Act for fiscal year 2007 on September 29, 2006, in a 412–6 vote in the House and a voice vote in the Senate. The president signed the bill five days later on October 4 with much fanfare at a bill signing event in Scottsdale, Arizona. The president said that the bill was "an important piece of legislation that will highlight our government's highest responsibility, and that's to protect the American people." He continued by saying that the bill "will also help our government better respond to emergencies and natural disasters by strengthening the capabilities of the Federal Emergency Management Agency."[109]

Signing the bill, however, was not the last action President Bush executed on the Collins-Lieberman bill. Like in many instances before, the president issued a "signing statement," a statement presidents make to clarify their understanding of the law or challenge its premise, just hours after the bill signing ceremony. The signing statement has become a Bush administration staple in its efforts to expand presidential power and protect presidential prerogative—Bush issued over eight hundred such statements during his first six years in office.[110] In this case, Bush used the signing statement to explain that he would not be bound by several of the provisions of the new law, including the provision requiring that the director of FEMA have "demonstrated ability in and knowledge of emergency management and homeland security" and "not less than five years of executive leadership." The president's signing statement specified that the law "purports to limit the qualifications of the pool of persons from whom the president may select the appointee in a manner that rules out a large portion of those persons best qualified by experience and knowledge to fill the office." The signing statement went on to argue that because the Constitution gives the appointment power to the president, Congress cannot encroach on that power—and the president would not be bound by such encroachment. Members of Congress in both parties objected to the president's decision and interpretation and were quick to point out that such limitations are placed on other appointees, such as the solicitor general or the director of the Fish and Wildlife Service. Even with the president's refusal to comply with the limitations on appointments, the Senate will have the last say in the matter because the president must win Senate confirmation for future FEMA directors. In the words of David Marlin, a spokesman for Representative Thomas Davis, "Good luck getting someone confirmed who doesn't meet these standards."[111]

The signing statement is the last example of the president's unilateral strategy in this case. In the face of overwhelming support from both the House and Senate, the president chose to follow his own path on reorganizing FEMA and the emergency management system. With changes in the emergency management system coming from Congress and the executive branch, only time will tell if the system has been improved or which changes will be fully implemented.

THEMES OF INDIVIDUAL LEADERSHIP ON KATRINA

The story of Hurricane Katrina, with respect to the relationship between Congress and the president, is one of unilateralism. As in the legislative histories of homeland security and intelligence reform, President Bush elected to pursue a unilateral strategy early in the process, but unlike in these other cases, he managed to maintain unilateralism on Katrina. While our other case studies offer examples of how bipartisanship often serves as the mechanism that allows meaningful policy change in a highly charged partisan environment, this case study provides an opportunity to observe meaningful change when bipartisanship and institutional cooperation were hard to come by.

The first example of unilateralism is that both Presidents Clinton and Bush used executive orders, not congressional statute, to make many of the changes to FEMA and the emergency management system. With FEMA so dependent upon presidents for guidance, scholars have characterized FEMA as a "presidency-serving agency" rather than a "Congress-serving agency."[112] Bush's reorganization of FEMA's budget and mission was therefore very much consistent with FEMA's history. Once Katrina struck, and it became clear that the response would not meet expectations, the president continued the tradition of unilateralism by refusing requests from congressional leaders to participate in an investigation, preferring instead to order an internal executive branch investigation separate from Congress. Finally, once the investigations were concluded, the administration proceeded to rectify problems within FEMA and the DHS without waiting for congressional action, and even when Congress provided statutory guidance, the president pursued a unilateral strategy with a signing statement announcing his intention to defy the law Congress wrote.

Direction, with respect to Katrina, came from different sources for different purposes. The president provided clear direction on Katrina—that the administration would handle the investigation of what went wrong and make the necessary changes to fix the problem. Once the White House identified problems, the president provided direction to the bureaucracy on implementing solutions. Without a role in the president's unilateral strategy, Congress sought direction from committee chairs with jurisdiction over the emergency management system. Ultimately, when House and Senate leaders could not agree on the formation of a bicameral, bipartisan investigation, the two chambers each carried out their own investigatory efforts with the prospect of rejoining each other after the conclusion of the investigations. While Representative Davis provided direction in the House investigation, it was Senators Collins and Lieberman who led not only the Senate investigation but also the entire Congress in implementing solutions through their legislation.

As in cases in this book, the House leadership was much less flexible than the Senate in terms of embracing bipartisanship, refusing to compromise with Democratic leaders over the composition of the panel or subpoena power, leading to a refusal by the Democratic leadership to cooperate with, or even name Democratic members to, the House investigation. In the Senate, where bipartisanship has been much more readily achieved, the investigation was a bipartisan effort led by a Republican, Senator Collins, and a Democrat, Senator Lieberman, who partnered in an effective tandem that had provided interparty leadership in the past.

The president moved from a unilateral investigation to a unilateral implementation of findings, instructing Secretary Chertoff to implement an eleven-point list of top priorities, on which the DHS immediately began working. Without a presidential request for congressional action in the form of a policy proposal and competing ideas of how to fix the emergency management system, congressional action moved slowly. The best example of the coherence void in Congress is that when House leaders faced a choice between two radically different approaches to dealing with FEMA, one bill that would carve FEMA out of DHS and another bill leaving FEMA inside DHS, Republican Party leaders expressed no preference between the two bills and solicited the opinion of their caucus to reach consensus. While this is an egalitarian approach, it is dramatically inconsistent with the House leadership's behavior on most other issues; they usually have a well-defined agenda, and this indecisiveness might have been in part due to a lack of coherence. It was Collins and Lieberman who provided *coherence* to the emergency management redesign—their bill provided a framework that members in both chambers could work on and negotiate over to find an amenable compromise.

The final leadership skill, *energy*, was provided by the president and members of Congress fearful of losing their jobs in the 2006 midterm election. Congressional committee chairs also provided energy by moving forward with their independent plans to investigate the Katrina response. Representative Davis, chair of the House Governmental Reform Committee, in particular motivated quick congressional action. When congressional party leaders disagreed over whether the Congress would use a joint bipartisan investigation, with Democrats holding out for equal representation and subpoena power, Davis and his committee began scheduling independent hearings. With Davis's committee moving quickly, House Republican Party leaders were forced to move quickly as well, lest they be blamed for dragging their feet or obstructing the investigation.

Since the days after Katrina's landfall, the administration and Congress have been working steadily to identify and fix problems. It should be noted that while considering the creation of the DHS and intelligence reform in 2002, both parties had incentive to delay action until after the midterm election since both thought they would win the election and be able to dictate their terms in the subsequent lame duck session or with an emboldened majority in the next Congress. With Katrina, the House Democratic leadership dragged its feet over the investigation, possibly to score political points over the lack of an independent investigation—but in the end the Republican-led congressional investigation handed heavy criticism to the administration. The House Republicans and the Senate moved quickly through their investigations and into deliberation as the 2006 hurricane season approached, and the president and the Congress were able to implement a meaningful redesign of the emergency preparedness system within one year of Hurricane Katrina.

NOTES

1. Summary of details reported in U.S. Congress, Senate, Committee on Homeland Security and Governmental Affairs, *Hurricane Katrina: A Nation Still Unprepared*, 109th Congress, 2nd Session.

2. U.S. Department of Homeland Security, *The Federal Response to Hurricane Katrina: Lessons Learned*, February 2006, 129.

3. U.S. Department of Homeland Security, *The Federal Response to Hurricane Katrina*, 129.

4. See Bruce B. Clary, "The Evolution and Structure of Natural Hazard Policies," *Public Administration Review* 45 (1985): 20–28; and Barry J. Barnett, "U.S. Government Natural Disaster Assistance: Historical Analysis and a Proposal for the Future," *Disasters: The Journal of Disaster Studies, Policy & Management* 23, no. 2 (1999): 139–55 for a discussion of the history of emergency management in the United States.

5. Daniel Franklin, "The FEMA Phoenix," *Washington Monthly*, July–Aug. 1995.

6. Gary L. Wamsley, Aaron D. Schroeder, and Larry M. Lane, "To Politicize Is NOT to Control: The Pathologies of Control in Federal Emergency Management," *American Review of Public Administration* 26, no. 3 (1996): 263–85.

7. Richard T. Sylves, "President Bush and Hurricane Katrina: A Presidential Leadership Study," *Annals of the American Academy* 604 (March 2006): 35.

8. Sylves, "President Bush and Hurricane Katrina," 33, 35.

9. Jason Mycoff, "Congress and Katrina: A Failure of Oversight," *State and Local Government Review* 39, no. 1 (2007).

10. U.S. Congress, Senate, Committee on Governmental Affairs, "*Rebuilding FEMA: Preparing for the Next Disaster*," 103rd Congress, 1st session. 18 May 1993: 2.

11. Franklin, "The FEMA Phoenix"; and Stephen Barr, "One Reason FEMA Is No Longer a Disaster Area," *Washington Post*, 19 January 2001, B2.

12. Rebecca Adams, "FEMA Failure a Perfect Storm of Bureaucracy," *CQ Weekly*, 12 September 2005, 2378.

13. Bill McAllister, "Chief Given Cabinet Status," *Washington Post*, 27 February 1996, A17.

14. Nathan Abse, "FEMA Plan to Grid for Disasters Expanding; Project Aims to Stem Losses," *Washington Post*, 8 June 1998, A21.

15. Bob Kappstatter, "W Targets Quake Program," *Daily News*, 1 March 2001, 4.

16. Adams, "FEMA Failure a Perfect Storm of Bureaucracy," 2378.

17. Kappstatter, "W Targets Quake Program," 2.

18. Tania Anderson, "Bush Proposes Elimination of Two Major Projects in Worcester," *States News Service,* 1 March 2001.

19. William Claiborne, "Disaster Management Cuts Raise Concerns; Some States Fear Bush Budget's Actions on Preparedness May Signal Policy Shift," *Washington Post,* 8 May 2001, A21.

20. Christopher Marquis, "Man in the News; A Tough-Talking, but Self-Effacing, Loyalist; Joe Marvin Allbaugh," *New York Times,* 5 January 2001, A14.

21. Bennett Roth, "Tropical Storm Aid Wins Praise for Bush," *Houston Chronicle,* 1 July 2001, <http://www.chron.com/disp/story.mpl/storm2001/957422.html> (6 September 2006).

22. Claiborne, "Disaster Management Cuts Raise Concerns," A21; Mike Ferullo, "Bush Designates Allbaugh FEMA Director, Rove as Senior White House Advisor," *CNN.com,* 4 January 2001, <http://archives.cnn.com/2001/ALLPOLITICS/stories/01/04/bush.announce/> (6 September 2006).

23. Ferullo, "Bush Designates Allbaugh FEMA Director."

24. Claiborne, "Disaster Management Cuts Raise Concerns," A21.

25. Claiborne, "Disaster Management Cuts Raise Concerns," A21.

26. Spencer S. Hsu, "Leaders Lacking Disaster Experience," *Washington Post,* 9 September 2005, A01.

27. Adams, "FEMA Failure a Perfect Storm of Bureaucracy," 2378.

28. U.S. Congress, House, Select Bipartisan Committee to Investigate the Preparation for and the Response to Hurricane Katrina, *A Failure of Initiative,* 109th Congress, 2nd Session, 30.

29. Congressional Research Service, "Transfer of FEMA to the Department of Homeland Security: Issues for Congressional Oversight," 17 December 2002.

30. Senator Clinton was also the only senator voting against Chertoff's nomination to serve in the Justice Department. Vincent Morris, "Bitter Hill Lone 'Nay' Vote vs. Judge," *New York Post,* 10 June 2003, 22.

31. U.S. Congress, House, *A Failure of Initiative,* 59.

32. U.S. Congress, Senate, *A Nation Still Unprepared,* 2.

33. U.S. Congress, Senate, *A Nation Still Unprepared,* 1-6.

34. U.S. Congress, Senate, *A Nation Still Unprepared,* 1-7 through 1-8.

35. U.S. Congress, Senate, *A Nation Still Unprepared,* 1-11.

36. U.S. Congress, Senate, *A Nation Still Unprepared,* 5-6 through 5-15.

37. Peter Baker, "FEMA Director Replaced as Head of Relief Effort," *Washington Post,* 10 September 2005, A01.

38. Anne Kornblut and Carl Hulse, "Bush Promises to Seek Answers to Failures in Hurricane Relief," *New York Times,* 7 September 2005, A17.

39. Daren Fonda and Rita Healy, "How Reliable Is Brown's Resume?" *Time Magazine,* 8 September 2005, <http://www.time.com/time/nation/article/0,8599,1103003,00.html> (30 August 2006).

40. Editorial, "Congress, Heal Thy Self," *Washington Post,* 12 September 2005, A18.

41. Peter Baker, "An Embattled Bush Says 'Results Are Not Acceptable,'" *Washington Post,* 3 September 2005, A01.

42. Jamie McIntyre, "Rumsfeld Twice Offered to Resign during Abu Ghraib Scandal," *CNN.com,* 5 February 2005, <http://www.cnn.com/2005/ALLPOLITICS/02/03/rumsfeld.resign/> (5 September 2006).

43. Baker, "An Embattled Bush," A01. While there is also considerable blame to be given to state and local governments, we focus on the federal government, which is consistent with the purpose of our book.

44. Baker, "An Embattled Bush," A01.

45. David D. Kirkpatrick, "Competition Starts in Congress to Aid Victims and to Investigate the Response," *New York Times,* 6 September 2005, A20.

46. Joseph Curl and Rowan Scarborough, "GOP Begins Damage Control," *Washington Times,* 7 September 2005, A01.

47. Curl and Scarborough, "GOP Begins Damage Control," A01.

48. Baker, "An Embattled Bush," A01.

49. Kornblut and Hulse, "Bush Promises to Seek Answers," A17.

50. David D. Kirkpatrick, "Competition Starts in Congress to Aid Victims and to Investigate the Response," *New York Times,* 6 September 2005, A20.

51. Kirkpatrick, "Competition Starts in Congress to Aid Victims," A20; Kornblut and Hulse, "Bush Promises to Seek Answers," A17.

52. Daphne Retter, Alex Wayne, Joseph J. Schatz, and Susan Ferrechio, "Revamped Agenda Focuses on Relief," *CQ Weekly,* 12 September 2005, 2416.

53. Peter Baker, "An Embattled Bush," A01; Adam Nagourney and Anne E. Kornblut, "White House Enacts a Plan to Ease Political Damage," *New York Times*, 5 September 2006.

54. Stephen Dinan, "Congress OKs $51.8 Billion; Lawmakers Vow To Hold FEMA Accountable," *Washington Times,* 9 September 2005, A01.

55. "Washington in Brief," *Washington Post*, 16 September 2005, A05.

56. Martin Kady II, "Conservatives Challenge Rebuild of Gulf Coast," *CQ Weekly*, 23 September 2005, 2564.

57. Shailagh Murray, "Storm's Costs Threaten Hill Leaders' Pet Projects," *Washington Post*, 22 September 2005, A13.

58. Murray, "Storm's Costs Threaten Hill Leaders' Pet Projects," A13.

59. Shailagh Murray, "For a Senate Foe of Pork Barrel Spending, Two Bridges Too Far," *Washington Post*, 21 October 2005, A08.

60. Michael Grunwald, "Pork by any Other Name . . . ." *Washington Post*, 30 April 2006, B01.

61. Emily Pierce, "Parties Divided over Katrina Response," *Roll Call,* 7 September 2005.

62. Kornblut and Hulse, "Bush Promises to Seek Answers," A17.

63. Kirkpatrick, "Competition Starts in Congress to Aid Victims," A20.

64. Curl and Scarborough, "GOP Begins Damage Control," A01.

65. Curl and Scarborough, "GOP Begins Damage Control," A01.

66. Amy Goldstein, "House GOP Opens Slimmed-Down Inquiry into Katrina," *Washington Post*, 22 September 2005, A13.

67. Jennifer Yachnin, "Davis' Panel To Go Ahead with Its Katrina Hearings," *Roll Call*, 12 September 2005; Isaiah J. Poole, "Partisan Finger-Pointing over Katrina," *CQ Weekly,* September 12, 2005, 2414.

68. Dinan, "Congress OKs $51.8 Billion," A01; Peter Baker and Amy Goldstein, "Congress Approves $51.8 Billion for Victims; Bipartisan Accord on Aid, But Not on Investigation," *Washington Post,* 9 September 2005, A01; Poole, "Partisan Finger-Pointing over Katrina," 2414.

69. Yachnin, "Davis' Panel To Go Ahead with Its Katrina Hearings."

70. Carl Hulse and Philip Shenon, "Democrats and Others Press for an Independent Inquiry," *New York Times,* 14 September 2005, A23.

71. Hulse and Shenon, "Democrats and Others Press for an Independent Inquiry," A23.

72. Yachnin, "Davis' Panel to Go Ahead with Its Katrina Hearings."

73. Michael Barone and Grant Ujifusa, *The Almanac of American Politics* (Washington, DC: National Journal, 1997), 1468.

74. Poole, "Partisan Finger-Pointing Over Katrina," 2414.

75. Ben Pershing, "Hill Wants Details From Bush," *Roll Call,* 14 September 2005.

76. Pershing, "Hill Wants Details From Bush."

77. Pershing, "Hill Wants Details From Bush."

78. Martin Kady II, "Conservatives Challenge Rebuild of Gulf Coast," *CQ Weekly,* 23 September 2005, 2564.

79. Amy Goldstein, "House GOP Opens Slimmed-Down Inquiry Into Katrina," *Washington Post,* 22 September 2005, A13.

80. Goldstein, "House GOP Opens Slimmed-Down Inquiry Into Katrina," A13.

81. Kady, "Conservatives Challenge Rebuild of Gulf Coast," 2564.

82. Kady, "Conservatives Challenge Rebuild of Gulf Coast," 2564.

83. Kady, "Conservatives Challenge Rebuild of Gulf Coast," 2564.

84. Tim Starks, "Collins, Lieberman Pushing Bill to Increase Oversight of Katrina Spending," *CQ Weekly,* 14 October 2005, 2783.

85. James Dao, "Louisiana Sees Faded Urgency in Relief Effort," *New York Times,* 22 November 2005, A01.

86. Eric Lipton, "White House Declines to Provide Storm Papers," *New York Times,* 25 January 2006, A1.

87. Charles Babington, "Lawmakers Urge More Executive Branch Oversight," *Washington Post,* 3 February 2006, A03, Final Edition.

88. Lipton, "White House Declines to Provide Storm Papers," A1.

89. Lipton, "White House Declines to Provide Storm Papers," A1.

90. Lipton, "White House Declines to Provide Storm Papers," A1.

91. Joseph Curl, "Bush Claims Authority on War, Eavesdropping; Also To Ban Aides from Katrina Testimony," *Washington Times,* 27 January 2006, A04.

92. Lipton, "White House Declines to Provide Storm Papers," A1.

93. Eric Lipton, "In Reversal, Ex-FEMA Chief Will Answer Storm Questions," *New York Times,* 10 February 2006, A16.

94. Tim Starks, "Former FEMA Head Michael D. Brown Blames Departmental Setup for Hurricane Problems," *CQ Weekly,* 10 February 2006, 442.

95. Eric Lipton, "Homeland Security Chief Outlines FEMA Overhaul," *New York Times,* 20 October 2005, A22.

96. Leonard Greene, "Chertoff in Eye of the Storm," *New York Post,* 16 February 2006, 14.

97. U.S. Congress, Senate, *A Nation Still Unprepared,* 2.

98. The House investigation identified the following problems: design of the New Orleans levees; evacuation efforts; failure to follow the National Response Plan; lack of

preparation by DHS and the affected states; damaged communication systems and a lack of adequate backup systems; impaired command and control at all levels; lack of coordination with the military; collapse of local law enforcement; lack of preparation and communication in medical care; a lack of planning for emergency shelter; failure of FEMA logistics; and charitable organizations could not provide enough assistance for a storm that large (U.S. Congress, House, *A Failure of Initiative*, 2–5). The White House investigation identified what it called seventeen critical challenges: national preparedness; integrated use of military capabilities; communications; logistics and evacuations; search and rescue; public safety and security; public health and medical support; human services; mass care and housing; public communications; critical infrastructure and impact assessment; environmental hazards and debris removal; foreign assistance; nongovernmental aid; training, exercises, and lessons learned; homeland security professional development and education; and citizen and community preparedness (U.S. Department of Homeland Security, *The Federal Response to Hurricane Katrina: Lessons Learned*, 2–5).

99. Lara Jakes Jordan, "Disaster Response Improvements Lacking," *Associated Press*, 29 April 2006, < http://www.washingtonpost.com/wp-dyn/content/article/2006/04/29/AR2006042900655.html> (7 September 2006).

100. Tim Starks, "House Panels Take Differing Approaches to 'Fixing' FEMA," *CQ Weekly,* 22 May 2006, 1412.

101. Starks, "House Panels Take Differing Approaches to 'Fixing' FEMA," 1412.

102. Eileen Sullivan, "Storm's a-Comin', FEMA," *CQ Weekly*, 29 May 2006, 1447.

103. Sullivan, "Storm's a-Comin', FEMA," 1447.

104. Jordan, "Disaster Response Improvements Lacking."

105. U.S. Department of Homeland Security, <http://www.dhs.gov/dhspublic/interapp/editorial/editorial_0846.xml> (7 September 2006).

106. Federal Emergency Management Agency, "FEMA: Ready for 2006 Hurricane Season," 18 August 2006, < http://www.fema.gov/news/newsrelease.fema?id=29049> (7 September 2006).

107. "Homeland Security Committee Approves Senator Collins', Lieberman's Legislation to Implement Findings of Hurricane Katrina Report," *States News Service*, 27 July 2006.

108. "House-Senate Negotiators Reach Agreement on Collins-Lieberman FEMA, Hurricane Katrina Legislation," *States News Service*, 18 September 2006.

109. Charlie Savage, "Bush Cites Authority to Bypass FEMA Law; Signing Statement Is Employed Again," *Boston Globe,* 6 October 2006.

110. President Bush has used signing statements on such high-profile issues as bypassing a statutory ban on torture in 2005 and disobeying oversight provisions in the PATRIOT Act reauthorization in 2006. Savage, "Bush Cites Authority to Bypass FEMA Law."

111. Spencer S. Hsu, "Bush Balks at Criteria for FEMA Director; Signing Statement Asserts Right to Ignore Parts of New Homeland Security Law," *Washington Post*, 7 October 2006, A02.

112. Richard Sylves and William R. Cumming, "FEMA's Path to Homeland Security: 1973–2003," *Journal of Homeland Security and Emergency Management* 1 (2004): 4–6.

7

Social Security Reform and Leadership in American Government

During the press conference that followed his successful reelection campaign in 2004, President George W. Bush famously described his victory as having earned him "political capital."

> I earned capital in the campaign, political capital, and now I intend to spend it. It is my style. That's what happened in the—after the 2000 election, I earned some capital. I've earned capital in this election—and I'm going to spend it for what I told the people I'd spend it on, which is—you've heard the agenda: Social Security and tax reform, moving this economy forward, education, fighting and winning the war on terror.[1]

This statement left little doubt that reforming Social Security stood at the top of the president's second-term priority list. And the political planets seemed aligned to enable him to achieve a historic goal: modifying for the twenty-first century the cornerstone New Deal program originally signed into law in 1935. After a hard-fought campaign, Bush's victory in the 2004 election was convincing if not overwhelming—a three million popular vote plurality and fifteen-vote margin in the Electoral College. His party retained control of the Congress, adding five seats in the House and four in the Senate. His White House staff and administration were battle-tested and ready for action, having scored several major successes in the first term and survived difficult challenges both at home and abroad. Past dealings with Congress had produced valuable experience in how to win support from a balky legislature or retreat when absolutely necessary. In short, Bush and his aides were ready to assume the challenge. But by the end of the year, Social Security had disappeared from the administration's plans, and reform had not been achieved. What went wrong? And how can this case provide additional perspective that helps us understand the leadership issues addressed in this book? Before turning to the general issues, we will examine the effort to reform Social Security more closely.

BACKGROUND: PROGRAM DESIGN AND EARLY REFORM EFFORTS

Social Security: FDR through Reagan

President Franklin Delano Roosevelt convinced Congress to establish Social Security in 1935 in response to the Great Depression which left over half of all senior citizens in poverty. The original program, still largely in place today, had two primary components of social insurance: financially supporting retirees and their survivors as well as the disabled. In 1935, lawmakers debated whether this program should be a pay-as-you-go program, in which workers and their employers pay taxes into a collective account to support all beneficiaries or a personal account system with workers and employers depositing funds into personal accounts managed by the government. The Congress chose the former and began collecting payroll taxes to pay for benefits through the Old-Age and Survivors Insurance Trust fund and the Disability Insurance Trust fund. Since 1969, whenever payroll taxes have exceeded the amount needed to pay benefits, the trust funds have invested the excess deposits in nonmarketable U.S. treasury bonds, earning interest while lending the money to the government to pay for other government programs. The Congress has borrowed a cumulative total of $1.3 trillion from the trust funds over the years, excess contributions that were not needed for current beneficiaries.

For its first few decades, Social Security operated with a large surplus and relatively low tax rates because sixteen workers supported each retiree in the 1950s. But since the 1970s, when the worker to retiree ratio dropped to between three and four workers per retiree, revenues have occasionally come perilously close to falling short of benefits, and elected officials took action to correct anticipated shortfalls in Social Security revenues. Unlike other government programs, the legislation that created Social Security requires that planning be completed with a seventy-five-year time horizon. When benefit payouts increased too rapidly, the number of retirees grew, or retirees lived longer than expected, adjustments were made on the revenue side.

Facing a projected funding shortfall in 1982, President Ronald Reagan created a bipartisan commission chaired by Alan Greenspan to develop solutions to the funding problem.[2] In 1983, the Greenspan Commission proposed, and the Congress implemented, a number of short-term solutions. First, the Congress raised the retirement age to reduce the number of new retirees receiving benefits. Second, they increased the payroll tax to the current level of 12.4 percent of a worker's earnings, with the worker and employer each paying 6.2 percent.[3] Third, they increased the number of employees covered to expand revenues by collecting taxes from more employees. Finally, they made a portion of Social Security income potentially taxable, based on the recipient's income. These modest changes avoided an immediate shortfall and were intended to delay the need for serious reforms for at least twenty years.

Clinton Tackles Social Security Reform

The next round of reform efforts came in 1998 when President Clinton announced that the nation needed a conversation on Social Security to prepare for serious action, and he held several town hall meetings to discuss the impending Social Security crisis. Then in January 1999, during his State of the Union address, Clinton made Social Security reform the domestic centerpiece of his final two years in office, though at the time, he had been impeached by the House of Representatives and was waiting for the Senate to complete its role in the constitutional process. After the Senate voted not to remove Clinton from office, Social Security became the top issue. Clinton proposed three steps: invest a portion of Social Security's surplus in the stock market to generate higher returns that could help close the gap in necessary funding; dedicate 62 percent of the projected federal budget surplus to Social Security; and create additional incentives for low-income workers to save toward retirement.[4] On the one hand, most Republicans rejected the idea of government investment in the stock and public bond markets as creating excessive government intrusion in the nation's economy. On the other hand, Republicans supported several budget proposals in 1999 that dedicated more budget resources to "save" Social Security, and the principal response of Republican Party leaders was to adopt a procedural hurdle to using Social Security surpluses for general government obligations, something referred to by politicians and the press as a "lockbox."[5] In truth, while "lockbox" made it sound like Social Security revenues were being put into a locked vault to cover future needs, it really meant that Congress and the president would have to go through extra steps to redirect Social Security funds to pay for general government obligations—more of a symbolic than a real protection. Finally, some legislators, mostly Republicans, explored creating individual retirement accounts, an idea that had been developed and advocated mainly by the Cato Institute, a D.C. think tank with a strongly libertarian leaning. Although there were several versions of how such a system might work, the plan proposed by John Kasich in June 1999 as part of his campaign for the

Republican presidential nomination would allow individuals to invest a portion of their Social Security payroll taxes in stocks and bonds, a precursor to Bush's later plan.

Republican congressional leaders cautioned their members to move slowly on Clinton's Social Security proposals. This warning targeted, among others, Bill Archer (R-TX), chair of the House Ways and Means Committee, who was eager during his last year in Congress to make progress on this problem that fell within his committee's jurisdiction.[6] In general, Republicans feared the electoral consequences of getting out in front on Social Security questions. Budget hawks, those members who placed balancing the annual federal budget above all other policy concerns, feared that plans to restructure Social Security might endanger the budget surpluses that Congress had worked so hard over the previous fifteen years to create and had only achieved in the late 1990s. Liberals, almost wholly Democrats, were concerned that the prospect of individual retirement accounts, which attracted support from a few moderate Democrats, was the first step toward privatizing Social Security, a step that would undermine the basic purpose of the program. The new push for individual retirement accounts posed a central question: "Should Americans save for old age collectively as a nation, or as individuals through private savings and investments?"[7] This issue would be addressed more directly by President Bush's proposals in 2005.

An Alarmingly Expensive Problem Takes Center Stage

While the Greenspan Commission reforms made in the 1980s delayed the problems associated with Social Security, namely a shrinking worker to retiree ratio and ballooning benefit payments, they did not solve the problems. President Bush argued that Social Security was heading toward certain bankruptcy by 2042 (2052 according to the nonpartisan Congressional Budget Office)[8] and questioned whether young Americans would ever see a dime of the money they were contributing to the program. But the more immediate problem is that somewhere shortly before 2020, current revenues will not be able to meet the program's benefit commitments. At that point, money will be drawn from the trust funds to meet current obligations but those, too, will be exhausted leaving an estimated $3.7 trillion shortfall over the next 75 years.[9] Once the trust funds are exhausted, Congress would then have to start paying back bonds, borrow more money, or raise taxes to meet Social Security's obligations.

The fundamental problem looming over the system that policymakers frequently debated but never seemed to solve was that seventy-seven million "baby boomers," those Americans born between 1946 and 1964 to the veterans of World War II after they returned home and started families, will begin to retire in 2011 and thereby put enormous strain on the retirement system. Not only will the number of Social Security beneficiaries swell to record numbers, but they are expected to live longer due to progress in medical science—good news for the retirees and their families but bad news for the program.[10] At the same time, the number of workers who pay into Social Security is shrinking, meaning that the number of tax-paying workers per beneficiary is declining—now about 3.3 workers for each retiree and projected to decline to 2:1 in 2033.[11] How will fewer workers be able to support the payments to more, longer-living retirees unless taxes are dramatically raised, a step that might endanger the well-being of the boomers' children and grandchildren? If no other changes were made to the system, meeting current benefit commitments to all the baby boomers would require that payroll taxes increase another six percentage points.[12]

PRESIDENT BUSH ENTERS THE FRAY

President Bush's First-Term Effort to Reform Social Security

President Bush's commitment to Social Security reform was clear. During both the 2000 and 2004 presidential campaigns, candidate Bush promised to "fix" Social Security so that younger workers could hope to derive benefits from a program described by the president as headed for "bankruptcy." In 2000, Bush listed the essential principles to be included in such a fix:

> First, we must not change Social Security for those now retired, or nearing retirement . . . Second, all Social Security funds in the federal surplus must stay where they belong, dedicated to Social Security . . . Third, the payroll tax must not be raised. We cannot tax our way to reform . . . Fourth, reform should include personal retirement accounts for young people—an element of all the major bipartisan plans . . . A young worker can take some portion of his or her payroll tax and put it in a fund that invests in stocks and bonds. We will establish basic standards of safety and soundness, so that investments are only in steady, reliable funds.[13]

With one exception, the president's solution went largely unchanged throughout the first term. A bipartisan Commission on Social Security cochaired by former Senator Daniel Patrick Moynihan (D-NY), a longtime defender of Social Security, presented President Bush with three options for reform in late 2001; all three options included a version of private accounts. But President Bush did not launch the effort to reform Social Security until early 2005. Getting Social Security reform onto the national agenda (that is, exercising leadership by setting a direction) was a problem. As noted in our discussion of earlier cases, the attacks of September 11, 2001, dramatically transformed the legislative agenda, and security-related issues like intelligence reform, triggered by the terrorist attacks, lingered well into 2004. But there were reasons other than 9/11 to delay action. The stock market recorded a substantial decline in 2002 and corporate scandals wiped out the retirement savings of employees in several major firms, developments that boded ill for a proposal designed to draw on stock investments as a way to boost Social Security returns. Moreover, the administration realized that modifying a program that directly affects forty-nine million Americans a year—a substantial number are retirees (about 60 percent) but a large number are disabled, children of deceased workers, and widows— would be both politically difficult and dangerous.[14] Even more Americans, an estimated 162 million or 96 percent of all workers in the United States, are covered under Social Security, contributing to its trust funds and expecting to qualify for benefits when needed in the future. Any program with such wide-ranging effects would prove difficult to change.

As elections throughout the 1980s and 1990s had shown, both political parties would pounce on proposals to change Social Security as a way to mobilize beneficiaries, particularly elderly voters, to vote for their own candidates. Congressional Republicans had been badly bruised in previous battles over Social Security, most recently in 1996 when Democrats used Republican proposals to reduce benefits as a way to rally support from elderly voters. The political battle lines were clear. Congressional Republicans were understandably reluctant to risk their careers in pursuit of a legacy for George Bush who would never again run for political office. Democrats could be expected to defend the program as a critical part of their party's heritage. Most Republicans embraced the program's principal features, but some supported restructuring ideas developed in the 1990s. The elderly were both politically active and well organized: as they turned fifty, Americans were routinely recruited to join the American Association of Retired Persons (AARP), the nation's largest interest group, with an estimated thirty-five million members. A week after the 2004 election, the AARP announced that it would oppose the principal component of Bush's reform plan—individual retirement accounts funded with Social Security wage taxes. In short, there were numerous reasons to delay action until the time was right, and that meant when the president's political clout was maximized.

President Bush's Second-Term Effort to Reform Social Security

President Bush sought passage of his signature issue in his second term by providing all three elements that we have identified as necessary for political leadership—*direction, coherence,* and *energy.* The first step was to get his recommendations on the nation's agenda. As Bush's 2004 campaign policy director explained to the *New York Times,* the administration recognized that a successful effort in Congress to reform Social Security would require a bipartisan approach that followed an election victory. "It's such a big issue that it almost requires an election to give the president the political capital and the ability to frame the issue so that he can get his conceptual solution through a divided Congress."[15] Much as he had with education reform in 2001, President Bush decided to pursue a "blueprint strategy" for Social Security reform, a strategy we also found in other cases and discuss more extensively later in this chapter. After setting forth several essential elements that he insisted should be incorporated in the final legislation, congressional leaders would be able to fill in the details as needed in order to mollify reluctant Republicans and hesitant Democrats. The core elements to a solution—Bush's effort to provide coherence—were discussed throughout Washington during the weeks that followed the 2004 election and preceded the launching of a new legislative agenda.

Bush's State of the Union address, delivered two weeks after the inauguration, explicitly laid out this blueprint strategy:

> Fixing Social Security permanently will require an open, candid review of the options . . . we have to move ahead with courage and honesty, because our children's retirement security is more important than partisan politics. I will work with members of Congress to find the most effective combination of reforms. I will listen to anyone who has a good idea to offer.[16]

As the State of the Union address continued, the president's nonnegotiable positions echoed those of his speech in 2000 (noted earlier) with one major exception:

> We must make Social Security permanently sound, not leave that task for another day. We must not jeopardize our economic strength by increasing payroll taxes. We must ensure that lower-income Americans get the help they need to have dignity and peace of mind in their retirement. We must guarantee there is no change for those now retired or nearing retirement. And we must take care that any changes in the system are gradual, so younger workers have years to prepare and plan for their future.
>
> As we fix Social Security, we also have the responsibility to make the system a better deal for younger workers. And the best way to reach that goal is through voluntary personal retirement accounts.

By 2005, Bush's list of principles no longer included the "lockbox" for Social Security trust funds, an important element that had signaled fiscal responsibility in 2000 but which fell victim to several forces. First, the tax cuts passed in 2001 reduced the size of the budget surplus that had grown under Clinton; then, the surplus was transformed into budget deficits as a result of several factors. The attacks on September 11, 2001, triggered a new round of expenditures for homeland security and the war on terror. Moreover, after nearly a decade of continuous growth, the economy slowed down in 2001–2002, an economic recession exacerbated by the disruptions of 9/11, and budget revenues shrank dramatically. (During the 2004 election, President Bush promised to cut the annual budget deficit in half by the end of his term, from roughly $500 billion to $250 billion.) In this new budgetary setting, the Democrats' solution to Social Security's financial problems, forged by Bill Clinton during his last two years in office, suddenly disappeared. As Clinton had argued, the lion's share of the federal budget surplus was to be channeled into funding the future shortfalls in Social Security and Medicare. That option was suddenly gone—along with the lockbox for the surplus in Social Security revenues that was now needed for the war on terror. Thus, Bush's list of fundamental principles had changed; taking the place of protecting tax surpluses was the concern with low-income citizens, potentially an appeal to Democrats and to an important segment of their voters.

From the Democrats' perspective, the president left little room for negotiation. Over the years, analysts had divided Social Security solutions into two broad categories—benefit reductions and tax increases. The government could reduce or slow the outflow from the trust funds by reducing benefits—an action sure to generate widespread objections—or increase the inflow by increasing taxes. But under Bush's proposal, these options were either largely (benefits) or totally (taxes) off the table. And the new element that attracted Democrats' suspicions in the past was now nonnegotiable; Bush insisted that any solution must include personal retirement accounts, which he promised would generate additional revenues without the need for higher taxes.

Defenders of Social Security insisted that the administration was exaggerating the extent of the problem. They pointed to the modest changes made in the wake of the Greenspan Commission discussed earlier in the chapter as a model of needed reform. They recommended modest changes that tweaked the Social Security system so that the dire forecasts could be avoided by fine-tuning a few elements, for example, raising the full-benefit retirement age beyond sixty-seven (for those born after 1959), raising the wage cap on which taxes must be paid beyond the $90,000 maximum in 2006, slowing the rate of benefit growth by tying it to price inflation rather than wage inflation, or phasing in benefits depending on past income so the wealthy (who need them less than the poor) receive lower Social Security payments.[17] Such a balanced solution would make changes in both benefits and revenues in order to spread the impact broadly across the public. Instead, Bush argued that the program needed a fundamental overhaul for the twenty-first century, though he might also be willing to accept some modest tinkering in other areas so long as taxes were not raised.

As the politics in Congress unfolded, Democrats remained united in their refusal to enter discussions so long as personal retirement accounts, a favorite solution of Republican conservatives, were on the table.[18] As discussion of the president's Social Security proposal moved forward, polls showed that Bush succeeded in convincing "the public that Social Security is in trouble but has not persuaded them to back his solution for fixing it,"[19] further fueling the Democrats' intransigence. For example, an early August 2005 poll by the Associated Press showed that 63 percent of those surveyed opposed Bush's solution and 33 percent approved.[20] Nor were all Republicans happy with the president's proposal. Introducing voluntary personal accounts would actually make the projected shortfall in Social Security revenues worse because contributors could direct up to 4 percent of their Social Security contributions into personal accounts. This would reduce the program's current revenue and substantially increase the revenue deficit. If benefits were not to be reduced for current retirees and near-retirees, the significant "transition costs" (estimated at $1 to 2 trillion, if not more) could only be met through borrowed funds, anathema to an increasingly vocal group of congressional Republicans concerned about the growing size of the federal budget deficit.[21]

Immediately after the 2005 State of the Union address, the White House launched an aggressive public campaign to frame and energize the public debate while at the same time forcing Democrats to enter negotiations by highlighting long-run problems and winning public support for the president's preferred solutions. This effort, dubbed "60 Stops in 60 Days,"[22] was reminiscent of Clinton's efforts in 1999 but many times greater. By July 22, 2005, President Bush had addressed Social Security during visits to twenty-nine states and multiple times to different audiences in the District of Columbia.[23] Described by the White House as "town hall meetings," most of these events were similar to campaign rallies in which the goal was for the candidate to deliver a clear message, not engage the public in debate.[24] The president also discussed Social Security seven times during Saturday radio addresses in 2005 (three times in February alone) and the vice president hosted several events. A comparison between the public relations effort advocating Social Security reform and the president's "going public" strategy in 2001 on behalf of No Child Left Behind (NCLB) is instructive: during that earlier successful effort, President Bush addressed NCLB during visits in only eight states and three radio addresses. Even if one considers Mrs. Bush's additional three visits on education-related subjects during 2001, one gets a sense of the far greater White House effort made on behalf of Social Security reform. But there were also greater efforts by opponents. Both the AARP and organized labor invested heavily in a series of television spots that challenged the administration's diagnosis and prescription for fixing Social Security.

The differences between NCLB and Social Security did not end at the public strategy, however. Even more significantly, the president's "inside strategy" on Social Security was dramatically different from NCLB. In the earlier effort, President Bush had worked assiduously to develop a bipartisan group in Congress that could squire his proposals past opponents in both parties and in both houses. Bush recruited both George Miller and Ted Kennedy, liberal Democrats, into the "Big

Four" group of congressional advocates for NCLB. In the case of Social Security, however, the president's proposal sought to box in the Democrats rather than meet them halfway, as he had done on education in 2001. Trips designed to pressure Democratic moderates to break ranks with the majority of the party may have backfired, as in the case of Ben Nelson (D-NE) who was reportedly amenable to seeking a compromise on individual retirement accounts until the White House set up a visit to his home state without alerting him of the plan.[25]

ACTION IN CONGRESS

House and Senate Republicans developed their own retirement proposals, partly as a way to explore avenues for building a bipartisan coalition. The administration's key ally was Representative Bill Thomas (R-CA), powerful chair of the House Ways and Means Committee, with jurisdiction over Social Security. Unfortunately for the president, Thomas was better known for his unpredictability than for his loyalty to the president, though he had helped to deliver the Bush tax cuts in 2001 and Medicare prescription drug program in 2003. Thomas set about to craft a comprehensive retirement bill that dealt with Social Security as well as the related subjects of private pensions and personal savings. This broader approach departed from the White House's and House Republican Party leadership's preferred strategy, but Thomas persisted, much as his predecessor Bill Archer had sought a major Social Security breakthrough in 1999, knowing that his term as committee chair would expire in 2006.[26] After holding committee hearings in May and June, action on legislation was delayed into September but never resumed. Several rank-and-file House members also sought to advance the reform agenda and proposed pieces of legislation that prominently included individual accounts. Only one had a Democrat as cosponsor (Allen Boyd from Florida).[27]

Representative Bill Thomas (R-CA)

First elected to Congress in 1978 with a 59 percent victory margin after serving four years in the California legislature, Bill Thomas came to Washington as a moderate who quickly chafed at the frustration of being in the minority. All of his subsequent election victories were secured by safe margins (60 percent plus), and he ran unopposed in 2004. When Republicans won a House majority in 1994 for the first time in forty years, Thomas was given several critical assignments by his roommate when he first came to D.C., Newt Gingrich, the new speaker of the House and engineer of the Republican electoral success. Even after Gingrich's departure from the House, Thomas continued to play an important role and became chair of the Ways and Means Committee in 2000, arguably the most powerful policy committee in the House of Representatives. Again, Thomas delivered victories. He spearheaded the push for tax reforms in 2001 (tax legislation is the major legislative responsibility of his committee), for renewed authority for the administration to negotiate trade agreements, and for Medicare reform in 2003 that produced the prescription drug benefit. Floor votes on his committee's legislation frequently passed by the narrowest of margins, an indication that he was pushing controversial policy proposals. These successes came at a cost. Thomas's bruising tactics during negotiations with Senate conference committee members—both Democrats and Republicans—became legendary, and the same bruising methods soured his relations with Democrats on his own committee. The latter relationship came to a breaking point in July 2003 when Thomas sought to hold a committee vote on a proposal that members had not had time to read. After he rejected the minority party's objections, the Democrats walked out of the meeting and gathered in an adjoining room. Harsh words were exchanged, and Thomas called on Capitol police to remove the Democrats—they refused. Partisan rancor rose in the House over the incident until Thomas was forced to apologize for his short temper, poor judgment, and lack of moderation. Despite this personal admission of error, interparty relations on the committee remained tense, hardly a setting conducive to constructing a bipartisan coalition on Social Security.

Under rules adopted by the House Republicans, committee chairs serve a single six-year term rather than becoming chair for life, a status that prevailed for most of the twentieth century. Knowing that his term would expire in January 2007, Thomas was eager to engineer a solution to the nation's retirement dilemmas, but he viewed the issue more broadly than President Bush. Not only did he want to address Americans' access to private pension plans and improve their ability to accumulate personal retirement savings, but he also wanted to consider shifting Social Security funding away from the payroll tax to a controversial value-added or national sales tax. Thomas's views merited consideration; he was the only Republican member of Ways and Means who had been on the committee when Social Security had last been restructured in 1983 and brought two decades of policy knowledge to the task of reform. But the administration never endorsed this broader definition of the problem that would have linked its two top-priority domestic agenda items, and Thomas's more comprehensive approach to the issue did not prevail.

In the Senate, Charles Grassley (R-IA) chaired the Senate Finance Committee, but moderate members of the Senate—both Republicans and Democrats—were unenthusiastic about individual accounts, making progress unlikely. The potential "tandem" of Grassley and Max Baucus (D-MT), ranking minority member of the Finance Committee and a frequent partner with his committee chair in bipartisan efforts, could not materialize so long as Democrats remained united against individual accounts.[28] Moreover, the Senate leadership was largely focused on securing approval of Bush's judicial nominees, a battle that became heated several times during the year. Most observers saw the House as the critical battleground because Democrats would be able to block action in the Senate with a filibuster. In the Senate, both Lindsey Graham (R-SC) and Rick Santorum (R-PA) convened work groups to seek compromise solutions, but these efforts failed.

With progress on his proposed reforms bogged down, Bush endorsed a specific plan during a news conference on April 28, 2005, that would establish "progressive indexing" of Social Security benefits, a proposal that would tie the adjustments in benefits to prices rather than wages, and would likely have the effect of lowering benefits for middle- and high-income wage-earners. Because wages rise at a faster rate than prices, adjusting benefits to keep pace with the latter would reduce the growth of benefits over time. Endorsing the plan was considered a bold step since reducing benefits was expected to be politically unpopular. For example, the AARP came out squarely against price-indexing proposals as did other liberal and labor groups, portending problems for such a proposal as a basis for crafting a bipartisan compromise.[29] And sure enough, most Democrats rejected the suggestion. Another attempt to reenergize the reform effort came in late June 2005 when House sponsors of various reform proposals consolidated their efforts behind a single plan to create individual accounts, and Senate conservatives led by Jim DeMint (R-SC) proposed a similar plan.[30] Nonetheless, other congressional business began to reduce the time and effort that could be devoted to Social Security: the Central American Free Trade Agreement, an energy bill, a Supreme Court nomination, and annual appropriations were other pressing pieces of business that required congressional attention.

At the end of July 2005, Republican leaders in the White House and Congress announced plans to address Social Security legislation when they returned in September from the summer break and predicted that action would begin in the House. Roy Blunt, the House majority whip, Karl Rove, the White House deputy chief of staff, and Charles Grassley, chair of the Senate Finance Committee, indicated a similar timetable.[31] The unexpected then intervened to change the legislative agenda. As detailed in chapter 6, when Hurricane Katrina struck the Gulf Coast on August 29, 2005, the congressional agenda shifted to recovery efforts, triggering concern over the new strains such expenditures would pose for the federal budget. Within ten days of the storm, Congress appropriated $62 billion in relief aid; the federal share for rebuilding New Orleans was projected at $200 billion. Less than a month later, the House Republicans' driving force behind the administration agenda, Majority Leader Tom DeLay (R-TX), was forced to resign from his party leadership role after being indicted by a Texas grand jury. House Republicans immediately fell into uncertainty and disarray.[32] Furthermore, prosecuting the war in Iraq was costing more, not less as everyone had hoped. With the new national priority, an ongoing war, and disarray in the House majority party, Social Security reform receded quietly from the national stage, though die-hard congressional supporters of reform continued to explore ways to advance their agenda even without the president's help.[33] Unlike the bipartisan cooperation that flourished in the wake of 9/11, partisan rancor blew through the halls of Congress after the Katrina disaster; Democrats refused to participate in a bipartisan House investigation that they feared would seek to cover up rather than reveal administration mistakes.[34]

Thus, despite unprecedented effort and commitment, President Bush was unable to secure passage of his proposed reform. Many forces no doubt contributed to this unsuccessful outcome. There was the unexpected event—Katrina—that suddenly dominated the legislative agenda; the administration no doubt made some mistakes in strategy and tactics; like other second-term presidents, Bush lost a good deal of his influence in Congress, even with his own supporters, as his lame-duck term began winding to a close; President Bush's public approval ratings steadily declined during 2005, partly influenced by bad news from the war in Iraq and partly by the Democrats' unrelenting attack on Bush's war motives and questionable honesty in sharing information with the public before launching the war; prospects for constructing a bipartisan coalition were poor given the partisan warfare that prevailed on the House Ways and Means Committee and the Democrats' rejection of the president's principal policy proposal; and opponents (for example, the AARP) raised questions about the administration's proposed solution and actively campaigned against it in contrast to the support they had provided for Bush's Medicare reform proposal in 2003.

INDIVIDUAL LEADERSHIP ON SOCIAL SECURITY REFORM

Bush sought to provide *direction, coherence,* and *energy* largely on his own and found the political system highly resistant to presidential direction. From the outset, Republican leaders were concerned about placing Social Security at the top of the agenda. The experience of being politically burned during the Clinton years remained vivid. Similarly, Bush defined the policy proposal launched in his State of the Union message; it reflected the best thinking of one segment of the Republican Party created during the 1999–2000 period but remained controversial because of the potentially great costs of transitioning from the old to a new system. Bush's key congressional ally—Bill Thomas of the Ways and Means Committee—never fully endorsed the president's plan and sought a different, broader solution. But neither Bush's proposal nor Thomas's was likely to produce the bipartisan coalition needed to reform a program with such a vast impact. Early in his term, Bush had tried to broaden the base of support for Social Security reform by soliciting support from several Democrats—particularly former Senator Daniel Patrick Moynihan (D-NY) and Senator John Breaux (D-LA)—but both had since retired from Congress, leaving the president with virtually no cross-party support and divided support within his own party. His cross-country efforts to build public acceptance of how he defined the Social Security problem and support for his proposed solutions represented a major effort to generate and maintain energy, but one that ultimately proved unsuccessful.

ORIGINS OF LEADERSHIP: EVIDENCE FROM SIX CASES

In each of the six preceding case studies, we focused on the political figures who provided *direction, coherence,* and *energy* in setting the agenda, developing policy options, and assembling the necessary support to gain passage of important legislation, although success is not always guaranteed, as illustrated by the case of Social Security. In this chapter, we seek to draw out the themes we developed across the separate cases. What can we hope to learn more generally about political leadership and about how it operated during the first six years of George W. Bush's tenure as president?

As set out in chapter 1, we relied on a definition of leadership that is a composite of direction, coherence, and energy, a conceptualization found in the work of Bert Rockman. Briefly summarized, direction refers to setting the nation's or an institution's agenda of issues to address. This step directs the attention of political officials and helps them concentrate their efforts. Coherence recognizes the critical step of developing tangible policy proposals that serve as the starting point for policymaking. There is a twofold challenge: addressing the substantive needs of the problem at hand while simultaneously framing the proposal with an eye to the political context so as to attract sufficient support for passage and acceptance. In a system like America's where power is broadly fragmented, the political challenge faced in policymaking is every bit as important as the substantive challenge. Finally, energy is creating and maintaining interest in a policy area among those responsible for setting the agenda or among enough lawmakers to force political action.

Presidential Preeminence

As we explained in chapter 1, popular perceptions of national leadership typically concentrate on the president, and our case studies suggest that Bush provided leadership across the broadest range of issues of any official during his first six years in office. Although members of Congress also exercised leadership in the policymaking system, several factors made the president preeminent.

President Bush took a central role in determining the outcome on four of the six case studies; he and his aides were largely responsible for directing the agenda on education reform, and even in cases in which the agenda was largely shaped by others or by events (intelligence reform, homeland security, Katrina), the administration was able to avoid undesirable results and achieve a preferred outcome. They tried to do the same on Social Security reform, but failed, and campaign finance reform moved in a direction contrary to White House preferences.

The president's focus on education during the 2000 presidential campaign provided Bush with the closest thing he could claim as an electoral mandate; he used this leverage to make education reform the first major issue addressed in 2001. With this momentum behind his efforts, Bush was able to keep education as the top domestic priority while guiding the Congress to a compromise that had seemed impossible prior to his election. On intelligence reform, the president's advantage in national defense policy allowed Bush to decide on the timing and process of reorganizing the nation's intelligence gathering agencies. Although the administration was forced to take action after a year of delay and dissembling, it was able to secure relatively modest changes consistent with its own preferences rather than imposed by congressional reformers. Much the same occurred in creating a Department of Homeland Security and responding to the devastation of Hurricane Katrina. In both instances the president seized the initiative from others and guided the process to a result more to his liking and on his own terms. In both cases, Congress deferred to presidential leadership. After Democrats first suggested the need to abandon Bush's preferred organization for homeland security, the president adopted their solution as his own and reshaped it to his own liking. In the wake of Katrina, the administration was able to fend off aggressive congressional investigations and define the structural reforms that Bush was willing to embrace, a clear example of "unilateralism." We can even see something similar in the effort to reform Social Security. President Bush boldly pushed the issue onto the agenda, defined the policy debate, and sought to sell his proposals to the American people, though the effort ultimately failed. In five of these cases—all except Katrina—the administration's strategy was not to start with an elaborate plan; rather, the president identified a set of essential features to be included in the final solution that could then be supplemented by the priorities of others. We examine this *blueprint strategy* in greater detail below.

Only one of the cases—Social Security—demonstrates how presidents might keep an issue alive until a more favorable political context establishes the foundations for action. Most often, presidents are expected to overcome the problems that make action difficult, but they may also keep issues alive, that is,

provide sustained energy until such time as action becomes possible. Among
our cases, this was true only of Bush's effort to reform Social Security, a policy goal delayed until the second term. As the comments from a campaign operative made clear,[35] the administration believed that action on Social Security
required an unambiguous electoral mandate, something unavailable after the
2000 election but secured in 2004. Until his political hand was strengthened,
Bush was able to keep action on Social Security alive through a presidential
commission (2001) and then launched related efforts on health care that were
geared toward creating an "ownership society" that would ultimately be defined
to include individual retirement accounts. When the president and his advisors
considered their political capital strong enough, they advanced the Social Security reform proposal that was ultimately unsuccessful. Rather than dropping the
effort completely, however, Bush included further discussion of Social Security
reform as one topic for a commission on entitlement reform proposed during
the 2006 State of the Union address.[36]

Leadership from Congress

While it may seem that presidents are preeminent, they are not the nation's only
source of political leadership, as our case studies make clear. Congressional
party leaders have also provided *direction*, *coherence*, and *energy*. The speaker
of the House and the Senate majority and minority leaders, in particular, hold
a significant amount of formal agenda-setting power—while they may not have
as firm a grasp on the nation's agenda as the president does, they can set their
chamber's agenda and often dictate the manner in which agenda items will be
discussed on the floor. No member of Congress has as much influence over the
national agenda as the president, but party leaders are in a better position than
most to exercise influence. Often, party leaders work in concert with the president on a common agenda as was the case in consideration of No Child Left
Behind. Party leaders are much more likely to work closely with a president
from the same party, but every party leader has a certain amount of responsibility to work with, rather than against, the president in order to keep the lawmaking process from grinding to a halt. At other times, party leaders force the
president to accept a new agenda item; we saw evidence of this in our case studies of intelligence reform and the creation of the Homeland Security Department. Majority Leader Daschle played a leading role in motivating the president
to accept a new Homeland Security Department by using his position as party
spokesperson and repeatedly called attention to Congress's concern over the
White House Office of Homeland Security. On another front, Daschle was initially unwilling to force action on intelligence reform, but later in 2002, he
became an outspoken supporter of the independent effort of the 9/11 Commission, helping to provide the momentum needed to launch the investigation.

Providing coherence is a critical responsibility of party leaders. When party leaders support a bill, they are almost always responsible for negotiating with groups of their colleagues and holdouts in order to find a compromise that will ensure passage. Whether they are seeking the combination of provisions that make action possible or literally negotiating the language that establishes a viable compromise, party leaders are seldom far from the center of action in reconciling the solutions to public problems with politics. Part of the job description for a congressional leader is that they are responsible for keeping the party unified and the chamber working efficiently. The best way to do this is by using leadership tools like the whip organizations to gather intelligence on which members support or oppose a bill and why, and then using the organization to win passage for the bill by revising it to expand the coalition of support.

One finds examples of party leaders providing coherence in each first-term case study. In education reform, favorable treatment of the proposed package on the House floor, a strategy set after consultation with the party leadership and reflected in decisions of the Rules Committee, precluded the many battles that had to be fought in the Senate to resolve members' policy disagreements. Speaker Hastert guided House action on intelligence reform through a task force of committee chairs, and he later worked in conjunction with the White House to address the objections of conservatives in his caucus who rejected the Senate/White House version of reform. Senate party leaders, in particular Senator Daschle, were responsible for avoiding a potential filibuster by Senator Robert Byrd by delaying consideration of homeland security legislation. In the House, where party leaders have stricter control over the lawmaking process, leaders simply imposed their will and replicated President Bush's proposal by granting final authority to write the bill to a select committee comprised of Republican and Democratic Party leaders. Finally, throughout consideration of campaign finance reform, Democratic leaders had a hand in shaping the text of the bill and of amendments to help win support—while Republican leaders were working to weaken and defeat the legislation.

Social Security reform offers further evidence about the importance of congressional leadership. Republican Party leaders, worried about the electoral consequences of such a push, never appeared to be enthusiastic supporters of a major reform effort. It fell to President Bush to provide congressional Republicans with "cover," that is, generate a groundswell of public support for the reform effort and for Bush's specific proposals that would reassure nervous legislators. When polls showed that the public embraced his critics' position more than the president's, Social Security reform was unlikely to emerge from the congressional labyrinth. The Republicans' discomfort with Bush's effort was reflected in the lack of party unity; multiple reform proposals came forward in the House and Senate, and the key figure on the House Ways and Means Committee, Representative Bill Thomas, wanted to pursue much more comprehensive reform than did the White House. In the face of unified Democratic opposition and new national pressures, Social Security simply disappeared, a fate about which only a few Republican members of Congress seemed genuinely distressed.

Party leaders provide energy to policy issues by using their institutional positions to keep potential agenda items from dying. They can use speeches or press conferences to keep attention on an issue—even a peripheral issue. Second, party leaders can use their scheduling power to reserve floor time for issues; debating the issue on the floor alerts members to its importance and signals to the press that the issue remains unaddressed. Finally, party leaders can pressure a committee chair to hold a hearing on a policy issue or schedule votes on a bill that might otherwise die a silent death in committee. Some of these activities, like mentioning an issue in a press conference are easy to observe, while lobbying a committee chairman will go unnoticed by outside observers. In our case studies, then, where we rely heavily on the public record, we are not as likely to see many internal efforts made by party leaders to provide energy, but we are able to see the product of their labor in the public action that is taken.

Likewise, committee chairs can take similar actions on their own volition without prompting from the party leadership. Senator Thompson used his position as committee chair to provide energy to campaign finance reform when he redirected his committee's investigation from campaign finance violations during the 1996 presidential election to identifying more general problems in the system and their potential solutions. His institutional position enabled him to highlight an issue, campaign finance reform, that other members of the formal leadership had no interest in bringing to the agenda.

Rank-and-file members of Congress have the least leverage to exercise over direction, coherence, or energy—they do not have the institutional advantages enjoyed by presidents, party leaders, or committee leaders. Legislators compete with hundreds of others in the House and the Senate to win agenda space for their favored issues and must wait for opportunities to arise. The quintessential example of rank-and-file members providing leadership can be found in the efforts of Senators McCain and Feingold and Representatives Shays and Meehan in their joint crusade to pass campaign finance reform. These four legislators went to extraordinary lengths over a sustained period to keep their issue alive despite multiple legislative setbacks and to bring the issue back to the agenda until final passage, made possible by changes in the political environment that fragmented opposition. Extraordinary individual, tandem, or group efforts do not always succeed. Representative Thornberry worked on the Homeland Security issue for many years, but it was not until the September 11, 2001, attacks that he was able to become an important player once homeland security reached the top of the agenda.

In summary, while presidents hold the greatest influence in national leadership and can provide direction, coherence, and energy on nearly any issue in which they have interest, party and committee leaders also play vital roles in providing leadership. In fact, presidents will find it difficult to succeed—as in Social Security reform—when they fail to secure the support they need for concerted action. While rank-and-file members have the fewest advantages for exercising leadership, they, too, can make a contribution. The next sections in this chapter extend our discussion of two other factors critical to understanding leadership: context and individual leadership skills.

LEADERSHIP THEMES

Context

Our six case studies revealed how individual lawmakers used their institutional positions as well as leadership and political skills to provide energy to an issue, set the agenda, and pass agenda items. Each issue presented political officials with a different set of conditions that formed a context within which they sought to exercise leadership; time pressures, partisan balances, and previous legislative battles put different leaders in position to lead on different issues using different leadership skills. While our discussions of leadership in each case study identified examples of leadership, broader themes emerge by comparing leadership efforts across the case studies. By comparing and contrasting leadership across the six case studies, we identify five recurring leadership themes: the role of moderates, the influence of tandem leadership, the impact of trigger events, the role of issue networks, and electoral calculations.

Moderates

Moderate members of Congress played important roles in each of the four first-term case studies but were less prominent in our two second-term case studies. The role of congressional moderates received intense scrutiny during the Bush administration in large part because of the president's unexpectedly aggressive legislative strategy and the subsequent reaction of moderate Republicans—in particular Senator Jim Jeffords (I-VT). The picture that emerged in journalistic accounts was that moderate Republicans had been pushed to a peripheral position in the lawmaking process. Many moderate Republicans, Senator Jeffords included, welcomed President Bush's bipartisan record in Texas and initially thought that he would bring much-needed bipartisanship to Washington. But when the administration began pressing the thin Republican majorities in Congress to stick together, it became clear that Bush intended to win by using partisan unity. Many concluded that the Republican majority in Congress had little use for moderates except as loyal votes in support of President Bush's agenda. Much of this impression was based on the relationship between Jeffords and his party's leadership, which quickly stretched to the breaking point less than six months after Bush's inauguration. Jeffords's party shift triggered discussion of whether the Republican Party and its conservative agenda had room for other moderates who represented critical voting blocs in both the Senate and the House. The issue was far from merely academic; in a Congress with narrow majorities, 221–212 in the House and 50–50 in the Senate, moderates held a critical position, giving them the capacity to determine outcomes and therefore to negotiate better terms for their support. Our research suggests that moderates availed themselves of these strategic advantages: in the four first-term case studies, moderate members of Congress served as a bridge between the parties and often between coalitions within each party. The absence of such a role in reforming Social Security explains much about the failure of that effort.

As discussed in chapter 1, the Bush administration, despite a controversial election victory that rested on an electoral vote majority without a popular vote plurality, chose to pursue an aggressively partisan Republican agenda rather than a more moderate or bipartisan agenda. Because of the narrowly divided Congress, passing this agenda required a great deal of unity on the part of the Republican Party. While Republicans in Congress with issue agendas close to President Bush's were ardent supporters, less enthusiastic party members were less inclined to provide the support needed to win passage. Rather than negotiate for support from these reluctant colleagues, party leaders often sought to enforce unity by limiting the freedom of moderates to abandon the party's common agenda and by using increasingly heavy-handed measures, much like Newt Gingrich had done during his speakership when party members felt increasingly burdened and ill-treated.[37] Ironically, this was more manifest in the Senate than in the House where leaders more frequently exercise an extensive array of formal powers to enforce unity. Many moderate Republican senators—confronted with a dramatic departure from the norm—complained about the lack of consideration for their concerns about President Bush's agenda. The relationship between party leaders and these moderate members became increasingly cool.

The pressure put upon moderate members, and the marginalization of their concerns, eventually led to dire consequences for Republicans in the Senate. Senator Jeffords announced that he would leave the Republican Party and no longer vote for its leadership because, he claimed, the party had become much more conservative and closed-minded in its dismissal of moderates' agendas. As the Senate was equally divided between Republicans and Democrats, leaving Vice President Dick Cheney to break the tie in the Republicans' favor, Jeffords's withdrawal from the party and announced intention to vote for the Democratic leadership meant that the Democrats regained control of the Senate. Partisan warfare on Capitol Hill lay at the heart of this change.

Our case studies reveal the important role moderates played in deciding the outcomes for four policy issues; the moderates served their parties and chambers as negotiators between coalitions and built the agreements that resulted in final passage of major legislation. For example, Senators McCain and Feingold and Representatives Shays and Meehan, all moderates within their parties, played the central leadership role in passing campaign finance reform legislation. Because the Democratic leadership supported campaign finance reform and had agreed to let Democrats Feingold and Meehan lead the party's effort, it was the Republicans, McCain and Shays, who emerged as the critical sponsors. They were able to use their Republican credentials to lobby fellow party members in search of the Republican support needed to pass the bill against the wishes of the majority leadership in each chamber. The sponsors built a coalition of supporters that featured additional moderates—most importantly moderate Republicans—who reached out to their Republican colleagues to find additional support.

During the creation of the Department of Homeland Security, while the House relied heavily on formal leaders to write a bill consistent with President Bush's vision, the Senate relied on Senator Lieberman, a moderate member of the Democratic Leadership Council, to guide the legislation through the committee stage and onto the floor. Lieberman, and other moderates like Representative Thornberry, were vital contributors and frequently met with party leaders and President Bush at the White House to iron out details of the new department and negotiate on behalf of their chambers. In fact, one of the striking features of these four cases is the omnipresence of Senator Lieberman. Though not a member of the Big Four that guided education reform, he had identified the central ingredients of a compromise formula in 2000 and became a critical player on the 2001 conference committee. With John McCain, he introduced the initial proposal for an independent 9/11 inquiry and later helped Susan Collins (R-ME), another moderate, squire the 9/11 Commission's proposals through a difficult, three-way conference negotiation with House conferees and the White House. In this instance, Republican moderates in the House were largely pushed aside by party and committee leaders who insisted on a partisan response reminiscent of the strategy they pursued on homeland security during the lead-up to the 2002 election. Thus, Lieberman consistently was an important player in forging compromise solutions with party leaders, House conferees, and the president.

Finally, moderates played an important role in passing No Child Left Behind, though the core coalition symbolized by the Big Four represented a partnership between liberals and conservatives rather than moderates. Representative George Miller (D-CA) and Senator Ted Kennedy (D-MA) were well-known liberals just as Representative John Boehner (R-OH) and Senator Judd Gregg (R-NH) were recognizably conservative members of their party. On the periphery, Senators Lieberman, Bayh (D-IN), and Jeffords as well as Representatives Tim Roemer (D-IN) and Mike Castle (R-DE) played important supporting roles at various stages of the process. Although they were less central to developing strategy, their positions on issues were important because they represented important voting blocs that the Big Four had to factor into their calculations.

Tandem Leadership

Closely related to the role of moderates was the influence of leadership pairings that spanned party lines—tandem leadership, an underappreciated feature of Washington politics, which appeared frequently in our case studies. These partnerships of a Democrat and a Republican working closely together were instrumental in forging compromise legislation and a winning coalition. The sponsors of campaign finance legislation, Republican John McCain and Democrat Russ Feingold, and Republican Chris Shays and Democrat Martin Meehan, worked across party lines as well as across chambers to achieve success. Education reform saw the odd-couple pairings of Republican John Boehner and Democrat George Miller as well as Democrat Ted Kennedy and Republican Judd Gregg. As in the case of campaign finance reform, these four met regularly to chart progress and discuss strategy, and they reflected the more traditional pattern of committee chairs and ranking members working in concert, advantages that were not available to the party rebels seeking campaign finance reform. Democrat Lieberman and Republican Collins continued to work effectively on intelligence reform even after party control shifted in January 2003 and produced a reversal of their roles as chair and ranking member. Republican Tom Kean and Democrat Lee Hamilton gently guided a potentially fractious group of colleagues on the 9/11 Commission and conducted delicate negotiations with a suspicious and frequently uncooperative administration. Lieberman and Collins partially repeated their earlier performance in investigating Katrina, but their efforts were frustrated by an indecisive congressional response. Similarly, the potential tandem of Charles Grassley and Max Baucus, chair and ranking member on the Senate Finance Committee, might have been able to craft a bipartisan solution to Social Security reform if the president had been willing to forgo personal retirement accounts or if Democratic leaders had been less intransigent in refusing to negotiate.

Tandem leadership is important in building coalitions and transforming a policy proposal into a bill that can be considered in the committee and on the floor. During an era of partisan warfare, bipartisan tandem leadership allows a bill's sponsors to send a clear signal to both committee chairs and rank-and-file members that the proposed bill is an attempt at compromise and should be taken seriously. Tandem leadership lends credibility to the motivation behind a bill and its contents—the effort is not primarily intended to gain attention or score partisan points. By including a member of each party in a leadership tandem, the team has access to both sets of party leaders and a better chance of attracting support from members of both parties. The proposed bill is not immediately labeled a Democratic bill or a Republican bill but a bipartisan bill seeking to address a common problem. In contrast, when one party sought to claim a proposal as its own, tandem leadership efforts were absent or failed. Thus, House Republican leaders prevented Representatives Shays and Maloney (D-CT) from exercising influence over intelligence reform, and the Lieberman-Collins partnership was not replicated. Despite the president's rhetoric about seeking cross-party support, no tandem leadership pairing emerged on Social Security in either chamber that could give the administration's proposal a bipartisan cast. This ensured that the president's proposal would be seen as a purely partisan initiative. Tandem leadership also has the benefit of dividing the labor of sponsoring and squiring a bill through the legislative process. Instead of one member working to provide the requisite levels of energy, direction, and coherence, work can be divided among members and staffs with different skill sets.

Trigger Events

Trigger events were vitally important in each of our case studies. A trigger event causes voters to change their perspective on which issues should be at the top of the national agenda. Getting issues on the policy agenda is far from automatic; one must actively lobby party leaders for consideration. The agenda can be stable or unstable based on the political environment. When disaster strikes, scandal erupts, or the public otherwise demands political action, established agenda items can fall from the top, rise precipitously from the bottom, or exit the agenda altogether.

During George Bush's first term, several trigger events changed how the public, and subsequently lawmakers, perceived the importance of homeland security, intelligence reform, and campaign finance reform. The terrorist attack of September 11, 2001, was the most important trigger event during Bush's first term. This event put national security issues at the top of the national agenda after their significance had steadily declined in the wake of the Soviet Union's disintegration in 1991. Nine months after a presidential election in which national security was barely discussed, it emerged as the top national concern. A second trigger event during Bush's first term was the Enron scandal in 2002, which made passage of campaign finance reform possible after many years of marginal agenda status. Katrina played a similar role in the second term; by demanding immediate action from both the president and Congress, projected to cost hundreds of billions in new budget commitments, Katrina pushed Social Security reform off the legislative agenda and ensured that "government competence" would be an important issue for the next national elections. In each case, an event redirected the prevailing political wind, and both congressional leaders and the president had to reprioritize items on the national agenda.

In the aftermath of the September 11 attacks, the public expected an immediate response to the new collective insecurity that so suddenly emerged. Americans began following national and international news more closely, expressed concern about their personal security, and sought answers to the question "How could this have happened?" Pressure mounted on public officials to ensure that the same mistakes made prior to September 11 would not be repeated. In this setting, creation of a new Department of Homeland Security and reforming the collection and evaluation of intelligence rose to the top of the agenda from the obscurity of congressional subcommittees, agency conference rooms, and little-known commissions. In a similar fashion, until the Enron corporate accountability scandal, support for campaign finance reform had been tepid. The scandal enraged voters and motivated officials to move the issue to the top of the agenda for consideration and ultimate passage. It is possible that the continuing efforts of supporters would have eventually put these issues at the top of the agenda without trigger events, but these events created an opportunity for supporters to push their recommendations forward.

Two case studies also illustrated how a trigger event might put the existing agenda into question. After 9/11, education reformers, led by John Boehner, managed to prevent their hard work from disappearing from the legislative agenda. Even this leading domestic issue suddenly fell to second-tier importance, and party leaders wanted to delay the hard work that remained to be completed in resolving House-Senate differences. Boehner successfully argued that two factors demanded continuing the investment of scarce time and energy: progress would signal normalcy—terrorists could not disrupt the normal operation of America's democratically elected officials—and continued effort would signal bipartisan cooperation, a quality that Americans wanted during a time of national tension. President Bush, the most important player Boehner had to convince, agreed. In contrast, when Hurricane Katrina redirected the nation's focus to the devastation of a major American city, Social Security never made it back onto the agenda, and the administration allowed its proposals to simply disappear quietly.

Issue Networks

Issue networks were important in our case studies, though they worked quite differently in each. We found that despite the existence of a well-developed issue network in education, successful passage of legislation depended on negating its involvement. In contrast, both advocates and opponents of Social Security reform were mobilized and became engaged even before the president announced his plan. Advocates of campaign finance reform developed a network that was integral to the legislation's passage, and the attacks on 9/11 spawned the creation of a new public network of victims' groups who latched onto intelligence reform as a major national demand.

A dense network of organizations surrounds education policy that represents the interests of teachers, administrators, school specialists, local school boards, state school boards, and many more specialized segments of the education community, such as charter schools and advocates of education vouchers. In addition, virtually all the many think tanks that populate Washington had taken positions on education reform as the issue rose in national prominence. State officials were also deeply concerned about what the redefined federal role in education might be, particularly given President Bush's campaign proposals that suggested a more intrusive strategy even as he denied any such intent. In light of this complexity, the education issue network represented a cacophony rather than a chorus of voices and contributed to the inability of Congress to reach agreement during the 106th Congress. All proposals had both proponents and opponents; no proposal went unchallenged, and the groups were highly effective in monitoring legislative action, communicating with their members, and mounting campaigns designed to combat what they regarded as undesirable changes. Thus, the network mirrored the fissures on Capitol Hill and ensured that efforts to bridge those differences would fail. One key, then, to education reform was keeping the education issue network at bay as long as possible. So long as the administration and the Gang of Four were able to negotiate their differences behind closed doors, members of the education issue network were unable to determine exactly what provisions should be encouraged or attacked. When the House and Senate conference committee began to resolve the many differences between the chambers' respective reform plans, members of the network began to have a better idea of what they needed to attack or support. By that time, however, most of the key legislative compromises had been reached. In the case of education reform, success depended on neutralizing the effects of a dense issue network.

In contrast, congressional supporters of campaign finance reform built an internal issue network critical to their success. It served much like a congressional whip organization with McCain, Feingold, Shays, and Meehan serving, in effect, as the party leaders in charge.[38] The BCRA issue network organized supporters by sharing information about policy alternatives with members when voting on amendments and procedure. The network also prevented the coalition from fragmenting under the pressure of splintering amendments. While other issue networks often use information to educate participants on substantive policy, the BCRA issue network was a strategic network primarily designed to help pass legislation on the floor of the House and Senate.

Journalistic observers suggested that intelligence reform would not have occurred without the efforts of the 9/11 Family Steering Committee. This assessment might be accurate, but it also signals the close alliance that was established between members of the Family Steering Committee and the media who thrived in describing and broadcasting the pathos of families suddenly torn apart. Emotional appeals for action directed to a reluctant administration packed enormous punch. Many family groups suddenly were created to meet the needs of the thousands of citizens who lost husbands, wives, fathers, mothers, sons, and daughters on 9/11. These groups were centered in the New York City area; consequently, legislators from New York, New Jersey, and Connecticut were the most engaged by their calls for action. A number of moderate congressional Republicans also hailed from this area and played an important role in mounting pressure on both the president and their party leaders to take more effective action. We believe the family groups played their most important role by making dramatic calls for creation of an independent commission and then calling for adoption of the Commission's recommendations. This was a citizen-based lobby effort that succeeded; housewives and accountants used the strategies of lobbyists to call the government to account for its actions and ensure that they would do better in the future. They supplemented press releases, press conferences, and committee testimony with many private meetings where they pressed their case with emotional intensity. Although it lacked formal status to represent the full network, the 9/11 Family Steering Committee had extensive overlapping membership with other family groups and committed itself to monitoring the progress of intelligence reform.

Electoral Calculations

Elections not only set the strategic context for decision-making by establishing the partisan balance within Congress and between Congress and the White House, but strategists also anticipate how issues will play in the next election and choose legislative tactics accordingly. At times, bipartisan negotiation and quiet cooperation is the best strategy to produce results, while attacking opponents and creating an election issue is preferred at other times. When do presidents pursue quiet, cooperative strategies, and when do they rely on combative ones?

Party leaders and party strategists decide which issues give them the greatest competitive advantage. As elections loom in the future, these party figures decide whether it is more favorable to produce results or accept a deadlock that prevents action. Thus, party strategists decided in 2000 to delay action on reauthorizing the Elementary and Secondary Education Act until after the presidential election rather than to conclude a compromise beforehand. The greater puzzle, however, is why the party calculus changed in 2001 so that advantages from delivering a bipartisan solution to the public's top domestic issue outweighed disadvantages.

"Politicians 'go bipartisan' when political circumstances make it electorally profitable for them to reach across the aisle."[39] As Trubowitz and Mellow's research has shown, bipartisanship is variable, has eroded badly since 1969–1971, and is more likely to occur when certain conditions prevail: the parties are nationally competitive rather than regionally distinctive; economic conditions are favorable rather than declining; and control of national government is divided. Significantly, the internal dynamics of party voting blocs has a strong impact. "When neither party completely controls the machinery of national government, moderates will exercise more power, making bipartisan cooperation more likely."[40] Finally, while "foreign policy continues to produce higher rates of bipartisanship relative to domestic policy," the difference narrowed in the post-Vietnam era and disappears during some periods, particularly when the opposition party has the opportunity to criticize a long-running military involvement.[41]

During the period covered by our case studies, many—but not all—factors discussed previously made bipartisanship more likely. The outcome of the 2000 election demonstrated the close national party balance, and while Bush prevailed in 2004, the outcome was, once again, closely contested. Republican control of the Senate was so tenuous that it was lost in mid-2001 though regained in 2002 and retained in 2004. Republicans maintained control of the House, but by a narrow margin that grew by eight seats in 2002. One factor that favored partisanship was the nation's economic condition, which eroded badly in 2001, producing greater incentives for parties to address the interests of their core constituencies. The terrorist attacks of September 11, 2001, encouraged bipartisanship in the short run but after the Bush administration launched a controversial strategy in the war on terror in 2003 with the invasion of Iraq, Democratic support largely evaporated. Although most factors seemed to support bipartisanship, our cases reveal that cross-party cooperation was seldom pursued by the White House, occurring in only one of six cases (see figure 7.1).

Figure 7.1. Bush Strategies and Party Strategists' Calculus

		Party Strategists' Calculus	
		Run on Results	Run on Issues
Bush Strategies	Confrontational	NCLB	
	Compromise	Intelligence Reform (2004) Social Security Reform Katrina Investigation	Intelligence Reform (2002) Campaign Finance Reform Homeland Security

Bush Strategies and the Strategic Calculus

Our six cases unfolded in the context of three election cycles: the 2002 and 2006 midterm elections and the 2004 congressional and presidential elections. In reviewing the legislative histories of our cases, it is clear that the Bush administration calculated that a cooperative, bipartisan strategy that delivered results on a campaign promise was more advantageous on only one issue—No Child Left Behind. A confrontational strategy that contributed to fulfilling a campaign promise (run on results) was found in three cases, including intelligence reform prior to the 2004 election. Adopting a strategy of confrontation that would create an electorally beneficial campaign issue (run on the issue) was more advantageous in three other cases, including intelligence reform prior to the 2002 midterm election.

With narrow majorities in each chamber and a close presidential election in 2000, leaders in both parties used the two subsequent elections to expand or regain the majority in Congress as well as control the commanding heights of the White House for the next four years. After the 2000 election, the Republicans held a 221–212 advantage over the Democrats in the House, and the Senate was split 50–50 with Vice President Cheney breaking ties in favor of the Republicans. After the subsequent election in 2002, Republicans had expanded their majorities to 229–205–1 in the House and 51–48–1 in the Senate with Senator Jeffords, a Senate independent and Bernard Sanders, a House independent also from Vermont, voting with the Democrats. In our final case studies, Democrats clearly staked out positions on Katrina and Social Security reform anticipated to influence the 2006 midterm elections; they wanted the administration's ineffective preparation and response to the storm highlighted by congressional investigations, and they worked with outside groups to emphasize the dangers in moving toward a restructured Social Security system. Thus, election considerations underlay the approaches of both parties to all our case studies. Both parties tried to use each issue to their electoral advantage, far from a new idea in American politics.

Elections are often described as representative mechanisms—by standing for reelection, elected officials have the opportunity to show voters that they have adequately represented the constituency's interest. Elected officials fear losing their reelection bids and invest a great deal of time and effort into winning reelection, part of which is satisfying the constituency's demand for policies that address important needs. Elections therefore give voters the chance to remove incumbents who fail to adequately meet the public interest. Lawmakers are under pressure to create new laws and programs that meet the public's expectations—lest they lose reelection.

Passage of education reform legislation best illustrates the classic pattern one expects if elections serve as a true mechanism of representation. Education reform had been on the congressional agenda throughout the 106th Congress (1999–2000); the timetable for reauthorizing ESEA required that action be completed before the 2000 election, but these efforts bogged down in disagreement and lawmakers failed to find a compromise solution for the public's number one domestic policy concern. It was not until George W. Bush entered the negotiations, after making education reform a centerpiece of his presidential campaign, that Congress was able to work out a compromise and pass a bill. While Bush came to Washington with a questionable victory, he was able to claim a mandate of support for education reform because it had been a central plank in his campaign platform. Even a tainted victory enabled Bush to win reforms that met his vision.

Bush hoped to reprise this same role on Social Security reform. For an issue that defied solution during the 106th Congress, Bush proposed a plan for dramatic restructuring during the 2000 campaign that was largely repeated in 2004; the Democrats took the diametrically opposed position that the program needed fine-tuning, not restructuring. Unlike education reform, Social Security did not stand at the top of the public agenda in 2000, and it was less critical that action be taken immediately. Moreover, the Bush administration realized that the political stakes would be much higher on Social Security and they waited to take action until their leverage was maximized with a clear election victory. But rather than facilitating a congressional compromise, Bush sought a Republican-defined restructuring that was made more difficult given divisions within his own party. The result was a disappointing failure.

Can elections serve as action-forcing mechanisms? Do legislators feel under pressure to complete action on high-visibility issues prior to Election Day in order to claim success? Two of our case studies suggest that this occurs less frequently than some might believe. During Bush's first term in office, elections created incentives for lawmakers to delay creating a new Department of Homeland Security and reforming the intelligence community, rather than complete action on major public problems, pending the outcome of the 2002 or 2004 elections. Even in the face of public pressure, policy disagreements were not resolved until after the elections were held.

While considering legislation to create a new Homeland Security Department, party leaders in both the House and Senate embraced the challenge of passing a bill by the first anniversary of the September 11 attacks—promising to meet public demand for a new department. But both parties had electoral incentives to delay the policymaking process until after the November midterm elections. Democrats could attack Republican candidates for the House and Senate as being unable to pass important homeland security legislation even when they also controlled the presidency. Republicans also saw advantages in delay; public opinion surveys revealed that voters considered Republicans better able to handle homeland security issues and terrorism than Democrats. So the longer homeland security stayed at the top of the agenda, the longer Republican candidates could run on the issue, blame Democrats for inaction, and avoid domestic issues on which the Democrats held the public opinion advantage. Despite overwhelming public support for creating a new department, both parties had an electoral incentive to delay its creation. In the end, a lame duck Congress that convened after the 2002 midterm election passed the bill. Once the Republicans picked up seats in both chambers, they quickly passed a bill creating a new department on their own terms. Elections can create incentives for lawmakers to avoid acting in the public's interests in a timely fashion.

A similar pattern emerged in connection with intelligence reform. During two election cycles, reform advocates tried to use the approach of elections as a means to pressure the White House and congressional Republicans to take action. This happened first in fall 2002 when pressure mounted to convene an independent inquiry. As the first anniversary of the attacks approached, and with midterm elections only two months away, the joint congressional inquiry finally held its first public hearing that included public denunciations of an uncooperative administration. Under widespread pressure from the media, Democrats, and a few prominent Republicans, the president reversed his earlier opposition to creating an independent commission. But rather than rushing to establish the commission before Election Day, the administration held out for better terms on how the inquiry would be conducted.

A similar scenario emerged two years later. With the 2004 election nearing, the administration was under pressure to embrace the 9/11 Commission's recommendations on restructuring the intelligence community. Reformers hoped to use the pressure from an advancing Election Day to secure more extensive changes. At least publicly, the administration agreed to the Senate's version of reform. This came after the president had already put most of the Commission's recommendations into operation through executive order. But House conferees proved unwilling to conclude a compromise and blocked action before Election Day. Both Democratic and Republican reformers suspected that the administration—Vice President Cheney and Secretary of Defense Rumsfeld, in particular—had encouraged the House conferees to remain recalcitrant. In the end, action was not completed until after the election, and the final product gave the president enormous flexibility to determine how reforms would be implemented.

Electoral calculations, therefore, can justify either taking or delaying action. In our cases, delay was more prevalent than action.

Individual Skills and Strategies

Our case studies made it clear that the strategies and skills of individual leaders make a decisive difference in promoting policy issues. This discussion will concentrate on distinctive strategies of the Bush administration and leadership skill sets found in Congress, particularly issue entrepreneurship and coalition building.

Bush Strategies

President Bush pursued a distinctive tactic to provide coherence that we call *blueprint policymaking*. In education reform, intelligence reform, the creation of the Department of Homeland Security, and Social Security reform, Bush provided a bare-bones proposal that set forth the president's primary concerns and then negotiated the details as needed to create the political coalition required for final passage, except in the case of Social Security when this strategy failed to work. In the case of homeland security for example, Bush wanted flexibility to reorganize the new department and redeploy its employees to confront threats facing the nation. Similarly, in intelligence reform, Bush wanted maximum flexibility to define the new director of national intelligence's responsibilities. In education reform, Bush's thirty-page outline was more than a thousand pages shorter than the final legislative product. While he included provisions on a number of issues important to Republican colleagues, such as vouchers, it was clear from the outset that his primary concern was the system of student assessments that would enable educators and policymakers to gauge student progress.

In case after case, Bush insisted that Congress develop a bill that incorporated his primary concerns, but he worked closely with Republican Party leaders in filling in the other details to create a workable compromise that could pass the Congress. By employing this strategy, Congress wrote bills that were consistent with Bush's principal objectives while providing a measure of independent input. Congressional party leaders were able to design bills that met the president's concerns and those of enough members to build a majority. Only on Social Security reform did this strategy fail to work when the president insisted from the outset that personal retirement accounts be part of any final plan, a feature that Democrats uniformly rejected as did some Republicans. Blueprint policymaking stands in marked contrast to the strategy pursued by the Clinton administration on health care during 1993–1994 when Clinton introduced a long-delayed, comprehensive plan that included minute policy details. In fact, Clinton's strategy overwhelmed Congress with details, helped establish an immediate coalition of opponents, and set up an environment in which party leaders did not have the flexibility to forge a coalition of support.

Another distinctive feature of Bush's strategy in working with Congress was the frequent use of *tactical reversals*. Consistency is one of the traits Americans value in a president—the sense that presidents provide strong, unswerving guidance to the nation based on a clear set of principles understood by the public. In this view, presidents should never change their minds or reverse positions on public policy.[42] In stark contrast to the public's views, however, seasoned politicians are more likely to recognize the need for artful flexibility. Not only can "foolish consistency [be] the hobgoblin of little minds,"[43] but it can also ensure political defeat rather than victory. Among the case studies we examined, there was ample evidence that Bush, the pragmatic politician, frequently reversed field on questions both large and small.

One can imagine a spectrum of reversals extending from the *calculated pivot* at one end to the *forced reversal* at the other. In the former, presidents decide to reverse course on their own due to the tactical advantage they might gain. We see the calculated pivot as a choice the president makes to control the terms of debate and win the best possible outcome. In the latter, reversal is forced on an administration against its will because of the costs incurred for continuing on the same path. The forced reversal is therefore done with little fanfare and the president does not seek to expand his leadership role. In reality, it may be difficult to disentangle the motives for such maneuvers, making it difficult to determine whether a reversal is one or the other. Our cases provide examples of both.

The Calculated Pivot

In reviewing the record, one would be hard-pressed to find a more dramatic reversal than Bush's endorsement of a Department of Homeland Security in June 2002 after he and his administration insisted for months that a Homeland Security Office headed by Tom Ridge would suffice.[44] In the nine months following the September 11 attacks, support for a new department grew considerably in the Congress and among the public. While Bush favored keeping control of homeland security in the White House, Congress preferred a larger role with oversight of a new department.[45]

As pressure increased in Congress, the president began planning for a new department with a small group of senior White House officials headed by Chief of Staff Andrew Card. This group met in secret to prevent a long, bitter turf war in Congress over which of eighty-eight committees and subcommittees would have oversight responsibility of the new department. The administration informed only Speaker Hastert and Majority Leader Lott of their intentions. By announcing the new proposal with no warning to the rest of Congress, and challenging Congress to pass a bill quickly, the administration was able to head off potential infighting and give the proposal the best chance of becoming law quickly.[46]

President Bush made the tactical choice to embrace a new department rather than keep control in the White House. This shift enabled the president to set the parameters of the new department rather than have them thrust upon him by a majority of Congress that might not include the Republican leadership. Blueprint proposals made this kind of reversal easier; by not ruling out positions that might have support in Congress, Bush was able to reverse course during negotiations. The shift to a cabinet-level department was never acknowledged as a tactical reversal because the president had never explicitly rejected the call of some congressmen for a new department.

Forced Reversals

During the process of crafting intelligence reform, Bush was pressured into several reversals. Most dramatically, he endorsed the creation of the 9/11 Commission in September 2002 after resisting such calls from Congress for eight months. In the face of increasing pressure from the Congress, the media, and 9/11 family groups, Bush endorsed a "focused inquiry" to be conducted by an independent commission. This reversal came two days after the joint congressional inquiry's first televised hearings and one day after the Senate called for such an independent, bipartisan effort. The administration's lack of cooperation with the inquiry frustrated members of Congress from both parties, and a skeptical media highlighted the criticisms from 9/11 groups that were a prominent feature of the first public hearing.[47] Nonetheless, protracted negotiations over the membership and rules under which the 9/11 Commission would operate delayed its creation until after the November elections.[48]

Once started, the administration quietly sought to contain the damage that the 9/11 Commission might produce, but in March 2004, Richard Clarke's nationally televised testimony charged the president with negligence, causing the administration to reverse its position on providing testimony. After resolutely refusing to allow presidential advisors to testify publicly and under oath to the Commission, the Bush administration decided to allow Condoleezza Rice, Bush's national security advisor at the time of the attacks and Clarke's former supervisor, to do so.[49] In a second reversal, Bush and Vice President Cheney met privately with Commission members in the White House on April 29 under notable restrictions.[50] Later in the summer, Bush also endorsed the 9/11 Commission's recommendation to create a new position—director of national intelligence—after initially opposing it. With the November election looming and the Democrats taking maximum advantage of the Commission's revelations, the administration concluded that the costs of noncooperation had become too great. The administration found ways to justify reversing its positions.

There were other examples of forced reversals in our case studies including a reversal on support for campaign finance reform. President Bush initially opposed the Bipartisan Campaign Reform Act (BCRA) and threatened to veto the bill if it reached his desk.[51] Bush's veto threat backstopped Republican efforts to kill the bill in the House and Senate in case those efforts failed. And while Bush never executed his veto, the threat emboldened Republican efforts to defeat the bill. With the Enron corporate accountability scandal came a backlash of support for BCRA and other efforts directed at reforming government.[52] As public pressure to pass and sign BCRA increased, and as more Republicans became weary of opposing such popular good government legislation in the face of massive corporate fraud, the president reversed course and dropped his veto threat.[53]

As these cases reveal, President Bush has used both the calculated pivot and the forced reversal to varying degrees. After recalculating the costs of silence, Bush allowed the 9/11 Commission to question administration officials, thereby halting the growing perception that he was obstructing the investigation. Bush also reversed his position on campaign finance reform in order to avoid criticism that he was preventing reform in the aftermath of one of the largest corporate accountability scandals in history. In other cases, Bush's reversal seems to have been a calculated repositioning, as when he decided to scrap the White House Office of Homeland Security in favor of a new cabinet-level department when congressional support grew for the idea even among his allies. In this case, Bush seized the initiative—and credit—by reversing field and endorsing Congress's demand for a new department. Making it his own proposal then allowed him to have more control over the new department's design and to use the issue effectively in the November midterm elections.

Issue Entrepreneurship

Rank-and-file members use issue entrepreneurship to provide direction and energy. Senators McCain and Feingold as well as Representatives Shays and Meehan achieved campaign finance reform even though they lacked the formal positions of leadership—either of party or committees—that usually increase the likelihood of legislative success. Congress has long had a history of "mavericks," isolated members who made a reputation by challenging the established ways of party and committee leadership. Oregon's Wayne Morse (1945–1969) served in the Senate as a Republican, an Independent, and a Democrat, always a thorn in the side of his party's leaders;[54] Wisconsin Senator William Proxmire (1957–1989) rose to become a committee chairman but waged a one-man battle against wasteful spending, frequently stepping on colleagues' toes.[55] Both Morse and Proxmire were earlier examples of how legislators can use their independence to attract media attention and advance their legislative projects. Rank-and-file members, therefore, can find ways to succeed, though the road is difficult.

The four main sponsors of campaign finance reform were issue entrepreneurs—demonstrating how long-term dedication to an issue can yield success. Over the course of several Congresses, BCRA's sponsors were personally involved in every step of consideration. McCain, in particular, used his personal access to the national media, an asset unavailable to most members of Congress, to lobby the public and officials to support campaign finance reform. According to Michael Malbin, noted campaign finance expert, "That a new law was eventually achieved, given this context, is more a testament to the determination and tenacity of the legislation's sponsors than to the success of the legislative process."[56]

Coalition-Building

Finally, as the profiles we highlighted in each case study suggest, many actors in Washington excel at the quintessential American political skill of coalition-building. As suggested by the arguments about America's fragmented system of power, the challenge for all political leaders in the American context is to assemble the votes needed to comprise a legislative majority. Fortunately, the necessary skill set is not in short supply.

We found that both President Bush and Vice President Cheney were effective players in the constantly shifting series of calculations that underlay legislative-executive politics. In focusing on one case study at a time, we lose sight of the linkages among these issues. Bargaining and strategic calculations related to homeland security moved forward at the same time that revelations emerged about intelligence failures and calls came forward for an independent inquiry. To exercise leadership, a political official must be adept not just on the usual chessboard of moves and countermoves but also at a version of three-, four-, or five-dimensional chess. This is especially true for those representing the president's interests and those occupying positions of party leadership. At a more mundane level, committee chairs, rank-and-file members of Congress, and representatives of major federal bureaucracies can limit their activities to a single board, the one most directly affecting their interests.

Our case studies demonstrated different ways to assemble coalitions. On No Child Left Behind, Democratic liberals and Republican conservatives cooperated in crafting a mutually acceptable result. As the frustration of similar efforts in 1999–2000 demonstrates, this outcome would not have emerged without Bush's intervention. Nonetheless, success required the dedication of the Big Four to work together through close coordination and mutual trust, as well as timely presidential interventions. Boehner and Kennedy, committee chairs, faced down the demands of their conservative and liberal colleagues, respectively, as the compromise outcomes moved in directions they did not prefer. Kennedy had long been recognized as a master of the legislative process during the latter stages of his long career; Boehner received similar recognition in January 2006 by being chosen House majority leader to replace Tom DeLay after he resigned from the leadership. Both Kennedy and Boehner had skillful assistance from their ranking member counterparts.

Bipartisan tandems were the pivots for success on intelligence reform, one in the Senate Committee on Governmental Affairs and Homeland Security and one in the 9/11 Commission. In this instance, President Bush was not a consistent ally of reform, though he came to endorse many of its tenets. In addition to modeling a way for Congress to achieve bipartisan agreement, Kean and Hamilton cajoled the president into cooperating with the inquiry. The Commission became the vehicle for constructing a three-way coalition among congressional Democrats and Republicans as well as the White House. The Senate followed the formula; the House balked at doing so until the cost of obstruction triggered White House pressure.

In campaign finance reform, coalition-building hinged on the efforts of McCain, Feingold, Shays, and Meehan. These four sponsors built a coalition of support over time by negotiating with their colleagues over acceptable terms. The sponsors also emphasized building their coalition by attracting new members of Congress. As BCRA's opponents retired, the sponsors targeted their replacements in order to build a winning coalition while the opposition weakened.

We found both informal and formal coalition-building in the struggle over homeland security. In the months immediately following the September 11 attacks, the Congress allowed the president to take the lead in addressing homeland security failures. The Congress, however, grew increasingly displeased with President Bush's decision to coordinate action through a White House Office and with the administration's refusal to allow Director Ridge to testify. Unlike coalitions in our other cases, the support for a new department arose from legislators' reactions to the administration rather than through formal effort. The coalition that supported the president's plan for a new department rested heavily on efforts of the House and Senate Republican leadership. The House leadership created a process that guaranteed a final bill that would reflect the president's initial proposal. In the Senate, where the Democrats held a narrow majority, support for the president's proposal coalesced quickly as key players like Lieberman and Daschle embraced the key elements and sought to change only a small number of issues.

On Katrina and Social Security, neither the House nor the Senate leadership team was able to create effective coalitions. A bipartisan, bicameral coalition failed to form when Republicans realized that Democrats were committed to painting the administration's performance both before and after Katrina as a miserable failure. But even without the Democrats' participation, Republicans were unable to construct a joint congressional investigation. As a result, Republicans launched three separate investigations that produced overlapping but nonetheless distinctive recommendations for action. On Social Security, without Democratic willingness to negotiate, there was no chance to create a bipartisan coalition, but Republicans were again badly divided, both within their respective chambers and between them. In the conventional view of the president as "director" of legislative affairs, Bush would have stepped in and imposed order on his party. For a variety of reasons, this did not happen. In these cases, the leaders who had shown considerable skill at coalition-building in the other case studies failed to do so. Thus, individuals' skills will not always be able to solve the political puzzles they confront.

LEADERSHIP IN AMERICAN NATIONAL GOVERNMENT

Our case studies illustrate an overriding reality: policymaking in the U.S. is severely fragmented and requires conscious, consistent effort to assemble the pieces needed for action. Such tasks fall to elected, and less often, appointed public officials who provide direction, coherence, and energy through calculated effort—it is not simply the byproduct of doing one's job. Party and committee leaders assemble the pieces in Congress while rank-and-file members can occasionally wield influence. Presidents, too, seek to influence congressional action, usually with the assistance of their own party's leaders but sometimes on their own.

In the process of exercising leadership, presidents cut the widest swath and sometimes appear to dominate the policymaking system. But playing a preeminent role is not the same as dominating. Presidents function as the first among a wide array of constitutional equals, and presidents derive advantage from their unitary status, whereas Congress is disadvantaged by its inherently fragmented structure. Because presidents receive priority media coverage, they have the greatest opportunity to influence public opinion and therefore provide more direction and energy than any other political figure. In recognizing this advantage, some political scientists have reevaluated the basic nature of presidential power, suggesting that it now rests on "going public" rather than on private bargaining as emphasized in more traditional studies. It is more likely, however, that presidents will be found somewhere in the middle of a spectrum that ranges from exclusively going public to exclusively remaining private. In other words, administrations are likely to pursue a mix of inside and outside tactics, and strategy is likely to vary from one issue to another.

Our case studies demonstrated that during his first term, President Bush's appeals to the public did not overshadow "remaining private." Although Bush made many public appearances that addressed education reform during his first year in office, especially early in his first year, progress on education reform was largely an inside game that relied on the protocoalition of four leaders that Bush began to assemble even before inauguration day and that was completed when Ted Kennedy joined in March. Bush continued these efforts to generate public backing for his education reforms, but they were largely a complement to the inside strategies. In fact, he was back on the road to urge action by a balky conference committee on the morning of September 11, 2001, when the terrorists attacked on the east coast.

We found a different presidential strategy in the aggressive schedule of trips and public speeches made by Bush in support of Social Security. The president hoped to create pressure on Congress to act, and as a complex, fragmented institution, Congress's best chance of acting would be to follow the president's proposals. In this case, however, the outside strategy was not fully coordinated with a viable inside strategy and the result was a major administration failure.

Presidents are not the only political leaders who can go public, as we saw in the cases of intelligence reform and campaign finance reform. The 9/11 Family Steering Group used sympathetic media coverage to build support on Capitol Hill and pressure the administration into accepting an independent inquiry into intelligence failures. Policy entrepreneurs John McCain and Joe Lieberman were instrumental in the effort. Similarly, a group of policy entrepreneurs, including McCain, Feingold, Shays, and Meehan, were able to energize campaign finance reform through heavy reliance on favorable media coverage. Although presidents have an important advantage in commanding media attention, they do not have exclusive media access and must face competitors also seeking to go public.

Our case studies suggest that President Bush's political skills are considerable. Politics is sometimes likened to playing cards. Using this analogy, Bush and his advisors have shown the ability to carefully read the strategic situation— the cards they were dealt—and skillfully play their hand. It remains unclear whether Bush personally guides strategy and tactics and the extent to which he relies on Vice President Cheney or Karl Rove, his principal political advisor. But the question is irrelevant if we do not expect presidents to be omniscient or wholly self-reliant, that is, we accept the reality that presidents should realize their own limitations and seek out the advice they need to succeed. Bush seems to have struck a balance between following his own political instincts and following advice from counselors he trusts.

We also observed across these six case studies that the Bush administration frequently pursues a unilateral strategy seeking to solve problems and implement solutions internally. This strategy was most evident in the intelligence reform, homeland security, and Katrina cases. In each case, the administration rebuffed efforts by Congress to include the president in negotiation or for executive branch testimony, at least initially. While the president successfully used a unilateral strategy in only one of the three cases from start to finish, the response to Hurricane Katrina, in all three cases the president issued a signing statement similar to the one discussed in chapter 6. Each of the three signing statements explicitly argued that the president would interpret the new law "in a manner consistent with the constitutional authority of the President."[57] These signing statements were meant to prevent congressional intrusion, but the lack of congressional oversight from Republican majorities in the House and Senate allowed the president's signing statements to go largely unchallenged. It is unclear whether these statements would be meaningful in the face of a Democratic majority in the House or Senate willing to challenge the president over congressional-presidential power.[58]

Finally, our cases demonstrate a basic truth that is often overlooked: Congress is a powerful partner in shaping important national policies. The Bush administration's most important successes were only achieved at the cost of significant compromises on policy substance. As the failed effort to reform Social Security demonstrated, without compromise, success is unlikely. In case after case, Congress did not simply approve the administration's opening policy gambits but found ways to refashion them more to the legislature's liking. This is partly illustrated by the administration's numerous reversals. The Bush administration frequently abandoned its initial positions, sometimes under pressure and sometimes to gain tactical advantage and salvage a situation. In making these tactical moves, the Bush administration demonstrated dexterity in its political footwork that would have been the envy of many earlier administrations, but the administration—particularly in our second-term cases—also sometimes displayed a stubbornness that made success impossible. We would probably find the same mix in most administrations—instances when compromise was embraced and others when it was rejected. The larger point is that political leadership will not consistently be either flexible or stubborn, but the two leading institutions of American government will always need to find ways to work with one another, not against each other.

NOTES

1. Transcript, Bush Press Conference, 4 November 2004, <http://www.whitehouse.gov/news/releases/2004/11/20041104-5.html> (10 September 2006).

2. Alan Greenspan served as chairman of the Board of Governors of the Federal Reserve from August 1987 to January 2006, an unprecedented length of service in a position that has enormous impact on the nation's economic health.

3. Self-employed workers have to pay the full amount themselves.

4. Sue Kirchhoff, "Social Security Compromise Appears Increasingly Difficult as GOP Critiques Clinton's Plan," *CQ Weekly*, 12 February 1999, 393.

5. Sue Kirchhoff, "Budget Plan Skirts Tough Decisions on Social Security Overhaul," *CQ Weekly*, 27 March 1999, 751; Andrew Taylor, "Senate Prepares to Vote on Social Security Lockbox That Echoes Existing Rules," *CQ Weekly*, 12 June 1999, 1369.

6. Sue Kirchhoff, "Archer Mounts Last-Ditch Effort to Overcome Political Inertia on Social Security," *CQ Weekly*, 12 June 1999, 1386; also see Sue Kirchhoff, "Social Security Overhaul Slows as GOP Leaders Oppose Plan for Private Investment Accounts," *CQ Weekly*, 24 April 1999, 967.

7. Edmund L. Andrews, "Tough Issues, Awaiting Their Turn," *New York Times*, 13 April 2004, G1.

8. Depending on economic assumptions—the rate of economic growth and productivity, the inflation rate, and interest rates—the projected date could be different. In mid-2004, the nonpartisan Congressional Budget Office identified the date as 2052, ten years later than in the White House estimate. Robert Pear, "Report Finds Social Security Is Better Off Than Forecast," *New York Times*, 14 June 2004, A21.

9. Adriel Bettelheim, "Bush's Rough Choice on Social Security: Backtrack or Take Flak," *CQ Weekly*, 7 March 2005, 550.

10. The average sixty-five-year-old retiree is expected to live seventeen more years today, up from 12.6 additional years when the program was created in 1935. "Saving Social Security: Will the System Go Broke?" *CQ Researcher* 8, no. 31 (2 October 1998): 857–880.

11. Estimates from the Social Security Administration reported in "Social Security Reform: How Should America's Retirement System Be Saved?" *CQ Researcher* 14, no. 33 (24 September 2004): 788.

12. Andrew Taylor, "Weighing Nip, Tuck vs. Total Makeover," *CQ Weekly*, 4 April 2005, 841.

13. Bush speech, 15 May 2000 in Rancho Cucamonga, California in *Renewing America's Purpose: Policy Addresses of George W. Bush July 1999–July 2000* (Washington, DC: Republican National Committee and Bush for President, Inc., 2000), 214–15.

14. Social Security Administration, Press Office Fact Sheet, <http://www.social security.gov/pressoffice/basicfact.htm> (11 September 2006). Also see Social Security Administration, *Annual Statistical Supplement 2004,* Table 5, A4.

15. Robin Toner and David Rosenbaum, "Bush Revisiting Social Security, And Fight Is On," *New York Times*, 18 February 2004, A1.

16. White House transcript of 2005 State of the Union address, February 2, 2005 <http://www.whitehouse.gov/news/releases/2005/02/print/20050202-11.html> (10 September 2006).

17. A long list of such modest adjustments and their dollar values can be found in Taylor, "Weighing Nip, Tuck vs. Total Makeover," 841.

18. Richard E. Cohen, "Congressional Chronicle—No Toes Crossing Party Lines," *National Journal*, 16 July 2005.

19. Bettelheim, "Bush's Rough Choices," *CQ Weekly*, 7 March 2005, 550.

20. Rachel Kapochunas, "Florida 22: 'Third Rail'; Voltage Still Dangerous," *CQ Weekly*, 15 August 2005, 2241.

21. Edmund L. Andrews, "Bush Says He Won't Raise Taxes for Social Security Overhaul," *New York Times*, 10 December 2004, A30.

22. Bettelheim, "Bush's Rough Choice," *CQ Weekly*, 7 March 2005, 550.

23. See the White House map and videos of the president's appearances at <http://www.whitehouse.gov/infocus/social-security/map.html> (13 September 2006). President Bush made multiple appearances in Florida (three), Kentucky (two) and Pennsylvania (two).

24. Craig Crawford, "Craig Crawford's 1600: Winning the 'Debate,'" *CQ Weekly*, 14 March 2005, 678.

25. Julie Kosterlitz, "Bush's Agenda—Maxed Out on Social Security," *National Journal*, 21 January 2006.

26. Adriel Bettelheim, "Going Beyond Social Security," *CQ Weekly*, 13 June 2005, 1566.

27. The only bipartisan proposal came from Representatives Jim Kolbe (R-AZ) and Allen Boyd (D-FL). Other legislation was proposed by Representative Sam Johnson (R-TX), Representative E. Clay Shaw (R-FL), Representative Paul Ryan (R-WI) with

Senator John Sununu (R-NH), and Senator Chuck Hagel (R-NE). Alex Wayne, "Five Legislative Proposals from Which to Choose," *CQ Weekly*, 9 May 2005, 1239.

28. Alex Wayne, "Trail to Social Security Overhaul Gets Murkier," *CQ Weekly*, 15 July 2005, 1975.

29. Alex Wayne, "Bush Takes New Tack on Social Security," *CQ Weekly*, 29 April 2005, 1147; Taylor, "Weighing Nip, Tuck vs. Total Makeover," 841.

30. Alex Wayne, "New Stabs at Social Security Plan," *CQ Weekly*, 24 June 2005, 1740.

31. Patrick O'Connor, "House First on Social Security, Rove Says," *Hill*, 27 July 2005; Jeff Bliss, "Pension, Social Security Measure Possible in '05, Grassley Says," *Bloomberg News*, 26 July 2005; Wayne, "Trail to Social Security Overhaul Gets Murkier," 1975.

32. John Cochran, "Debacles, DeLay and Disarray," *CQ Weekly*, 3 October 2005, 2636.

33. Alex Wayne, "GOP of Three Minds on Next Social Security Step," *CQ Weekly*, 31 October 2005, 2896.

34. Richard E. Cohen, "Special Report—A Turning Tide on the Hill," *National Journal*, 17 September 2005.

35. See note 15 above.

36. See President Bush's State of the Union message for 2006, <http://www.whitehouse.gov/stateoftheunion/2006/> (23 September 2006). Tax policy is another area where President Bush kept an issue alive and was more successful in achieving his goals.

37. Mike Christensen, "Anguished Transformation from Maverick to Outcast," *CQ Weekly*, 26 May 2001, 1242.

38. This issue network is separate from the cacophony of interest groups lobbying lawmakers to pass or defeat campaign finance reform. While these interest groups played a part in keeping voters aware of the issue, they did not play an integral part in organizing members on the floor as the internal issue network did.

39. Peter Trubowitz and Nicole Mellow, "'Going Bipartisan': Politics by Other Means," *Political Science Quarterly* 120:3 (2005): 450–51.

40. Trubowitz and Mellow, "'Going Bipartisan': Politics by Other Means," 443.

41. Trubowitz and Mellow, "'Going Bipartisan': Politics by Other Means," 448. Also see the discussion on 446.

42. James Pfiffner, *The Character Factor: How We Judge America's Presidents* (College Station: Texas A&M University Press, 2004), chapter 5.

43. Ralph Waldo Emerson, "Self-Reliance," found in *The New Dictionary of Cultural Literacy*, third edition. <2002 http://www.bartelby.net/59/3/foolishconsi.html> (23 September 2006).

44. Jill Barshay, "Lawmakers Might Put Some Muscle Behind Call for Ridge Testimony," *CQ Weekly*, 23 March 2002, 816.

45. Adriel Bettelheim, "Impatient Senate Drafts Its Own Homeland Security Plan," *CQ Weekly*, 25 May 2002, 1387.

46. Adriel Bettelheim and Jill Barshay, "Bush's Swift, Sweeping Plan Is Work Order for Congress," *CQ Weekly*, 8 June 2002, 1498.

47. McCain and Lieberman proposed S. 1867 in December 2001, but it had languished. See a discussion by Niels C. Sorrells, "Intelligence Panel Says Probe Into Failures Needs Independent Commission, More Time," *CQ Weekly*, 21 September 2002, 2468.

48. Carl Hulse, "How a Deal Creating an Independent Commission on September 11 Came Undone," *New York Times*, 2 November 2002, A8; also see Niels C. Sorrells, "Intelligence Authorization Clears, Creating Independent Panel To Probe Sept. 11 Terrorist Attacks," *CQ Weekly*, 15 November 2002, 3040.

49. On the reversal, see especially Alexis Simendinger, "Power Plays," *National Journal*, 16 April 2004.

50. Ned Zeman, David Wise, David Rose, and Bryan Burro, "The Path to 9/11," *Vanity Fair*, November 2004, 326 ff. The testimony was not given under oath, there was no official transcript of the discussion, the commissioners' notes were subject to White House review, and questions had to be submitted beforehand.

51. Andrew Taylor and Derek Willis, "As Campaign Finance Debate Nears, Maneuvers and Worries Intensify," *CQ Weekly*, 17 March 2001, 591–96.

52. Karen Foerstal, "Campaign Finance Bill Wins Its Day on the House Floor," *CQ Weekly*, 26 January 2002, 221.

53. Susan Benkelman, "Editor's Notebook: Under Cover," *CQ Weekly*, 16 February 2002, 434.

54. <http://www.infoplease.com/biography/us/congress/morse-wayne-lyman.html> (9 September 2006).

55. <http://www.infoplease.com/biography/us/congress/proxmire-william.html> (9 September 2006).

56. Michael J. Malbin, *Life After Reform: When the Bipartisan Campaign Reform Act Meets Politics* (Lanham, MD: Rowman & Littlefield, 2003), 25.

57. See: "President's Statement on H.R. 5441, the "Department of Homeland Security Appropriations Act, 2007," <http://www.whitehouse.gov/news/releases/2006/12/20061004-10.html> (11 October 2006); "Statement by the President," <http://www.whitehouse.gov/news/releases/2002/11/20021125-15.html> (11 October 2006); "President's Statement on the Intelligence Reform and Terrorism Prevention Act," <http://www.whitehouse.gov/news/releases/2004/12/20041217-15.html> (11 October 2006).

58. According to the *Boston Globe*, President Bush has issued over eight hundred signing statements since he took office. All previous presidents combined issued six hundred such statements. Charlie Savage, "Bush Cites Authority to Bypass FEMA Law; Signing Statement Is Employed Again," *Boston Globe*, 6 October 2006.

Index

Department of Homeland Security;
FEMA; leadership
Congressional Budget Office, 12, 216
congressional party leaders, 228–31;
agenda-setting power of, 228; control-
ling lawmaking process, 229; impos-
ing own will, 229; keeping chambers
working, 229; keeping issues alive,
230; keeping parties unified, 229;
negotiating responsibilities of, 229;
pressuring committee chairs, 230;
providing coherence, 229; providing
energy to policy issues, 230; scheduling power of, 230; using leadership
tools, 229; working with president,
228–29. *See also* committee chairs
Corwin, Edward S., 4
Craig, Larry, 132, 147
Cronin, Thomas E., 8

Daschle, Tom, 18–19, 75, 151, 161, 163,
165, 166, 170, 228, 229
Davis, Thomas, 195–96, 197, 205, 206
DeLay, Tom, 24, 92, 121–22, 126, 192,
225, 247; indictment of, 225
DeMint, Jim, 51, 224
Democrats. *See* Congress; Hurricane
Katrina; Katrina investigation
DeMott, Benjamin, 88–89
Department of Defense, 199
Department of Homeland Security, 101,
139–40, 244–45; bipartisanship in
forming, 150; changing structure of,
201; complying with Katrina investigation, 199; Congress demanding,
154, 169; congressional oversight of,
148–50, 152; Congress requesting to
organize, 151; creating National
Operations center, 202; creation of,
140, 227, 233, 236, 241; director's
authority, 148, 150–51; FEMA v.,
200; importance of legislation for,
154; improving disaster preparedness,
201–2; improving FEMA's response
capacity, 201–2; incorporating
FEMA, 183–85; integrating agencies,

184; Office of Homeland Security v.,
154, 169; removing FEMA, 201, 206;
status of, 144–54; as third-largest
agency, 152; top priorities for reforming, 206; updating National Response
plan, 202; White House v., 150. *See
also* emergency management system
Department of Homeland Security bill,
169; Armey's amendments to,
159–60; deadline advantages to, 157;
electoral incentives to delay, 241–42;
final passage of, 167–68, 169–71;
House adding pork projects to,
158; House amendments to, 158,
160–61; House authorizing committee
action, 158–59; House deadline on,
156–57; House debating agencies'
transfer in, 158, 160–61; House debating labor rules in, 159, 160; House
final passage of, 167–68; House floor
consideration of, 159–61; House passage of, 154–61; House removing
programs from, 159; House Select
Committee managing, 156, 159–61,
170; House's jurisdictional question
on, 158; reservations about final version of, 167–68; Senate amendments
to, 165–67; Senate Committee on
Governmental Affairs managing,
161–63, 170; Senate deadline on, 163,
166; Senate debating agencies' transfer in, 161; Senate debating authority
over intelligence agencies in, 162;
Senate debating budgetary control in,
164–65; Senate debating labor rules
in, 161–63, 165–66; Senate delay in
final decisions on, 162–63; Senate
diminishing presidential powers in,
162, 165; Senate final passage of,
167–68; Senate obstructing passage
of, 163–65; Senate passage of,
161–67. *See also* Bush proposal for
Department of Homeland Security bill
Department of National Intelligence
(DNI), 93, 99–100
Depression. *See* Great Depression

Index

About the Authors

JASON D. MYCOFF, assistant professor at the University of Delaware, teaches courses on American politics and research methods. His research focuses on congressional committees in the lawmaking process and institutional relationships between the legislative, executive, and judicial branches.

JOSEPH A. PIKA, professor at the University of Delaware, teaches American politics with a research specialization in the presidency. During his career, he has held several administrative positions and has received the university's excellence in teaching and excellence in undergraduate advising awards. Pika is coauthor (with John Maltese) of *The Politics of the Presidency*, now in its 6th edition, and *The Presidential Contest*. In addition to his academic career, Pika has served on numerous state committees and task forces including eight years on the Delaware State Board of Education, four as president of the board. He is currently working on a coauthored American politics textbook.